ONE QUARTER OF THE NATION

ONE QUARTER OF THE NATION

Immigration and the Transformation of America

NANCY FONER

PRINCETON UNIVERSITY PRESS

PRINCETON AND OXFORD

Published by Princeton University Press
41 William Street, Princeton, New Jersey 08540
6 Oxford Street, Woodstock, Oxfordshire OX20 1TR

press.princeton.edu

All Rights Reserved

Library of Congress Cataloging-in-Publication Data

Names: Foner, Nancy, 1945– author.
Title: One quarter of the nation : immigration and the transformation of
    America / Nancy Foner.
Description: Princeton : Princeton University Press, [2022] | Includes bibliographical
    references and index.
Identifiers: LCCN 2021019817 (print) | LCCN 2021019818 (ebook) |
    ISBN 9780691206394 (hardback) | ISBN 9780691206554 (ebook)
Subjects: LCSH: Immigrants—United States. | Ethnicity—United States. |
    United States—Emigration and immigration—Social aspects. | United States—
    Race relations. | United States—Ethnic relations. | BISAC: SOCIAL SCIENCE /
    Emigration & Immigration | SOCIAL SCIENCE / Race & Ethnic Relations
Classification: LCC E184.A1 F578 2022 (print) | LCC E184.A1 (ebook) |
    DDC 305.800973–dc23
LC record available at https://lccn.loc.gov/2021019817
LC ebook record available at https://lccn.loc.gov/2021019818

British Library Cataloging-in-Publication Data is available

Editorial: Meagan Levinson and Jacqueline Delaney
Production Editorial: Kathleen Cioffi
Text Design: Karl Spurzem
Jacket Design: Pamela L. Schnitter
Production: Erin Suydam
Publicity: Alyssa Sanford and Kathryn Stevens

Jacket art: Pacita Abad, *L.A. Liberty*, 1992. Acrylic, cotton yarn, plastic buttons, gold thread, and painted cloth on stitched and padded canvas. 239 × 147 cm (94 × 58 in). Courtesy of Pacita Abad Art Estate. Photographer: Max McClure

This book has been composed in Arno with Alverata and Civane

Printed on acid-free paper. ∞

Printed in the United States of America

10 9 8 7 6 5 4 3 2 1

CONTENTS

ONE QUARTER OF THE NATION

CHAPTER 1

Introduction

IMMIGRATION AND THE
TRANSFORMATION OF AMERICA

It came out of the 1960s. And like everything else in that fateful decade, it still echoes to this day. Along with civil rights and racial equality, new roles for women, gay empowerment, and the environment, there was one more watershed movement. Less noticed at the time but every bit as consequential was the first of a new wave of immigrants.

Alongside the civil rights acts and Lyndon Johnson's Great Society, Congress passed, in 1965, a statute that upended our immigration laws. In the half century that followed, tens of millions of new arrivals began transforming this country.

The numbers alone are extraordinary. By 2020, an unprecedented forty-five million immigrants were living in the United States. Together with their children they totaled nearly eighty-six million, accounting for 26 percent of the nation's population. It's the equivalent of absorbing the entire population of Germany—and then some. They are more than one quarter of this country.[1]

Their impact has been just as large. The tens of millions of post-1965 immigrants and their second-generation children represent an even bigger group than the baby boomers. With relatively little recognition, they have affected almost every part of the American experience, from the music we listen to and food we eat to the high-tech innovations we enjoy.

For most Americans the latest wave of immigration is a new experience. But the fact is that it is as American as apple pie. In 1910, an even higher percentage of Americans were immigrants than today. This was true in 1890, 1870, and most likely several times in the eighteenth century. First on the land from Europe were Spaniards (in the south and southwest) and English (in the east) as well as Africans, against their will, followed by, among others, Germans, Irish, Chinese, and Scandinavians, and at the turn of the last century, southern and eastern (often Jewish) Europeans. Today they are coming in large numbers from all over the world.

Like Canada and Australia, we are a settler society. But unlike people in Asia, Africa, or Europe, the majority of our ancestors lived—three centuries ago—not just in another country but on a different continent. Indeed, this country's founding myth—the Pilgrims and Thanksgiving—celebrates an ocean voyage to a new, more hopeful land.

Look back and immigration is entwined with the evolution of American society in every era of our history. The first colonizers, in Plymouth and Jamestown, were immigrants. Alexander Hamilton, born on the island of Nevis, was among the founding fathers. Urban politics were fueled by immigrant and ethnic passions—from William Marcy "Boss" Tweed, of Scottish ancestry, to Fiorello La Guardia, the child of an Italian immigrant father and Jewish mother from Trieste, to John F. Kennedy's grandfather "Honey Fitz," the son of immigrants who came from Ireland. In World War II, the brain trust of the Manhattan Project producing the first nuclear weapons—Edward Teller and John von Neumann, Enrico Fermi, and Leo Szilard—were immigrants and refugees. Two of our three most recent presidents had a parent who was born abroad. Barack Obama's Kenyan father met the future president's mother in Hawaii on a student visa; our forty-fifth president's mother, Mary Anne MacLeod, left a remote fishing village in the Outer Hebrides of Scotland in 1930 to immigrate to New York City, soon to marry Fred Trump, himself the son of German immigrants.

Throughout American history, immigration has driven fundamental changes in this country's culture, institutions, and values. This was never simply a matter of immigrants becoming Americans; it was also

American society itself evolving as new people came to settle. Take two examples from the past: Judaism and Catholicism, once widely despised religions, became part of mainstream America thanks to the incorporation of earlier Russian Jewish and Irish and Italian Catholic immigrant groups. We no longer see ourselves as a nation of White Anglo-Saxon Protestants or WASPs.[2] In the realm of politics, the nineteenth-century Irish, with their storied Democratic Party bosses and powerful political machines, transformed big-city politics, leaving behind a legacy of effective ethnic turnout at the polls that is alive and well today. Interestingly, even our national myth of origin has changed. This country was always peopled by immigrants, but it is only since the 1960s that the phrase "nation of immigrants" became commonly and popularly used to celebrate the United States. According to historian Matthew Frye Jacobson, Ellis Island joined Plymouth Rock in our foundational myths.[3]

Post-1965 immigrants have made equally consequential changes to American society, though in different ways. These changes go to our culture and institutions. Three examples help to tell the tale. Race—or racial perceptions—have always been part of the immigration story, but the remaking of the racial order since 1965 represents a modern-day transformation. Immigration has not only changed the way Americans view racial and ethnic groups but also created a new and highly diverse on-the-ground national demographic reality. Immigrants and their children have played a part in politics before; now they have helped create new political party coalitions and may potentially reshape the broader political landscape. In the economy too, immigrants have always played an important role, but as this country has evolved into a service-driven economy, immigrants (especially highly educated ones) have been at the forefront of the high-tech revolution—think Google's Russian-born cofounder Sergey Brin or eBay's founder Pierre Omidyar, born in France to Iranian migrant parents. To be sure, not all the changes in the past five decades in which immigrants have been pivotal loom so large, but none of them are without interest and indeed importance for the narrative in this book.

Not every observer of immigration sees it this way. There is legitimate scholarly dispute about the depth of immigration's impact. Sociologist

Alejandro Portes even argues that the basic institutional order in the United States has remained untouched by immigration, and that the fundamental pillars of society, including the nation's value-normative system, legal system, and class structure, have by and large remained intact.[4] I believe that post-1965 immigration has been a prominent source of profound and far-reaching changes in this country's institutions, altering the social, economic, cultural, and political landscape in many significant ways. The chapters that follow will make this case.

In discussing how large-scale immigration of the past fifty years has been changing the United States, this book differs in a number of ways from other works that consider this topic. While some of them recognize that the immigration of recent decades has played an important role in changing American society, their focus is instead on how immigrants themselves have changed. Even the landmark volume *Remaking the American Mainstream*, despite its title, is almost entirely about how immigrants assimilate to America rather than the other side of the equation: how they remake it as well.[5] The groundbreaking National Academy of Sciences report on immigrant integration into American society, published in 2015, is at pains to emphasize that integration is a two-way process, but again, the focus is on immigrants' experience with change as opposed to how the society itself changes in response to immigration.[6] In general, the bulk of the copious scholarly literature on contemporary immigration to this country concentrates on the lives of the newcomers and their children, and how they have been adapting to and making their way in American society.

To the extent that scholars explore contemporary immigration's impact on American society, their accounts tend to be fairly narrowly drawn, covering only one particular domain or institutional sphere, such as race or the economy.[7] The books that examine a range of institutional domains in some depth nearly always center on specific places, typically one city or one type of immigrant destination.[8] There is virtue in a broad view that looks in depth at a number of key economic, social, and cultural spheres affected by immigration, not just one or even two, and encompasses the nation as a whole.

Nor, it should be obvious, is this book an anti-immigrant polemic. Perhaps the most prominent scholarly account of contemporary immigration's impact on the United States is the late political scientist Samuel Huntington's *Who Are We?*, whose theme is that immigration has been eroding America's national identity and core values; various conservative journalistic screeds, Peter Brimelow's *Alien Nation* among them, contend that contemporary immigration undermines the economy, social infrastructure, and national unity.[9] The present book, it goes without saying, has a different orientation to immigration, but it is more than that. Although it highlights immigration's many contributions and positive impacts, it is not, it should be emphasized, a manifesto or treatise about whether immigration makes America great, to excuse this expression in the recent political climate.

The book's coverage is broad, but it does not of course include everything. The focus is on many of the ways immigration has been transforming the United States, from creating changes in how Americans think about race to playing a role in shifting political debates and party alignments. It considers immigration's impact on cities, towns, and suburbs as well as important aspects of the nation's economy. And it looks at immigration's effect on popular culture, from what Americans eat to the television programs and films they watch and novels they read.

As an interpretive synthesis of the existing literature, the book draws on a wide range of quantitative and qualitative studies. These include in-depth accounts of particular groups and places as well as census reports and surveys carried out by social science researchers. It is also informed by my own research and writings in a long career exploring immigration in the United States. The goal is to provide an analysis of changes that immigration of recent decades has wrought: to explain what these changes are, why they have occurred, and what their consequences have been. Although the focus is on contemporary immigration in the broad post-1965 period, the book reflects a deep concern with history, seeing changes today in light of those generated by immigration in previous eras.[10] Immigration has long been an intrinsic part of American society; the changes it has stimulated have given the nation an unmistakable and distinctive flavor and character—shaping, in truth, who we are.

1965 and After

Contemporary immigration is often referred to as post-1965 immigration, and for good reason. On October 3, 1965, at the foot of the Statue of Liberty in New York Harbor, President Lyndon B. Johnson signed legislation revolutionizing the American immigration system. The bill he signed set in motion powerful demographic forces that are still shaping the United States today and will continue to do so in the decades ahead.[11] The law literally changed the face of America.

Known as the Hart-Celler Act after its Democratic sponsors (Philip Hart, a senator from Michigan, and Emanuel Celler, a representative from New York), the law abolished the national origins quota system in place since the 1920s. That system heavily favored those from northern and western Europe; it drastically limited immigration from southern and eastern Europe as well as many other parts of the world, including Asian countries, which already had been subject to earlier statutory bars to admission.[12] After the 1924 Johnson-Reed Act, Germany had an annual quota of fifty-one thousand and Great Britain just over thirty-four thousand, while Italy, which sent about two million immigrants to the United States between 1900 and 1910, had around four thousand and the entire continent of Africa slightly over one thousand.[13] Overall, the combined effects of the restrictive 1924 law, Great Depression, and Second World War caused immigrant entrants to plummet from over seven hundred thousand a year in the first two decades of the twentieth century to less than seventy thousand a year from 1925 through 1945.[14] By 1970, after decades of low levels of new arrivals, only 4.7 percent of the nation's population were immigrants, or slightly less than ten million people (see figure 1.1).[15]

The framework introduced by the 1965 Immigration and Nationality Act defined the basic contours of the immigration system for decades, although there have of course been many modifications along the way. The law emphasized family ties with lawful permanent residents (known

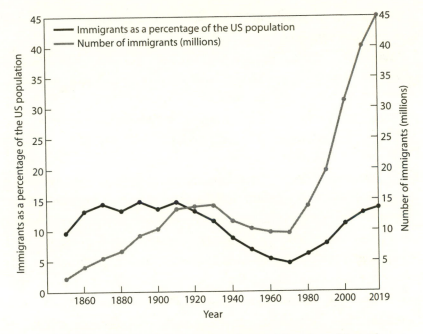

FIGURE 1.1. Number of foreign-born residents and their share of the total
US population, 1850–2019. *Source*: Batalova, Hanna, and Levesque 2021.

informally as green card holders) and US citizens, and to a lesser degree,
labor market qualifications, which were the basis for a minority of green
cards awarded. As a Migration Policy Institute report sums it up, while
the share varies from year to year, roughly two-thirds of permanent legal
immigration in the past few decades has been on the basis of family
relationships, with the rest divided among employment-based and humanitarian immigrants (refugees and asylees) as well as those arriving
through the green card lottery—a program established by the Immigration Act of 1990, bringing in immigrants from countries underrepresented in US immigration streams. There are annual numerical limits
on permanent legal immigration in most categories, although immediate relatives of US citizens—parents, spouses, and unmarried minor
children—have been exempt from them.[16]

By eliminating national origins quotas, the 1965 act paved the way
for sweeping changes. The United States "was in effect declaring," as

sociologists Richard Alba and Victor Nee noted, "that it was prepared to accept newcomers from all over the world."[17] Never before has the United States received so many immigrants from so many different countries. Since 1965, immigrants have come in remarkably large numbers from every region across the globe—mostly Asia and Latin America, but also Africa and the Middle East. While European immigrants are part of the mix, there has been a decisive shift away from Europe as the dominant source of new arrivals.

The 1965 law ended the immigration admissions policy established in the 1920s that had ensured that the United States was primarily reserved for European immigrants. In the first half of the twentieth century, the overwhelming majority of immigrants living in the United States were from Europe. In 1960, 75 percent of foreign-born residents were born in Europe; by 2018, the figure was 11 percent. In the same period, those born in Latin America and the Caribbean went from 9 to 50 percent of the foreign-born population, and with the 1965 law's elimination of the severe barriers against Asian immigration, Asians rose from 4 to 28 percent. Sub-Saharan Africans, virtually invisible among foreign-born residents in 1960 at four-tenths of 1 percent, had grown to 5 percent in 2018.[18]

The change in the top five source countries for immigrants living in the United States reveals the same pattern. In 1960, these were Canada, Germany, Italy, Poland, and the United Kingdom; in 2018, Mexico, China, India, the Philippines, and El Salvador headed the list. Mexicans have stood out as by far the largest foreign-born group for many decades, accounting for a quarter of the immigrant population in 2018, although the Mexican inflow slowed in the early twenty-first century given, among other things, an improving Mexican economy, a long-term drop in Mexico's birth rates, and stepped-up US border enforcement. In fact, from 2009 to 2014 more Mexican immigrants returned to Mexico than migrated to the United States. At the same time, there has been an increasing tilt toward Asian immigration, with more Asian than Hispanic immigrants having arrived in most years between 2010 and 2018.[19]

The change in source countries following the 1965 law was not a deliberate policy choice. Far from it. It was a case of unintended consequences, unforeseen by the authors and major supporters of the act who thought that its family reunification emphasis would favor the entry of European immigrants who had close relatives here, and not significantly alter the racial and ethnic composition of the nation's population. As Muzaffar Chishti and his coauthors tell the story in commemorating the fiftieth anniversary of the act, the prioritizing of immigrants with relatives already in the United States was a last-minute concession to influential conservative members of Congress allied with the House immigration subcommittee chair, who believed it would better preserve the country's predominantly European base.[20] They were wrong. In the years following the passage of the law, Europeans' interest in immigrating to the United States fell flat while it grew among people in non-European countries, many of them emerging from the end of colonial rule.

For millions of people facing limited economic opportunities in the Global South, the United States has held out the prospect of jobs, higher wages, and better living conditions. "Jamaica," one man told me when I was doing research in a rural community in the late 1960s, "is a beautiful country, but we can't see our way through."[21] In the Jamaican case, harsh realities in this small, resource-poor economy, plagued by high levels of unemployment and underemployment, and a population with needs and aspirations for standards of living that cannot be fulfilled at home, have spurred many to leave for the United States. Jamaica is not alone; variations on these themes have played out in many other countries of origin as well. In addition, political conditions in many places around the world, including oppressive governments and brutal civil wars, have driven people out of their homelands. So has everyday violence and the ravages of climate change. Loosened emigration controls in some source countries, perhaps most notably China, which opened its doors to large-scale exit in the late 1970s, also had a role in rising immigration to the United States. Once begun, migration tends to have a snowball or multiplier effect; network connections lower the costs, reduce the risks and uncertainties, and raise the benefits of moving to the United States.[22] By allocating most green cards on the basis of family connections, US immigration law reinforced and formalized the operation of migration family networks: as new immigrants from countries around the world established themselves in the United States, they became a channel for additional immigration through sponsoring family members.

The 1965 act and subsequent legislation had a dramatic effect on the number of immigrants entering the United States as well as where they have come from.[23] After the passage of the act, admissions of lawful permanent residents soared, increasing from around 250,000 a year in the 1950s and 330,000 in the 1960s to 450,000 in the 1970s and 600,000 in the 1980s. For almost all the years between 2001 and 2019, the United States annually issued about 1 million green cards to new lawful permanent residents.[24] In 2019, the nation had, at least until that year, the largest foreign-born population since Census records have been kept; by then the immigrant share of the US total (13.7 percent) had nearly reached the record high of 1890 (14.8 percent) (see figure 1.1).[25]

Refugees and asylees are a minority, though noteworthy, portion of permanent legal immigration: 13 percent of those obtaining green cards between 2013 and 2017. Individuals are granted refugee status or asylum, and given the right to live in the United States permanently, by demonstrating that they have experienced or have a well-founded fear of persecution. Legally, the difference between an asylee and refugee hinges on the person's physical location. Asylum is granted to people already in the United States, and refugee status to people vetted abroad and approved for resettlement. Large numbers of refugees were admitted in the 1970s and 1980s as a consequence of the Vietnam War, and over 100,000 a year in the early 1990s, many from the former Soviet Union; the numbers declined afterward, with most in the twenty-first century coming from Asia and Africa. Altogether, about 3 million refugees have been resettled in this country since 1980, with slightly more than 600,000 admitted between 2010 and 2020. The number granted asylum is smaller, averaging around 25,000 a year between 2007 and 2018.[26]

The immigration system developed after 1965 also includes those with nonimmigrant visas. They are here legally, but only have temporary visas, which in 2016, were held by an estimated 2.3 million foreign nationals living in the United States.[27] A great many have come for limited periods as international students and exchange visitors (about 780,000 visas issued in 2018). Others are temporary workers, whose numbers grew substantially between 1997 and 2018.[28] These include agricultural workers (nearly 200,000 visas issued in 2018, mostly to Mexicans) and high-skilled professionals in the H-1B program, which has allowed firms to petition for foreign workers with at least a bachelor's degree or the equivalent for "specialty" occupations for up to six years (although some have gone beyond the limit while waiting for a green card). Officially, the annual cap is 85,000, but additional visas have been approved in recent years; most H-1B workers are Indians, and most are in computer-related fields.[29]

Not all immigrants of course are legal residents. A remarkably high number are undocumented, who either entered without inspection, typically across the southern border with Mexico, or arrived at an airport or other port of entry with a temporary visa, but then overstayed the required departure date ("overstayers"). Despite all the attention to unauthorized border crossers, the fact is that overstayers made up an estimated 44 percent of the overall undocumented population in 2016, and most of the undocumented who entered between 2010 and 2017.[30] In total, the number of undocumented immigrants living in the United States was estimated at about 11 million in 2018, somewhat lower than the peak of around 12 million in 2007, but up from an estimated 3.5 million in 1990.[31] To put it another way, about one out of four immigrants in the United States is undocumented.

This situation is unprecedented.[32] Large-scale undocumented immigration is a new phenomenon. In earlier eras, there were so few restrictions on European immigration that hardly any European immigrants were unauthorized. To be sure, specific exclusion laws barred the entry of the Chinese as early as 1882. But until the 1920s, there were no numerical limits on European immigration or immigrant visas that had to be secured from the United States prior to arriving. At the turn of the twentieth century, European immigrants came by boat, and most got through the ports of entry easily because they already had been screened, mainly for disease, by steamship companies before embarking.[33] Of the more than 12 million immigrants who landed at Ellis Island between 1892 and 1954, only 2 percent were excluded from entry. Today, if you do not have proper documentation from American authorities, you cannot legally live and work in the United States. Getting this documentation is not easy. Those aspiring to become lawful permanent residents, for example, often lack the family or employment relationships that would make them eligible to apply.[34] Even if eligible, the annual numerical limits on green cards in most categories mean that in many countries where the desire to come to the United States is especially strong there is a long wait to get one—for Mexicans in some categories it was more than twenty years in 2019 and over a million were waiting.[35] As a result, many have arrived or remained without proper documents.

A growing share of the undocumented have been living in the United States for a long time. In 2017, a whopping two-thirds of undocumented immigrant adults had been in the United States more than ten years.[36] Paradoxically, this increase is partly due to beefed-up border enforcement. By making reentry more difficult, dangerous, and expensive, increased border enforcement ended up lengthening stays in the United States; in the case of Mexican workers, many who would have returned to Mexico periodically instead decided to settle in the United States and send for their families.[37] Although the number of undocumented Mexican immigrants has declined since 2007, Mexican immigrants still represent the largest proportion of undocumented, or about half in 2018. Mexico not only shares a nearly two-thousand-mile border with the United States but the 1965 act and later amendments created new restrictions on immigration from Mexico, which had not been included in earlier national origins quotas. Before 1965, Mexicans only faced qualitative restrictions, such as perceived illiteracy or lack of prearranged employment, not numerical limits. Indeed, legal Mexican immigration was considerable in the 1950s and early 1960s. Moreover, the Bracero program, which was established in 1942 and brought in several million Mexican agricultural workers on temporary work contracts, ended in 1964, closing off a major avenue for Mexicans to work legally, even if not permanently, in the United States.[38] Even though Mexicans dominate the undocumented population, other origin countries stand out too; three in Central America—El Salvador, Guatemala, and Honduras— and three in Asia—India, China, and the Philippines—together were estimated to be the source of a quarter of all the undocumented in 2018.[39]

Contemporary immigrants also stand out for the great diversity of their socioeconomic as well as national backgrounds. Although Europeans who came at the turn of the twentieth century included a sizable number who had worked in skilled trades in the old country, the bulk were low-skilled workers with little or often no formal education; professionals and the highly educated were scarce. On average, eastern, southern, and central European immigrants at that time had a little more than four years of education compared to eight years for the native born.[40] Today, many immigrants are still poorly educated and low skilled; in 2019, 26 percent of immigrants twenty-five years and older in the United States lacked a high school diploma. However, 33 percent had a bachelor's degree or higher, almost the same as US-born adults. In recent years, the share of immigrants with these academic credentials has risen significantly among the newly arrived—up to 48 percent among the foreign born who entered the country between 2014 and 2019. It is no exaggeration to say that never in the history of US immigration has such a large proportion of new arrivals been so highly skilled and educated.[41]

Road Map

The story of how immigrants and their families have been transforming America is complex and sometimes surprising, so much so that a road map is helpful in describing the plan of the book. Chapter 2 begins with the subject of race. Perhaps no change produced by the post-1965 immigration is as dramatic, profound, and far-reaching as the transformation of the nation's racial composition as well as ideas about race and ethnicity. How and why have East Asian Americans gone from the "yellow peril" to "model minority"? What explains the normalization and widespread use of the Hispanic and Latino labels? How has immigration affected the meaning of Whiteness? Is it having an impact on perceptions of Blackness? I also peer into the future: Can the analysis of recent changes as well as those in the more distant past help identify forces that may create additional transformations in the racial order in the decades to come?

Chapter 3 turns the focus to cities, towns, and suburbs, where the huge growth in the immigrant population has given rise to astonishing levels of ethnic and racial diversity, to say nothing of a host of other, sometimes unexpected changes. Immigration has fueled population growth in urban America, given a new vitality to many cities and parts of rural America, and even helped account for decreases in urban crime. Recent arrivals have always been drawn to ethnic neighborhoods, but what new features have become prominent in these neighborhoods today? In another development, how has immigration contributed to the decline of all-White neighborhoods in metropolitan America? Contemporary immigration has also led to changes in the institutional landscape in communities around the country, bringing new religions, and providing the impetus for innovative programs and policies in many mainstream local institutions.

Chapter 4 moves on to the economy. The many millions of new immigrant workers have been a force for change and innovation, fueling growth in the American economy, and helping to shape the development of businesses and whole industries. Among the topics I explore are how immigrants have played a role in the success and dynamism of the remarkable new high-tech sector, reinvigorated many businesses and created entirely new ones, and helped many service industries expand, even stimulating a demand for workers in some fields.

Popular culture, a topic given short shrift in the scholarship on immigration, is at the center of chapter 5. Once again, immigrants are remaking what we think of as our uniquely American culture. If earlier Jewish and Italian immigrants brought us bagels and pizza, today's newcomers have made salsa and tacos standard fare as they have introduced a wide range of new tastes and cuisines. In virtually every area of popular culture— from music, dance, and film to theater, television, and literature— immigrants and their children have been introducing new themes or reviving old ones in original ways, and inventing new styles and cultural forms. At one and the same time, they have broadened mainstream American culture while also often creating new multiethnic mixes.

Chapter 6 attempts to unravel the multiple ways the post-1965 immigration has helped transform electoral politics in the early twenty-first century. Not only has immigration emerged as a major focus of national political debates and campaigns; overt anti-immigrant rhetoric became a staple in the strategies of many Republican politicians, most notably Donald Trump, who gave it a legitimacy in political discourse at the highest levels. Immigration's impact has been felt as well in the reshaping of both the Democratic and Republican Parties' electoral coalitions—a shift with consequences in practically every corner of the political landscape. And a very different type of change stems from ethnic succession. Political figures with roots in the post-1965 immigration who have begun to win elected office are not simply new faces in old places but also have frequently introduced changes in the political sphere. Electoral politics of course is a fast-moving target, and among the many questions for the future is how the demographics stemming from immigration, including further shifts in the racial and ethnic composition of the electorate, will lead to additional changes in the political arena in the years ahead.

The concluding chapter has three main goals. One is to consider what we have learned about the impact of post-1965 immigration on this country. A second goal is to reflect on how—and why—the United States is distinctive in its recent experience with immigration-driven change as compared to western European countries. Finally, I raise questions about what may be in store in the future, with an eye, in particular, to the potential effects of the devastating coronavirus pandemic and recession. As millions of the US-born second generation grow up and enter adulthood, and as new arrivals settle in this country, they are destined to produce additional societal changes in the decades to come. In a time-honored fashion, we can expect immigrants as well as their children to continue to serve as a building block of the nation, molding and remolding it in new and sometimes unexpected ways.

CHAPTER 2

The Racial Order

Few subjects loom as large in America's history as race. And few things have changed America's racial picture more conspicuously than the last fifty years of immigration.

What was once a simpler racial hierarchy has grown much more complex. Indeed, for much of the twentieth century, race was largely a matter of Black and White. Turn the clock back to 1960 and Whites were the overwhelming majority. Fully 85 percent of Americans were White. When most people thought of minorities, they had Blacks in mind. That was not surprising since Blacks were three-quarters of the nation's minority population (nearly all of them descendants of enslaved Africans brought to this country in chains). In 1960, Hispanics were a mere 3.5 percent of US residents and Asian Americans were barely visible at less than 1 percent.[1]

Today when people view the racial order, they still see Whites on top—but Asian Americans and Hispanics have joined Blacks among those regarded as minorities. Whites, by 2018, had shrunk to only 60 percent of the nation's population; Hispanics, at 18 percent, had grown to become the largest minority group, Asians were at 6 percent, and the composition of the Black minority had changed. Although Blacks as a group had increased to 13 percent (from 11 percent in 1960), almost a tenth were newcomers, with the overwhelming majority from Africa and the Caribbean.

When talking of race, there is one distinction that is critical. Our subject is not race as physiognomy, it is race as a *perception*. What you look like and where your people came from, to be sure, are basic facts, but what people make of these distinctions is a social construct. Appearances and ancestry are real and concrete; how people interpret them is fluid and evolving.

Further complicating the story are the terms we use to tell it. Race and ethnicity sound like clear and differentiated concepts, but in the literature, they are very much intertwined.[2] "Asian" and "Hispanic" sound like ethnic terms, while "Black" sounds purely racial, but here again it is not that simple. For the purposes of this discussion, Asians or Asian Americans will be people of Asian origin, Hispanics generally people with Latin American roots, and Blacks those of sub-Saharan African ancestry, whether they have been in this country for generations, or arrived by way of the Caribbean or direct from Africa. Whites are what the Census calls non-Hispanic Whites.

Immigration, in this chapter, is the driving force. The central theme is the way it has transformed American perceptions of race: how definitions of groups and categories are changing, how boundaries are shifting, and how identities are new.

To set the stage, it is useful to look back to the last great wave of immigration. Americans now take it for granted that Jews and Italians are part of a broad White community, but a hundred years ago they were commonly seen in racial terms and thought of as racially inferior.

In our current era, other groups have been similarly transformed. Asians, for example, were once considered the yellow peril; now in the common popular view, they have become the model minority. Hispanics are another group whose position in the United States is new, and it is worth remembering that the very term "Hispanic" is a recent coinage. Fifty years ago, the term was rarely used. What is more, as we will see, the way that Blacks and Whites are viewed by others and themselves has also undergone change as a result of immigration's impact.

Lastly, there are questions about the future. Racial perceptions are still very much in flux, and the future is uncertain. Yet it is worthwhile to consider whether understanding the changes that have taken place so far, in the past as well as the present, provide any guides as to what may lie ahead.[3]

Looking Backward: Who Is a Racial Insider?

Most Americans today think of Jews and Italians as part of an all-inclusive White community of European heritage, but they didn't look that way to commentators at the turn of the twentieth century when millions were arriving from southern and eastern Europe. How Jews and Italians went from being racial outsiders to racial insiders is a tale of changes in the meaning of race as well as growing acceptance of their religions and ethnic origins. The story of their transformation raises questions about whether something similar is happening or will happen to some groups today or in the future.

Race today is basically a color word in the United States, but it was not that way a hundred years ago when race and color were not perfect synonyms, and a person could be "considered both white (color) and racially inferior to other whites (race)."[4] Jews and Italians were recognized as Whites in terms of legal and political rights. They were allowed to naturalize as US citizens at a time when American naturalization laws only gave "free white persons" or "persons of African nativity or African descent" the right to naturalize, and when the courts repeatedly denied Asian immigrants access to American citizenship because they were not, in legal scholar Ian Haney López's phrase, "white by law."[5] Jews and Italians were allowed to vote in states that restricted the suffrage to Whites; they were placed in the White category by federal agencies, including the Census; and they were not subject to miscegenation laws to prevent their marriages to other Europeans.

Yet at the same time, the Whiteness of Jews and Italians was sometimes questioned. And while to our contemporary ear Jews and Italians sound like different nationalities or ethnicities, many Americans in the first third of the twentieth century thought of them as different races, and viewed them as racially inferior to those of northern and western European origin on the basis of notions of stock, heredity, blood, and selectively chosen physical characteristics.[6] As historian Matthew Frye Jacobson aptly puts it, eastern and southern Europeans were both White *and* racially distinct from other Whites. Or in historian Erika Lee's phrase, they were White, but not White enough. They were also

religiously distinct; religion was a strong basis for the stigma attached
to Jews and Italian Catholics, who prior to the mid-twentieth century
were outside the core Protestant identity of mainstream America.[7]

In the early twentieth century, Jewish and Italian immigrants, who
then comprised more than half of the southern, central, and eastern
European immigrants in the United States, were widely seen as belonging to inferior "mongrel" races that would alter the essential character
of the United States, and pollute the nation's Anglo-Saxon or Nordic
stock.[8] They were commonly thought to have distinct biological features, mental abilities, and innate character traits, and many Americans
believed that they were physically identifiable; facial features (including
the "Jewish" nose) were often noted in the case of Jews, and "swarthy"
skin in the case of Italians, who were also sometimes maligned as "guin-
eas," an old slur for African Americans that referred to their origins on
the West African slaving coast. "One sees no reason," social scientist
Edward A. Ross wrote in the early twentieth century, "why the Italian
dusk should not in time quench what of the Celto-Teutonic flush lingers
in the cheek of the native American." Madison Grant's influential *The
Passing of the Great Race,* which had become a seminal text of American
life by the 1920s, argued that southern and eastern Europeans were di-
minishing the quality of the nation's Nordic stock and sweeping the
United States toward a "racial abyss."[9]

Far from being on the fringe, full-blown theories about the assumed
racial inferiority of eastern Europeans and southern Italians were well
within the mainstream of the scientific community. Openly propounded
by respected scholars, such views were also propagated and given the
stamp of approval by public intellectuals and opinion leaders in the press.
Articles with titles like "Will the Jews Ever Lose Their Racial Identity?"
(1911) and "Are the Jews an Inferior Race?" (1912) appeared in the most
frequently read periodicals.[10] The *New York Sun* (1893) argued that
Jewish racial features, "recognizable by sight," made them unassimilable.[11] As late as the 1930s, an American history textbook asked
whether it would be possible to absorb the "millions of olive-skinned
Italians and swarthy black-haired Slavs and dark-eyed Hebrews into the
body of the American people."[12] Not only was it acceptable a century

ago to speak about the inferiority of Jews and Italians in newspapers, magazines, and public forums, but discrimination against them—in housing, employment, higher education, and other institutions—was overt and, by and large, legal.

What factors eventually led Jews and Italians to become racial insiders and part of a broad White community—no longer set apart in the popular mind as inferior, in racial terms, from those with northern and western European ancestry?[13] Of critical importance were the economic and occupational successes of Jews and Italians, made possible by the remarkable economic prosperity in the post–World War II years, and growth of jobs in the middle and upper reaches of the occupational structure. The expansion of higher education also facilitated upward mobility for the children of turn-of-the-twentieth-century arrivals; the higher education system increased its capacities fivefold in just three decades, between 1940 and 1970, almost entirely due to public investment in state and municipal colleges and universities.[14] Government policies, such as the GI Bill of 1944 that provided low-cost mortgages and college tuition payments to veterans of the war, opened up opportunities for educational, job, and residential progress for the Jewish and Italian second generation. As they climbed the social and economic ladder, they simultaneously intermixed with those whose roots were in different parts of Europe in new suburban communities, at work, and eventually for many, in marriage.

Also relevant is that those with origins in eastern and southern Europe shared a safe haven of legal Whiteness with northern and western European groups from the beginning, and were not subject to the same kind of systematic legal and official discrimination facing Black, Asian, and Mexican immigrants. And because many Jews and Italians physically resembled members of the older European groups in skin color and other attributes, it was often possible for them to blend into the majority population ("to pass") if they shed cultural features such as distinctive dialects or dress.

Nor can we dismiss the ending of the massive eastern and southern European immigrant influx following restrictive US legislation in the 1920s that reduced the fears of old-stock Americans about the deluge of "racial inferiors," and contributed to cultural assimilation by preventing replenishment of Jewish and Italian communities with large numbers of new immigrants. Moreover, the massive migration of African Americans from the rural South to northern cities from World War I on likely facilitated the acceptance of Jews and Italians by changing the racial order in these cities from one marked by the multiplicity of White races to one focused on race as color.[15] As Blacks became a significant proportion of the population in cities like New York and Chicago (where they were less than 2 percent in 1900), Jews and Italians often sought to distinguish themselves from (and claim superiority to) African Americans by emphasizing their Whiteness.

Other developments played a role too. During the Second World War, the Nazi genocide made anti-Semitism less acceptable. What is more, the war occurred when the mass inflow of immigration had receded and the army was filled with US-born soldiers whose families had origins in all parts of Europe. Fighting in segregated White platoons "brought about a self-conscious wartime unity that transcended ethnic lines among whites"; the image of the multiethnic platoon became part of popular and official culture, with Protestant, Irish, Polish, Italian, and Jewish soldiers fighting side by side, or as one journalist puts it, "Kowalskis and Mancinis sharing foxholes with Mayflower descendants."[16] And there were struggles of the groups themselves to remove institutionalized impediments to their advancement. Especially after the war, organized efforts, most notably by Jewish organizations like the Anti-Defamation League, to eliminate exclusionary barriers in housing, elite universities, resorts, and social clubs were key in the passage of laws prohibiting racial and religious bias in employment as well as higher education.

Changes in Our Current Era

By now, the immigration of Italians and Jews along with the history of their successful assimilation are distant memories. It's a measure of how dramatic the transformation has been that most Americans have forgotten that Italians and Jews were once seen as separate and inferior

European races. What is striking is how the processes of reinvention and change have been occurring in the current era; perceptions of racial and ethnic groups have undergone significant shifts, and taken on new meanings in the context of the changed character of immigration.

Of course, immigration has not been the only transformative force in America's racial order in the post–World War II period. The civil rights movement coupled with legislation of the 1960s ushered in a new racial era, and a host of other social, political, and economic developments have contributed to changes in the meaning and impact of racial boundaries as well. Yet there is no denying the powerful role of immigration, and resulting new demographic features, in altering how Americans think about—and indeed the very words they use to describe—racial and ethnic differences.

Asian Americans and the Elasticity of Race

Views of Asian Americans have undergone a contemporary metamorphosis. Once looked down on as the yellow peril, East Asians are now often touted as a model minority. Indeed, when Whites stereotype Asian Americans today it is frequently for being economically successful.[17]

It is hard to imagine that the Chinese and Japanese in the United States used to be cast, as sociologist Yen Le Espiritu has put it, as "almost blacks but not blacks" since now they are frequently seen as "almost whites but not whites," and associated with academic success, hard work, and achievement.[18] In the past, racial prejudice against Asians was enshrined in restrictive immigration and naturalization laws. The Chinese Exclusion Act of 1882 singled out the Chinese as the first group to be excluded from the United States on the basis of race, ethnicity, or nationality, and by 1917 Congress had also banned the immigration of most other Asians. For much of the nation's history, Asian immigrants were denied the right to become citizens. Although the Fourteenth Amendment and a subsequent US Supreme Court decision in the late nineteenth century granted birthright citizenship to US-born Asians, it was not until 1943 that Chinese immigrants gained the right to become naturalized citizens and that the discriminatory immigration laws affecting Asians began to be relaxed. Only in 1952 was naturalization eligibility extended to all Asians.

Anti-Asian sentiments were particularly virulent on the West Coast, where California and Oregon adopted laws prohibiting Asian-White intermarriage. A 1913 California law, targeting Japanese farmers, barred Asian immigrants from owning land. When a California court held in 1885 that the public schools had to admit Chinese children, the state legislature passed a bill allowing school districts to set up separate schools for "Mongolians."[19] Most devastating of all, during World War II more than a hundred thousand Japanese Americans who lived on the Pacific coast, many of them US citizens, were forcibly evacuated and moved to remote internment camps. Although officially justified as necessary for national security after the bombing of Pearl Harbor, racism and xenophobia, as historian Erika Lee notes, were central in leading "the US government to commit this grave injustice."[20]

Changes in US immigration policy, foreign relations, and legal restrictions, including the abolition of the exclusion regime in the mid-twentieth century and revocation of Asian immigrants' ineligibility for citizenship, set the stage for altered perceptions of Asian Americans. Also, views of Asian immigrants' home countries have changed over time. Americans once saw Asia as a backward region; now China, South Korea, Japan, Taiwan, and India are modern advanced nations and world economic powers, held up for their business prowess and enormously successful companies, from Samsung to Alibaba, producing top-end global products. Of greater importance, however, in the changed racial status of Asian Americans is that a large proportion of post-1965 Asian immigrants are highly educated and highly skilled. Chinese and Korean as well as Asian Indian immigrants, who together are nearly half of all Asian immigrants, are what sociologists have called hyper-selected. They are more highly educated than nonmigrants in their countries of origin and more highly educated than the general US population.[21] In 2016, a remarkable 78 percent of immigrants aged twenty-five and older from India, 54 percent from Korea, and 52 percent from China had a bachelor's degree or higher—compared to 32 percent of the general US population.[22]

The extraordinary educational success of the second generation also helps explain Asian Americans' altered racial status—achievements that sociologists Jennifer Lee and Min Zhou argue can be traced back to the hyper-selectivity of Asian immigration. They emphasize that well-educated East Asian immigrants define success as earning a degree from a prestigious university and working in a high-status field while at the same time importing middle-class institutions from their home countries to provide supplementary education in the United States. Whatever the reasons, Asian Americans are significantly overrepresented in the nation's most competitive magnet schools and elite private universities, and at latest count made up around a fifth of the student body at Ivy League institutions. "Despite decades of institutional discrimination and racial prejudice," Lee and Zhou observe, "the status of Asian Americans has risen dramatically in less than a century. Today, Asian Americans are the most highly-educated [racial] group in the country, have the highest median household incomes, the highest rates of inter-marriage, and the lowest rates of residential segregation."[23]

The substantial rates of Asian American–White intermarriage in the current period not only reflect more positive views of Asian Americans; they have the potential to strengthen them, and loosen racial boundaries, as Asian Americans and Whites become more comfortable with as well as accepting of each other as spouses and close relatives. About one out of three US-born Asian Americans is married to a non-Hispanic White, with women more likely to intermarry, and Indians and Vietnamese having somewhat lower rates than other Asian nationalities.[24]

The frequent experience of marriage to Whites among the second generation does not mean that negative views of Asian Americans have disappeared; they have not. Asian Americans are still seen as racially distinct, differentiated from Whites by physical features—skin tone, hair texture, and the shape of their eyes—and still subject to incidents of racial prejudice and discrimination.[25] This was brought home to Asian Americans during the coronavirus pandemic when President Trump insisted on referring to it as the "Chinese virus," seeking to shift blame for his catastrophic failures in handling the outbreak by fanning fears of a foreign threat while also bolstering support from his base through xenophobia. In reigniting old racist tropes, Trump fueled and legitimated anti-Chinese sentiments; hate crimes were reported to spike against Asian Americans in the midst of the pandemic, following a long period between 2003 and 2017 when they had been in decline nationally.[26]

In addition, widely held contemporary stereotypes about Asian Americans have exclusionary elements. Regardless of how many generations their families have been in the United States, Asian Americans are commonly thought of as "forever foreign," a perception no doubt reinforced by the high proportion who are foreign born—roughly 70 percent of Asian American adults in 2019. Being assumed to be a foreigner is especially painful to those born here; they see it as a sign, as one Chinese American woman said, that "no matter how American you think you are or try to be," you are not fully accepted. Another prevalent modern-day stereotype is the model minority image, which as historian Ellen Wu states, labels Asian Americans as a racial group distinct from the White majority at the same time as they are lauded as culturally programmed for success, "well assimilated, upwardly mobile . . . and definitively not-black."[27] Hailing Asian Americans as a model minority, it has been argued, overlooks the heterogeneity among Asian immigrant groups, including the low educational levels among groups like the Cambodians, Hmong, and Laotians; diverts attention away from the existence of continued racism against Asian Americans, and the social and economic disadvantages that many experience; and pits them against Blacks and Latinos. Many Asian American intellectuals chafe at being used as a cudgel with which to criticize African Americans and other minorities, and seek to discredit what they often refer to as the *myth* of the model minority.[28] Still, the fact that Asian Americans are often now widely touted as a model minority reflects a positive change from the virulently negative caricatures of the past that depicted them as illiterate, undesirable, and unassimilable immigrants.[29]

How Asian Americans describe themselves has also changed in that the very term Asian has become more common in their own communities as well as widely used in popular discourse and the media. In the pre-1960s era, when the Asian population in this country was overwhelmingly of Chinese, Japanese, and Filipino origin, those with roots in Asia identified with their specific national origins, not in terms of a shared Asian label. National identities have not faded away. They remain strong among Asian Americans, especially the foreign born, and continue to supersede "Asian" much, perhaps most, of the time, if only because Asian immigrants come from countries with distinctive languages, cultures (including religion), and even in a few cases long-standing nationally rooted enmities, such as between Korea and Japan. Those from the Indian subcontinent sometimes describe themselves and their compatriots as South Asian, while to many Americans the term "Asian" is often understood as East Asian—that is, Chinese, Koreans, and Japanese.

Yet at the same time, many with Asian ancestry identify as Asian or Asian American at least in some situations. An inclusive, panethnic Asian identity, sociologist Dina Okamoto argues, has become established as a principle for building a community among groups of different ethnic origins, replete with many pan-Asian organizations, institutions, and political mobilizations.[30] Moreover, the adoption of the Asian / Pacific Islander racial category by the US Census Bureau in 1980—mainly in response to civil rights legislation, and the need to enforce equal opportunity and affirmative action policies—has led to its use by businesses, public agencies, educational institutions, researchers, foundations, hospitals, and industry to collect data, award grants, and allocate resources.[31] By now, in short, Asian and Asian American have become officially established and widely used racial labels in American society, and to a growing extent, markers of self-identity among those of Asian ancestry as well.

The Invention of Hispanics

The case of Hispanics also represents a contemporary sea change, in large part because the very category Hispanic is a modern-day invention. It is now normal to hear about the Hispanic vote and Hispanic organizations, but in the mid-twentieth century the press and pundits wrote about Mexicans or Puerto Ricans, not Hispanics.[32] A key development occurred in 1980 when the Bureau of the Census adopted Hispanic as an enumeration category. (Hispanics were not counted as a single group on the decennial Census before 1970, and in that year a Spanish origin question was only asked of a small sample.) The decision to adopt Hispanic as a category on the 1980 Census form sent to all households reflected changes in American society, including civil rights legislation requiring statistical documentation of minority groups' disadvantages; at the same time, the Census entrenched Hispanic as a legitimate official category, contributing to its importance as an identity label for Hispanics as well as its use by non-Hispanics. The normalization of the labels "Hispanic" as well as "Latino" to refer broadly to people of Latin American ancestry in the United States, and the increasing use in some circles of the gender-neutral "Latinx," have occurred in a context in which the Hispanic population has exploded, going from about 9.6 million in 1970 to a whopping 59.9 million in 2018—a growth, as demographers show, that is mainly due to immigration before 2000 and since then mostly to US births among Latino immigrants as well as US-born Latinos.[33]

But it isn't just a matter of numbers. The emergence of Hispanic (and Latino) as established categories of identity in this country is to a large degree the result of the politics of ethnic and racial classification.[34] As Cristina Mora tells it in *Making Hispanics*, the creation of this new identity label in the 1970s and 1980s involved a combination of factors: activists seeking political clout, government funds, and philanthropic support by uniting under the Hispanic banner; Spanish-language television broadcasters seeking a larger national market; and activists and politicians successfully campaigning to have the Census adopt the Hispanic category. To this day, Mora argues, the web of media, state, and activist networks has upheld the notion of Hispanic panethnicity.[35]

A key question is the extent to which those with origins in Latin America actually identify as Hispanic or Latino. It is not an either-or situation. Although many, or perhaps most, Latin American immigrants prefer to be known by and primarily identify in terms of their national origins, they also often identify as Hispanic or Latino. The two identities, in other words, are not mutually exclusive but instead complementary. Individuals may invoke or put aside a Hispanic or Latino identity at different moments and for different purposes, with its use fostered by such factors as regular daily interaction among Latin American nationality groups, shared linguistic and cultural roots, reports in the media, and political appeals and campaigns.[36] What seems clear is that what started out as a statistical term of convenience or tool to bring those of Latin American origin together has been transformed into a real social entity. Legitimized by the state, and diffused in daily and institutional practice, the Hispanic label, as sociologist Rubén Rumbaut notes, has become "internalized . . . as a prominent part of the American mosaic."[37]

Are Hispanics now a racial or ethnic group? On the ethnic group side, the Census classifies Hispanics in terms of ethnicity, not race, and as a group, they have varying skin tones, with many phenotypically White and more than half checking their race as White on the 2010 Census. Hispanics who are of light skin color and with European features, educated, or occupationally successful may gain acceptance as Whites in some contexts and places; by the same token, dark-skinned Hispanics may suffer many of the same disadvantages as African Americans.[38]

Yet a scheme that treats Latinos as a race between Whites and Blacks, as sociologist Wendy Roth puts it, is winning out in the United States today.[39] In the media, public discourse, political arena, some government reporting standards, and everyday language used by Latinos and non-Latinos alike, the view of Latinos as a separate racial group has increasingly come to dominate. Indeed, by treating Hispanics as a group equivalent to Blacks in anti-discrimination and affirmative action policies, the federal government also contributed to raising Hispanic to the status of a racial category.[40] Ideas about skin color are involved too. The terms Hispanic or Latino tend to conjure up images of people who are brown or tan skinned as well as foreign in speech and manner. As sociologist Nazli Kibria and her colleagues observe, notions of intrinsic difference from and inferiority to Whites are long-standing features of the stigmatization of Latino populations in the United States.[41]

The case of Mexican Americans is especially pertinent, if only because those of Mexican origin are by far the largest portion, almost two-thirds, of the Hispanic population in the United States. Mexican Americans stand out as "the descendants of the largest and longest lasting immigration stream in U.S. history"; their origins can be traced to the 1848 treaty ending the Mexican-American War when approximately eighty thousand Mexicans living in the conquered Mexican territories, including present-day California, Texas, New Mexico, Arizona, Nevada, and Utah, became "Americans" after the region was ceded to the United States.[42]

Looking back to the first half of the twentieth century, Mexican Americans straddled the White–non-White boundary. With the exception of a onetime Mexican race category in 1930, the Census classified Mexican Americans as White until the Hispanic question was introduced.[43] During World War II, official instructions called on local draft boards to classify Mexican Americans as White; no state miscegenation laws specifically barred unions between Whites and Mexican Americans, as they continued to do in many southern states for Blacks until the 1960s; and at a time when Asian immigrants could not become citizens, the federal government accepted Mexicans as White for the purposes of naturalization. Yet in the early decades of the century, the boundary between Whites and Mexicans, as sociologist Cybelle Fox and historian Thomas Guglielmo point out, appeared bright "in the sense that a wide range of individuals and nonstate institutions recognized Mexicans as nonwhite. Many race scientists categorized the vast majority of Mexicans as nonwhite. Numerous Anglos did as well, a point that became most obvious when Mexicans [in parts of the Midwest and especially the Southwest] found themselves excluded from white-only public accommodations, when realtors refused to sell them homes in white neighborhoods, or when school officials excluded them from white schools."[44] For the "masses of working class mexicanos, many of them first generation," historian Neil Foley writes, "the idea that they were members of the white race would have struck them as somewhat absurd. Anglos were white; mexicanos, well, were mexicanos."[45]

Fast-forward to the present, and most Mexican Americans are viewed as occupying an intermediate status between Black and White, although the details are subject to debate in the scholarly world. Some scholars

maintain that Mexicans, like other Latinos, should be labeled a racialized ethnic group since they are often stigmatized as inferior, illegal, and
foreign, and regarded as non-White.[46] Another view, focusing on Mexican Americans, stresses that they are targets of prejudice and discrimination because of nativism, or intense opposition based on their foreign
connections, rather than because of, or simply because of, beliefs about
their racial inferiority. According to one argument, Mexican Americans
experience a racialized form of nativism in which their presumed for-
eignness is central and their right to be in the country is questioned;
third- and later-generation Mexican Americans, in this perspective, may
encounter discrimination because they are associated with and frequently mistaken for new Mexican immigrants, and often assumed to
be undocumented.[47]

Pigmentation and other physical features add further complications
to the picture. Skin color among Mexican Americans and other Latinos
has been shown to matter for socioeconomic standing and residential
integration. At the same time, as an in-depth interview study shows,
Mexican Americans, including those who have attained middle-class
status, may experience discrimination in their daily lives because of
their skin color as well as surnames.[48] Indigenous ancestry, manifested
in physical features such as facial appearance and height as well as skin
color, can also pose challenges. As sociologists David López and Ricardo
Stanton-Salazar have put it, speaking of Mexicans, "Those who fit the
mestizo/Indian phenotype, who 'look Mexican,' cannot escape racial
stereotyping any more than African Americans, though the stigma is
usually not so severe."[49]

Blackness: Change and Persistence

This brings us to those who are labeled Black. As the title of a recent
book proclaims, immigration has been remaking Black America as millions of foreign-born Blacks have come to live in this country.[50] A central question is whether this inflow has altered the meanings associated
with Blackness and the way Black people fit into the nation's racial order.
The changes are perhaps best conceived as "tweaking" or modifying

notions of Blackness, since color-coded race remains an impermeable social barrier for those labeled Black and anti-Black racism remains a powerful force.[51] It is a case of change, but also to a significant degree of persistence.

Certainly, the huge Black immigration of the last five decades has led to growing ethnic diversity in the nation's Black population. In 1960, before the United States opened the door to large-scale immigration from the West Indies and sub-Saharan Africa, less than 1 percent of the country's Blacks were foreign born. By 2016, it was roughly 10 percent, or a little over four million people. Half of these people were from the Caribbean and nearly 40 percent from sub-Saharan Africa; most of the Africans arrived after 2000, many as refugees or beneficiaries of the diversity visa program created in 1990 for those from countries underrepresented in the immigrant population.[52]

This increasing diversity of national origins, along with an expansion of the Black middle class, has contributed to some diminution of the monolithic conceptions of Blackness held by many Whites and other non-Blacks.[53] The greater awareness of ethnic differences within the Black population is especially evident in cities where Black immigrants have become a significant presence, most notably New York City and the Miami–Fort Lauderdale–West Palm Beach metropolitan area where about one in three Blacks are foreign born, or in places such as the Twin Cities of Minneapolis–Saint Paul, Minnesota, and Lewiston, Maine, where Black African newcomers are highly visible drivers of increases in the overall Black population. The Twin Cities are now home to the largest Somali immigrant population in the nation, with an estimated twenty-two thousand foreign-born Somalis and other East Africans living there; Lewiston, a small, overwhelmingly White city of thirty-six thousand in south-central Maine, has been transformed in the last two decades by the influx of several thousand African, mostly Somali, refugees.[54]

The Caribbeanization and Africanization of New York City's Black population is striking, and particularly evident to Blacks themselves. The large African and West Indian populations in New York City now provide the scope for ethnic identities to thrive within their own communities in private interactions and public spaces as well as in neighborhoods, schools, and workplaces where Africans, Afro-Caribbeans, and African Americans come into close contact. This is the case in some heavily Black middle-class suburbs in the New York City area that have drawn in a mix of Black Americans and Haitian and English-speaking Caribbean immigrants. Sociologist Orly Clerge describes how within these suburbs, national origin distinctions are central to "Black identity making"—remaking the category of Black imposed on them is the way she puts it—as the residents have constructed nationality narratives about how each group stacks up against the others. Interestingly, in the communities she studied, Black Americans' identity in terms of roots in the American South—as southern people—has been strengthened through direct contact with Black immigrants; they defined themselves as "authentic" Black people while Jamaicans saw Black Americans as lagging behind them culturally and Haitians as "beneath" them.[55] Black ethnicity also figures more in New York City's political world than it used to. In the early twentieth century, at a time of the first and much smaller West Indian immigration, Afro-Caribbean politicians in New York played down their ethnic identity in the quest for office, putting themselves forward as representatives of the broader Black community.[56] Today—when the number of West Indian immigrants in the city is more than ten times larger than it was in 1920—several neighborhoods with large concentrations of West Indians have provided the base for Afro-Caribbean politicians to use ethnic appeals to gain support in campaigns for local office.[57] Something similar has happened in South Florida, where efforts to woo the ethnic vote have played a role in the political campaigns of a growing number of Haitian and Jamaican Americans running for local and state positions.

Whites in cities like New York and Miami with large Afro-Caribbean populations have also become more attuned to national origin differences among Blacks. In the Miami area, with the largest Haitian community in the country and well-known Little Haiti neighborhood, Haitians have established "a solid and visible presence as full members of the ethnic mosaic." They are increasingly in evidence in the Miami-Dade political arena, with one of their own, for example, winning a seat in 2010 on the county commission and a few years later rising to become its chair.[58] In New York, research reports that White employers prefer West Indian immigrants over native Blacks for lower-level service jobs.[59] Beyond particular cities, the fact that around a quarter of Black students at the nation's colleges and universities are now immigrants or children of immigrants has no doubt sensitized a considerable number in the larger student body to ethnic distinctions in the Black population.[60]

In the context of increased Black ethnic diversity, new cultural mixtures have been developing. Some second- and later-generation West Indian New Yorkers have been actively forging ties with younger African Americans, trying to create a hybrid identity, based in part on melding aspects of Caribbean and African American popular culture. African immigrants have introduced their own cultural elements into New York's minority youth culture, including African-inspired clothing and hairstyles.[61] Looking ahead in New York as well as beyond, and at the potential for continued Black immigration from Africa and the Caribbean, it has even been suggested that the very meaning of African American could eventually change to reflect the growing ethnic complexity within the Black population so that the children and grandchildren of Black immigrants "will . . . become part of an African American population with fewer roots in centuries on American soil and that has been made more hybrid through intermixing with black immigrants."[62]

This is just a possibility, of course, and in the future. At present, immigration's ethnic diversification of the Black population has taken place in an era that has witnessed more dramatic change owing to civil rights–era laws and policies that, even in the face of enduring racism, made the United States a less overtly discriminatory country. To the extent that the position and views of Blacks have changed for the better in recent years—and there is no question that they have in many ways— this has much more to do with the effects of the civil rights movement and legislation than immigration. Post–civil rights America has seen an expansion of opportunities for Black Americans; the growing presence and visibility of Blacks in elite positions, from the heads of large companies and well-known media personalities to the 2008 election of the first Black president; a rise in the number and proportion of mixed-race (Black-White) individuals; and changing racial attitudes to Blacks, including evidence of a greater recognition among Whites of class differences among African Americans as well as more acceptance of middle- and upper-middle-class African Americans.[63]

And yet despite civil rights gains and large-scale Black immigration, anti-Black racism has had a tenacious hold in American society and stark social cleavages involving people of African ancestry remain. Continuity, in other words, is a critical part of the story. The history of Blacks in the United States—slavery, Jim Crow, ghettoization, and most recently massive incarceration—has led to the persistence of a strong color line and hard boundaries associated with Blackness. Whether native or foreign born, Blacks are still highly residentially segregated from Whites in the United States, more so than is the case for Asians and Hispanics.[64] The New York City metropolitan area, home to the largest Black immigrant population in the country, is one of the most segregated; most non-Black New Yorkers, as Clerge notes, never even visit Black urban areas, let alone heavily Black middle-class suburbs.[65] Rates of Black intermarriage with Whites in this country may have risen appreciably in recent decades, but they are lower than for Asians and Hispanics. This difference is not surprising. Anti-miscegenation laws forbidding Black-White marriage were still on the books in sixteen states in 1967 when the Supreme Court declared them illegal, and informal social barriers to the formation of intimate relationships between Blacks and Whites remain particularly strong. In line with these patterns, second-generation Afro-Caribbeans are much less likely than US-born Hispanics and Asians to have White partners.[66] According to a recent study, Black Caribbean and African immigrants who were unmarried when they arrived were more likely to marry native-born Blacks than White Americans, once again indicating the continuing power of race.[67] Regardless of where they or their parents were born, Blacks are especially vulnerable to discrimination in anonymous encounters in public places on the streets, in stores, and as the Black Lives Matter movement has powerfully brought out, with the police; Black men find it especially hard to be seen as independent from the stereotype of Black criminality.[68]

Notions of a monolithic Blackness, along with its many negative connotations, have been hard to change. For most non-Black Americans, as sociologist Mary Waters notes, "the image of blacks as poor, unworthy, and dangerous is still very potent"—unless those labeled Black prove otherwise.[69] Even when Black immigrants' ethnicity is recognized in certain places and contexts, they are still seen as part of the larger Black population in the United States; their racial status as Blacks, in other words, is always salient. Indeed, some Whites single them out as "better Blacks." In the public arena, their ethnicity may not be recognized at all; in the "hustle and bustle of daily life," strangers resort to racial stereo-typing, seeing Black immigrants simply as Black or "as 'Black' as African Americans."[70] As sociologist Milton Vickerman puts it, American society still has a powerful tendency to homogenize Blacks or what he calls the reflexive habit of identifying "Black" with "African American."[71] Although Black immigrants often seek to distinguish themselves from and escape the stigma associated with Black Americans, they also iden-tify with African Americans on the basis of the shared experience of being Black in American society and a linked racial fate outlook.[72] Rac-ism, in other words, is a unifying experience among those labeled Black in America.

For the US-born second generation, identity issues take on special significance. They have difficulty "marshaling their West Indianness [or Africanness] in a society that racializes black people with little regard to ethnicity."[73] Second-generation Afro-Caribbeans and Africans who continue to strongly identify with their ethnic backgrounds are aware that unless they are active in conveying their ethnic status to others, they are seen as African Americans and the status of their Black race is what matters in encounters with Whites. If they lack an accent or other cues to immediately signal their ethnicity to others, it is difficult to make their national origins known. As one second-generation Nigerian said, "A lot of white people see us as one. At the end of the day, we are just black. They don't see the green-white-green colors of the Nigerian flag on your forehead or the Jamaican flag."[74] In being seen as Black Ameri-can, they are subject to the same kind of racial prejudice and exclusion as Black Americans, finding themselves at the bottom of the racial hierarchy and without the leeway to fully define their own identities in America.[75]

Whiteness in Flux?

Has immigration changed the meaning of Whiteness? To some extent it has. In part owing to the continued decline in the proportion of non-Hispanic Whites, sizable numbers of White Americans, around a fifth according to some evidence, have not just become more conscious of their Whiteness but also feel that Whites' dominant position is under threat.[76]

These are perceptions, of course, not actual realities. Whiteness has long been associated with privilege in the United States, and if you look at a broad range of measures, including the proportion of millionaires and the number who hold powerful political positions, Whites' dominant position persists. For many, probably most, Whites, their White identity is still something they take for granted; the social and economic advantages that come with Whiteness generally remain invisible to them. Some do not even think of themselves as having a race at all.[77] From the perspective of non-Whites, moreover, Whites—usually meaning those with European origins—are seen as maintaining their privileged place at the top of the racial hierarchy today, just as in the past. No doubt most Whites themselves see it this way too.

Still, it is not the same world, racially speaking, for Whites now as it was fifty years ago as many have become "increasingly aware of themselves as one racial group in an increasingly diverse America."[78] The political campaigns and presidency of Trump brought this shift into prominent focus given his appeals to portions of the White population, especially Whites with low levels of education, who feel that their "natural" privileges as Whites are in jeopardy, indeed under siege, in the context of demographic change fueled by immigration and the economic, occupational, and political gains of non-White groups in the post–civil rights era. Not surprisingly, the elections of the nation's first Black president and more recently a vice president of Afro-Caribbean (as well as South Asian) ancestry dramatically symbolize the threat many Whites feel to their racial status.

In the midst of growing ethnic and racial diversity that has reached into large swaths of the country—not only in long-term gateway regions such as California, New York, and Texas, but also states in the Mountain West and Southeast like Colorado, Georgia, and the Carolinas— Whiteness is becoming more salient to many White Americans who believe that Whites are being left behind as non-Whites are undeservedly receiving advantages from government and elites.[79] More generally, historian Nell Irvin Painter argues that in the current period, what it means to be White has "fundamentally changed, from unmarked default to racially marked . . . from *of course* being beauty queen and *of course* being the cute young people selling things in ads to having to make space for other, nonwhite people to fill those roles." Or as political scientist Ashley Jardina observes, "In the minds of a lot of white people . . . it's about the erosion of the ability to define mainstream America as white."[80]

In this context, social psychologists report empirical evidence of what they call group-status threat—that is, the perceived threat, or fear, by many Whites that they will lose their privileged and dominant position in America's racial hierarchy. Many White Americans believe that anti-White discrimination is on the rise—a concern that according to recent research, increases with exposure to information about the growth of the racial minority share of the national population.[81] Indeed, according to a study of the political meaning of Whiteness, the media narrative about changing demographics threatening Whites' majority status is one of the factors contributing to a growing consciousness of White identity among conservative Americans.[82] In another study of White identity politics, Jardina argues that the expanding non-White population, feared loss of Whites' majority status, and increasing political and economic power of people of color in the United States have combined to bring "to the fore, for many whites, a sense of commonality, attachment, and solidarity with their racial group" as well as a "desire to protect their group's interests."[83]

Another change, though unusual, is worth noting, involving cracks in Whites' privileged position in an affluent northern California city transformed by a huge high-skilled Asian immigrant inflow. Cupertino, a high-tech hub known for being the headquarters of Apple, saw Asian Americans go from 23 to 64 percent of the population between 1990 and

2013, and the White share from 74 to 29 percent. High academic achievement is no longer associated with Whiteness; Whiteness has come to
stand for lower achievement, laziness, and academic mediocrity, while
Asianness is linked with academic success, hard work, and high achievement. "If you're really studious and you're white, you're called 'Asian at
heart,'" said one White high school student with some Asian ancestry
(her paternal grandmother was Japanese). "Just like there's the white
people who act Asian, there's the Asians who act white. They're the
Asians who party."[84] Whether this kind of downgrading of Whiteness
is happening in other affluent communities where those of Asian origin
are also numerically dominant, highly educated, and well-off (and
where, as in Cupertino, Blacks and Latinos are virtually absent) is an
open question.

In the context of today's politics of race, an additional and quite different development has emerged: the attempt by some groups to leave
the official Census category of White. After decades of being classified
as White by the Bureau of the Census, Middle Eastern and Arab American advocacy groups have been pressuring, so far unsuccessfully, for the
adoption of a separate Middle Eastern and North African category.
Partly this is an effort to increase opportunities for government funding
and gain more political clout as a minority group. Identity issues are also
at play. Many Middle Eastern and Arab Americans do not see themselves as White, nor do they feel comfortable checking White on Census forms because of their skin color, identification with their home
country, region of origin, or religion, and experiences with public sus-
picion and discrimination, especially among the many who are Muslim.
"I've always identified as not white," said a young woman of Iranian origin who grew up in Seattle, "and so the expectation to check off 'white'
on forms has never felt accurate to me."[85] The White designation on the
Census is seen by many people of Middle Eastern or North African
descent as an inaccurate description of their groups' position in American society. As the president of the American-Arab Anti-Discrimination
Committee put it a few years ago, "We're counted as 'white,' but we're
not treated as 'white.' . . . We're subjected to heightened security wher-
ever we go. Yet we're considered 'white.' That's our problem. We are

considered 'white' without the privileges of being 'white.'"[86] The desire to break away from official Whiteness thus reflects a belief by many North African and Middle Eastern Americans that unlike Whites, who continue to occupy a place at the top of the racial hierarchy, they are not really accepted as belonging there.

Looking Ahead

And so we come to the future. If the mass immigration of the past fifty years has been fundamental in transforming America's racial order, what about changes in the decades ahead? An understanding of the changes that have occurred in the recent as well as more distant past can provide some clues about what lies ahead—and sharpen our ability to identify forces that may generate changes in racial boundaries and meanings in tomorrow's America as well as the part that the descendants of post-1965 arrivals are likely to play. Those with recent immigrant roots are not, of course, the only ones whose experiences and trajectories will help to stimulate racial change in the future, but they almost certainly will have an outsize role, if only because they represent such a large share of the country's minority populations.

If there is one thing we can learn from the past, it is that the way Americans think about racial differences is highly changeable. To put it somewhat differently, we cannot assume that the views about race we take for granted today will persist, or that current racial and ethnic categories will have the same meaning in the future. In looking ahead, what seems plausible is an evolution toward a more fluid racial system in which the boundaries distinguishing non-Whites and Hispanics from Whites of European descent will depend less on phenotype than they do now. Racial distinctions will not disappear, nor will prejudice and discrimination. We are not about to become a postracial society, at least in the foreseeable future. But social class will become more important than observable physical features, including skin color, in how many people are seen and treated in a range of social settings and situations. For Asian Americans and Hispanics "who possess favorable [social] characteristics, such as high-status occupations," Alba has written, "and who interact with whites of equal status at work and in more informal settings, ethno-racial distinctions could fade into the background much of the time. This doesn't mean that they will be entirely forgotten or that such individuals will be immune from the insults of racism."[87] But they may be accepted in many contexts in the mainstream—a term Alba uses to refer to institutions, social milieus, and cultural spheres where the dominant group, Whites in the present time, feel "at home." For some parts of the minority population, race and ethnicity could be less about limitations and handicaps mainly imposed by the powerful majority on minority-group members, and more about identities over which they have greater control in their daily lives.[88]

At the same time, the growing rates of intermarriage between Whites and Asians, Blacks, and Hispanics, and the rising number of mixed-race Americans, seem destined to reduce the salience of current racial and ethnic boundaries, giving many mixed-race individuals the ability to move between racial categories, and indeed in some cases to be viewed by others as White. Perhaps we will even see the creation of altogether new racial categories along the lines of mestizos in Latin America.

A deeply troubling prospect is that Blacks will face greater exclusion than people in other racial groups—a legacy of this country's history of African slavery, and generations of legal segregation and systematic racial oppression. The barrier dividing those with visible African ancestry from other Americans seems especially intractable, and will make it harder for their racial identity to fade into the background. Moreover, for Asian Americans and Hispanics with lower social class status (in combination with phenotypic features such as darker skin color), ethnic and racial distinctions seem bound to remain an obstacle to inclusion.

Whatever the exact course, timing, and extent of change, what mechanisms will drive it? There is no question that a lot will be different from the past. Some factors that operated in an earlier era for the descendants of southern and eastern Europeans are unlikely to recur in the near future. Even if federal policies severely reduce immigrant inflows, it is doubtful that large-scale immigration will sink to the low levels of the 1930s and 1940s, when the ending of the massive inflows from eastern and southern Europe reduced fears of old-stock Americans about the deluge of "racial inferiors," and played a part in cultural assimilation. Nor is a huge expansion of higher education in the cards like the one facilitating upward mobility for the second generation after World War II. Jews and Italians were classified as White by the federal state in various contexts from the start—something that is not true for Black, Asian, and many Hispanic immigrants today. And in a pre–World War I era of virtual open immigration from Europe, Jewish and Italian immigrants who arrived then did not suffer from the disadvantages of undocumented status that currently affect about a quarter of the immigrant population, and have negative effects for the socioeconomic mobility of their American-born children.[89]

Still, there are some functional parallels with the past that may well play a role in the future. The remarkable economic prosperity of the post–World War II years may not be on the horizon today—indeed in the twenty-first-century US economy, low employment growth and rising or persistent economic inequality are worrisome prospects—but impending demographic changes will have positive effects for many in the second and third generations. The large, overwhelmingly White cohort of baby boomers born in the two decades after World War II is rapidly aging; as of 2020, they were between the ages of fifty-six and seventy-four. At the same time, a growing number of children and grandchildren of post-1965 immigrants will have college and university degrees.[90] As the baby boomers exit from the labor force and leadership positions, the shrinking number of native Whites in the working-age population is bound to create opportunities for a substantial number of the descendants of the post-1965 immigrants to move up the occupational ladder at least for several decades to come, including into positions at the top tiers of the workforce. Admittedly, this mobility is likely to be less sweeping and inclusive than it was in the mid-twentieth century, if only because of much higher levels of economic inequality today; nonetheless, there is every indication that it will be significant.[91] In fact already by 2015, more than 30 percent of those under the age of fifty in this country in the best-paying occupations were minorities, and a high proportion of them were Latinos or Asians of immigrant origin.[92]

In the past, as the children and grandchildren of southern and eastern European immigrants climbed the social and economic ladder, they increasingly mixed with those whose roots were in northern and western Europe in neighborhoods, at work, in colleges and universities, and eventually in marriage. In the process, as Alba and Nee note, "their perceived distinctiveness from the majority faded. . . . Intermarriage both marked the shift and accelerated it."[93] Looking ahead today, the increased interaction of non-Whites of immigrant origin with Whites on an equal basis in the very same settings may loosen racial boundaries in a similar way. So will the inevitability of their greater representation over time in prominent positions, from high-ranking political officials to media celebrities and corporate leaders.[94]

Intermarriage is likely to be an even more significant generator of racial change than it was in the mid-twentieth century. Whereas in the mid-twentieth century, Jews and Italians were transformed from inferior European races into White ethnics without undergoing alterations in phenotype, today when the language of color is so prominent in racial discourse, intermarriage and the blurring of pigmentation and physical differences among mixed-race offspring are often predicted to be key agents of change. "In a society characterized by increasing rates of movement, mixing, and intermarriage and by growing numbers of persons who assert their multiplicity," sociologists Stephen Cornell and Douglas Hartmann write, "[racial and ethnic] boundaries become difficult to maintain." A great many of the multi- or biracials are, and will be, the product of unions involving at least one child or grandchild of immigrants.[95]

Already, mixed-race unions have risen sharply. About one in six marriages contracted in 2015 involved partners of a different race or ethnicity—more than twice the rate in 1980—and most involved a White person with a minority partner. Equally revealing is another statistic: a little over 10 percent of infants born in the United States in 2017 had one White and one minority parent—a figure that has been rising steadily in recent decades and, like mixed unions, is expected to continue to increase.[96] We do not know how many of the children of mixed unions will identify themselves and be viewed by others as Whites, although research suggests that many will, at least some of the time, especially when it comes to those who are a combination of non-Hispanic White and Hispanic or non-Hispanic White and Asian. Much depends on physical appearance and whether a person is seen as looking like a member of the White group. A darker-skinned Pakistani American pediatrician in a mixed marriage, to give one example, writes of her three-year-old mixed-race daughter's "privilege of choice," being able to identify as Asian American or "easily pass for White," given her fair skin, auburn hair, and light brown eyes that "do not even hint at her Pakistani background."[97] The opportunity to choose is key. Mixed-race individuals who "look White" may, at least in some circumstances, opt to be recognized as White, if only to reap the advantages that Whites gain from being at the top of the racial hierarchy and avoid the disadvantages associated with being seen as a minority.

For many multiracials, the shift to Whiteness, to the extent that it happens, is a multigenerational process—often a product of two generations of mixed unions given that those with White and minority backgrounds frequently marry someone who is White.[98] Biracial cultural critic Thomas Chatterton Williams writes about his own and his daughter's racial position in American society—his as a Black man, and his young daughter as someone who looks and is treated as White. Williams, the son of a White mother and Black father, grew up thinking of himself as Black and is generally seen this way by others; he even once argued that Blacks of mixed-race heritage have an ethical obligation to identify as Black. Meanwhile, he produced a blond-haired, blue-eyed, and extremely fair-skinned daughter with his White French wife; most people who meet his daughter, he said in a recent interview, will—and will want to—call her White. Sociologist Herbert Gans predicts that two generations from now, many of the children resulting from mixed unions will be perceived by others and counted as Whites.[99]

It is too early to tell how Williams's daughter will identify—and be identified by others—when she becomes a teenager and then adult. The same goes for the three-year-old child of the Pakistani American pediatrician. Nor can we say, more generally, how extensive a trend toward Whitening will be among later generation mixes where neither partner is exclusively White but one or both have White ancestors. We need to keep in mind that the identities of mixed-race individuals, particularly those with single-race parents, are fluid and vary over time, no doubt more so than among those who are "unmixed" ethnically and racially. Many biracials identify themselves, and can appear to others, as mixed, minority, or White depending on the context and situation. At the same time, research indicates that the children of Black-White unions, with single-race Black and single-race White parents, face greater constraints in how they identify than other mixed-race Americans.[100] In an interview study with interracial couples and their children, Asians and Hispanics married to Whites felt that their US-born children had the option to identify along ethnic lines or as Whites without their decisions questioned by outsiders or institutions. Not so for the children of Black-White couples. Blacks married to Whites said that their children were often seen as Black only; they emphasized that nobody would take them seriously if they tried to identify their children as White, and their children chose to identify as Black rather than as multiracial or non-Black.[101]

Although a recent Pew Research Center survey on multiracial Americans found that nearly the same proportion of adults with a White-Asian (70 percent) and White-Black (61 percent) background identified as mixed race or multiracial, it was a different story when it came to how they thought others saw them. Six in ten with a Black-White background said a person passing them on the street would see them as Black (only 7 percent said a stranger would see them as White), while around two-fifths of those with an Asian-White background said they would be seen as White and a quarter as Asian. Multiracial adults with a Black background were much more likely than those without one to say they had been treated unfairly by an employer or unfairly stopped by the police. Having Black ancestry also meant less involvement with White relatives and friends. Black-White biracial adults had more Black than White close friends, much more contact with Black than White family members, and felt a much greater sense of acceptance from Black people than from Whites. By comparison, biracial Asian-White adults had more close friends who were White than Asian and more contact with White than Asian family members; most said they felt very well accepted by Whites.[102] One young Black-White biracial man summed up the feelings of many others like him in the survey: "No matter how I see myself, at the end of the day I'm still black."[103]

The experiences of mixed-race adults, in short, underscore the continued stigma attached to African descent, and suggest that those with visible Black ancestry will continue to confront more everyday prejudice and discrimination than other multiracials, lending support to concerns about the difficulties for Blacks well into the future. Meanwhile, many more, perhaps most, of the children of White-Asian and Anglo-Hispanic unions will find it easier to assert a mixed and even at times White identity.

In good part because of these identity patterns, some scholars have challenged Census projections of the end of a White majority by the mid-twenty-first century; they argue that the Census practice of classifying people with one White parent and one from an ethnoracial minority group as not White in its public presentations of data has exaggerated the decline of the White population.[104] Because many with a mixed background, especially Asian-Whites, Anglo-Hispanics, and those with one mixed-race and one White parent, are likely to present themselves as Whites at least some of the time—and because the number of mixed-race children is likely to increase in the near future—Alba predicts that the White majority in the United States will not end anytime soon. While some children with mixed origins could turn up in future Census and survey data as minority or non-White, others, he concludes, could turn up as White.[105]

Exactly how the future will unfold is of course hard to say. The processes of change are likely to be gradual, and involve struggles and divisions, as some groups attempt to alter existing racial boundaries and categories while others resist. Yet we can say with some certainty that the racial order will look different in forty or fifty years from the way it does now. Just as the incorporation of eastern and southern European immigrants and their descendants into mainstream American society stimulated changes in the meaning of race in the mid-twentieth century, so too the incorporation of the children and grandchildren of post-1965 immigrants will play a role in reshaping America's racial future. A hundred years ago, Americans would never have imagined that Jews and Italians would be thought of, in racial terms, in much the same way as old-stock White Anglo-Saxon Protestants. As many in the second and third generation achieve economic and occupational success, as the number of mixed unions inevitably grows, and as unforeseen economic and political changes occur, there will no doubt be equally astonishing surprises in the years ahead.

CHAPTER 3

Changing Cities and Communities

When I was growing up in the 1950s and 1960s, my neighborhood in the New York City borough of Queens was all White, or in current Census terminology, non-Hispanic White. The neighborhood was filled with homeowners who were mainly the children or grandchildren of Jewish, Italian, and Irish immigrants who had moved there for the relatively spacious houses with backyard gardens as well as the good schools. By now, more than fifty years later, the neighborhood has undergone a remarkable transformation, owing to a large degree to immigration. The White population has steadily shrunk as the descendants of earlier European immigrants grew old, many moved elsewhere, and few new Whites moved in. Post-1965 immigrants and their second-generation children have taken their place. By the second decade of the twenty-first century, non-Hispanic Whites were only around a third of the neighborhood's population, which had become nearly half Asian American (mostly Chinese and Korean) and a little over 10 percent Hispanic.[1]

This of course is just one neighborhood in one city, but it points to a basic fact: immigration, especially from Latin America and Asia, has been a fundamental force in changing America's cities, towns, and suburbs. In practically every city in the country, immigrants are now a visible presence—a marked difference from half a century ago. This is hardly surprising given the remarkable increase in the foreign-born population in the post-1965 years after a many decades-long hiatus in large-scale inflows. But the new demography—and geography—of immigration have also led to less expected shifts that have played a significant role in altering, and bringing renewed dynamism to, much of the nation's urban landscape and some rural communities as well.

The astonishing growth of the foreign-born population is evident not only in traditional urban gateways like New York City and Chicago but also in places with little history, or only a distant one, of immigration. The Dallas–Fort Worth–Arlington metropolitan area, to give one example, had about 34,000 immigrants in 1970; by 2014, the figure was 1.2 million. In metropolitan Orlando, Florida, in the same years, the immigrant population went from 13,000 to 391,000.[2] Indeed, immigrant growth in the Sun Belt and Midwest, including rural communities and small towns as well as larger metropolitan areas, is one of the big stories of immigration since the 1990s.

These growing numbers and new settlement patterns themselves ushered in or played a role in creating additional transformations. One is the revitalization of cities, including declines in urban crime in recent decades, and another is giving new life to parts of rural America. Immigration has also led to remarkable racial and ethnic diversification nearly everywhere in the country. New ethnic neighborhoods have sprung up, replete with a range of institutions catering to immigrants from particular countries and regions. Well-off Asian ethnoburbs are new on the scene. At the same time, polyethnic neighborhoods of incredible diversity in which long-established Whites and multiple immigrant groups live in close proximity are increasingly common. In fact, the all-White neighborhood has sharply declined in metropolitan areas around the country.

And there is a further type of change in cities and local communities: established mainstream community institutions in many places have been changing in form, organization, and character as, among other things, they introduce alterations, modifications, and innovations to adjust to newcomers' needs and demands. At first glance, some of these changes may seem relatively minor, but they should not be dismissed as trivial or simply surface-level adaptations or responses to immigration. They may well have long-lasting effects and implications. In some locations, altogether new institutions have emerged too. Certainly in the religious sphere, the mosques and temples newly created by Muslim and Hindu immigrants are notable additions in many cities and local communities. While the presence of new Muslim institutions in particular has often led to unease and sparked conflicts with long-established residents, an open question is whether eventually these institutions, like those introduced by Jews and Catholics of an earlier era, will come to be accepted as a normal feature of the religious landscape.

A New Urban Geography

The ethnic and racial changes that occurred in the New York City neighborhood of my childhood, as it went from all White in the mid-twentieth century to majority non-White today, reflect shifts in immigration patterns that have affected communities all around the country. I grew up in the years that followed many decades of low immigration levels. Together with the post–World War II baby boom (of which I was a part), this meant that in 1960, the nation was almost entirely native born—and overwhelmingly, 85 percent, non-Hispanic White. Once immigration picked up after 1970, especially in the 1990s and into the twenty-first century, traditional gateway cities like New York and Chicago saw their immigrant populations swell, in New York City going from a century low of around 1.4 million in 1970 to a little over 3 million in 2010, and in the city of Chicago increasing by roughly 70 percent between 1970 and 2000, from 374,000 to 629,000.[3] Immigration's impact on the two cities' ethnic and racial composition was nothing short of profound, especially as many established White New Yorkers and Chicagoans were leaving at the same time. New York is now a majority-minority city where non-Hispanic Whites, who made up 63 percent of the city in 1970, are now about a third; similarly, Chicago's non-Hispanic White population has declined in the last five decades from around 60 to 33 percent.[4]

But it is not just many traditional or long-standing immigrant cities that have seen their immigrant populations explode. So have cities that only began to become major immigrant destinations in the second half of the twentieth century like Miami, Los Angeles, Houston, and Washington,

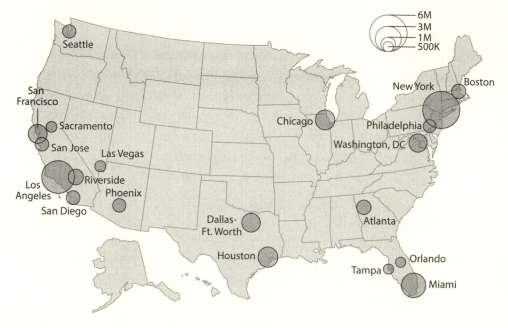

FIGURE 3.1. Twenty metropolitan areas with the largest number of immigrants in 2018.
Source: Budiman 2020.

DC. Indeed, the Los Angeles metropolitan area, along with New York's, are the two largest immigrant meccas, together home in 2014 to around a quarter of all the country's immigrants. All told, the five largest metropolitan area gateways, which also included Miami, Chicago, and Houston, housed nearly 40 percent of the total immigrant population.[5]

Other types of cities have also attracted large numbers of immigrants, with some of the newcomers arriving directly from abroad, and others moving from places in the country where they initially had settled. Metropolitan areas that sociologist Audrey Singer labels reemerging gateways, such as Minneapolis, Philadelphia, Baltimore, and Tampa, had many immigrants a century ago, but only again began to experience substantial immigration growth at the tail end of the twentieth century.[6] A striking development, as figure 3.1 shows, is the dispersion of immigrants to rapidly growing metropolitan areas in the Sun Belt that have become significant destinations for immigrants only recently. The Atlanta metropolitan area's foreign-born population grew by a whopping

817 percent between 1980 and 2000, from less than 50,000 to over 400,000, and by 2014 had almost doubled to 750,000. The Las Vegas area had only 35,000 immigrants in 1980; by 2000, there were about 260,000, and by 2014, there were 460,000. In the Phoenix area, the number of immigrants catapulted from 87,000 in 1980 to almost 500,000 twenty years later, and rose to over 650,000 by 2014—altogether a 653 percent increase. Whatever the exact numbers, the fact is that immigrants have been a growing fraction of the population in virtually all major metropolitan areas in the country. Moreover, in almost half of the central cities with more than 200,000 people, the foreign born represent at least 15 percent of the population.[7]

Today's immigrant settlement patterns, it should be noted, differ in some important ways from those of the past. In the early twentieth century, the majority of immigrants lived in the industrializing cities of the Northeast and Midwest, with New York, Chicago, Boston, and Philadelphia among the top destinations. By 2010, metropolitan areas in the South and West had become home to more than half of all immigrants, reflecting broader population shifts in these parts of the country.[8] Large numbers of immigrants now live in metropolitan areas that have had little historical experience with extensive immigration. Also in another contrast with the past, many new arrivals head to the suburbs right from the start. A hundred years ago, immigrants went to cities where they could be close to jobs, but now housing and economic opportunities draw many to the suburbs as the dispersion of new economy services has led to job growth outside urban boundaries in suburban areas. The result is that immigrants have been diversifying suburbs in many significant ways.[9]

As of 2010, only a third of US immigrants lived in the central cities of the hundred-largest metropolitan areas, whereas 51 percent lived in the suburbs of these cities.[10] The post–World War II years witnessed a suburban explosion. This was a time when newly built and expanding suburbs became bastions for native Whites fleeing the problems and often ethnoracial diversity of central cities. What has been called Whites-only suburbanization was aided and abetted by government policies, from exclusionary local zoning ordinances to federal subsidies for subdivisons built on the condition that African Americans be barred.[11] Since the 1970s, suburbia has changed a great deal. The percentage of renters has increased, and suburban poverty has grown substantially. And many predominantly White suburbs have become much more ethnically and racially diverse, in good part owing to immigrant inflows. The suburban areas on the edge of Washington, DC, to take one region, have experienced a breathtaking pace of change: a number of suburbs that had been over 90 percent White in 1970 had become majority-minority areas by 2000, including large numbers of immigrants from Asia and Latin America who moved there for, among other things, the relatively affordable housing.[12] In metropolitan Atlanta, according to historian Mary Odem, 95 percent of the foreign born lived in the suburbs in 2005. Many Hispanic and Asian immigrants were drawn to once largely White inner-ring communities north of the central city that experienced rapid job and population growth in the 1980s and 1990s. A common path for Latin American as well as Vietnamese and Korean immigrants was to start out in less desirable suburban areas as renters in apartment complexes built in the 1970s, and later leave for better housing districts when their economic position improved; they often pooled resources with family members as a way to purchase one- and two-story ranch houses in formerly all-White subdivisions that are now home to increasingly diverse racial and ethnic populations.[13]

Urban and Rural Revitalization

Immigrants, it has often been said, fueled the growth of urban America at the turn of the twentieth century. Between 1900 and 1920, New York City grew by more than two million; Chicago, then the second city, grew by one million; and Philadelphia, the third-largest city, expanded by over half a million, in good part owing to huge immigrant inflows from southern, eastern, and central Europe. Immigrants literally built the roads, bridges, tunnels, and subways in these and other major cities at that time, and supplied the workforce that helped turn many into flourishing industrial economies.

In recent decades, immigrants once again have been a boon to cities and their larger metropolitan areas. They played a key role in the growth of places such as Las Vegas, Nevada, and Orlando, Florida, that were becoming major metropolitan centers for the first time. They also helped to revive a number of cities that were losing population, with a dramatic case being New York City, where the population declined pre-cipitously in the 1970s by over 800,000 as "White flight" to the suburbs and other parts of the country escalated. From 2000 to 2006, according to the Census Bureau, without immigration the New York metropolitan area would have lost almost 600,000 in total population, while metro-politan Los Angeles would have declined by more than 200,000, San Francisco by 188,000, and Boston by 101,000. Of the ninety-one large metropolitan areas that gained population between 2010 and 2018, fif-teen, including New York and Philadelphia, would have lost population were it not for immigration. At the same time, immigration helped to mitigate population decline in many smaller cities and metropolitan areas, such as Rockford, a city of around 150,000 in northern Illinois where it reduced population loss and began to revitalize an aging workforce.[14]

The added numbers of immigrants boosted the economies of metro-politan areas, providing labor for growing sectors and propping up some existing ones. Immigrants created an array of new businesses every-where. They contributed to the support and expansion of public and private sector jobs because they not only provide but also purchase goods and services. In this sense, they have been an important force for change—and especially in good times, economic health and prosperity (see chapter 4).

And then there is crime. A common belief is that rising immigration leads to rising crime rates, but this is a myth, not reality. One can even say that immigration has made the United States safer. "If you want to be safe," sociologist Robert Sampson comments, "move to an immi-grant city."[15]

Immigration, experts agree, was a factor behind the decline in violent crime in urban America from the late 1990s and into the early 2000s. By the second decade of the twenty-first century, murder rates in the country, the most reliable indicator of violence, were back to those of the early 1960s, and in fact like those of the tranquil 1950s. In 2014, New York City had fewer than 330 murders, then the lowest number since comparable records were kept, and despite a population larger than in 1990; violent crime in Los Angeles declined markedly too, as it did across the country.[16] To be sure, a range of factors are responsible for these dramatic drops, including aggressive policing, the decline in crack cocaine use, increased prison populations, and the aging of the population. But in cities with large numbers of new arrivals, immigration is also at play.[17]

What accounts for immigration's role in reducing urban violent crime? For one thing, immigrants are much less likely to commit crimes than the native born mainly because they are a favorably self-selected population predisposed to low crime: ambitious, motivated to work, and concerned with avoiding deportation. Something else is also going on at the neighborhood level, where research indicates that the presence of large numbers of immigrants seems to lower rates of crime and violence. The neighborhood context of concentrated immigration itself may have a protective effect, perhaps because of population growth and the reduction in housing vacancies—and hence more "eyes on the street" for informal neighborhood monitoring.[18]

Immigrants have brought other positive changes to urban neighborhoods. Many northern cities had fallen on hard times in the post–World War II years as large numbers of White residents moved away to the suburbs and the Sun Belt, and their populations declined. Without immigration, it is likely that many apartments and houses in the neighborhoods left behind would have been vulnerable to abandonment. Or to put it another way, immigrants helped many deteriorating neighborhoods make a comeback in the latter part of the twentieth and early years of the twenty-first century.

In bringing new vitality and helping to reestablish a commercial base in local areas that were in disrepair in cities like Minneapolis and Philadelphia, immigrants gave the neighborhoods a new character and critical economic boost.[19] Brighton Beach is an example in New York City. By the mid-1970s, this oceanside neighborhood in the southern portion of the borough of Brooklyn was in decline; apartments stood empty as elderly eastern European Jewish immigrants who arrived in the early twentieth century died or left for Florida, and the main commercial avenue had turned into a decaying strip of old stores. The massive influx of Soviet Jews in the next two decades filled apartments and turned the avenue into a thriving commercial center, replete with Russian restaurants, nightclubs, state-of-the-art electronics stores, and clothing boutiques selling European designer clothing. In Chicago, in a not dissimilar way, Mexican immigrants breathed new life into the Little Village neighborhood on the southwest side that had suffered losses as White ethnics who had lived there for decades moved away. As the newcomers lifted the neighborhood's population in the 1970s, 1980s, and 1990s, they also spurred local economic growth and transformed a fading shopping district into one of the most active commercial corridors in the city.[20]

And we should not forget immigration's impact in revitalizing some parts of rural America as well. Without a doubt, the story of much of rural America, as one journalist puts it, is one of relentless economic decline or, in another phrase, the intensifying ruralization of distress.[21] Yet immigration is one of the bright spots, slowing the pace of population loss in many rural areas and in some cases enabling the population to grow. According to demographer Daniel Lichter, the new racial and ethnic diversity in rural America over the past few decades is one of the most important and least anticipated demographic changes in recent US history.[22]

This diversity has been overwhelmingly propelled by Latino (heavily foreign-born) in-migration, which rejuvenated many small towns, often in parts of the rural Midwest experiencing chronic population declines where Whites have been aging and dying, and in the case of young people, leaving for brighter prospects elsewhere.[23] Latino immigrants were drawn by job opportunities in clearly defined industries such as meat-processing or meatpacking plants, which have moved to rural American areas in search of low-wage labor.[24] Worthington, Minnesota, to give one example, is home to a pork-processing plant owned by JBS, one of the world's largest meat-processing companies. Thirty years ago many feared that Worthington would become a ghost town, but instead immigrants flooded in. The number of Hispanics went from 392 in 1990 to 4,521 in 2010, or from 4 to 35 percent of the population; over half of the Hispanics in 2000 were foreign born.[25] In Lexington and Schuyler, Nebraska, to mention two other towns with meatpacking plants, Hispanics are now the majority of the population. Certainly the rapid immigrant influx to towns like these has often sparked tensions with the local population, and placed demands on local services such as health and education. Still, immigrants have provided a lifeline in many distressed small towns in rural America, increasing or stabilizing the population, and providing a source of economic dynamism as they have added to the tax base, spent money locally, injected cash in housing markets, and helped keep schools viable.[26]

Immigrant-Driven Diversification

Immigration is so closely tied to ethnic and racial diversity that it is hard to separate one from the other. As I already indicated, ethnic and racial diversification is perhaps the most dramatic transformation that the post-1965 immigration has brought to America's cities and metropolitan areas. Given that around 45 percent of the nation's forty-five million immigrants are Hispanic and more than a quarter are Asian, this is not unexpected. Still, the extent to which immigration has led to new diversity in American cities, suburbs, and towns is remarkable. By 2010, 22 percent of the residents of central cities were Hispanic, up from 3 percent in 1970, while Asian Americans went from 1.5 to almost 8 percent over the same period; suburbs experienced a similar change, with Hispanics' share at 15 percent and Asian Americans' share at 6 percent in 2010—a huge increase from forty years before.[27]

Even in many large cities that have had substantial Hispanic populations for a long time, the numbers have exploded in the last half century owing to immigration and births; the countries of newcomers have multiplied as well. Consider just a few illustrations. Not only did New York City's Hispanic population double between 1970 and 2015, but its ethnic makeup has been transformed. The days are gone when Hispanic meant Puerto Rican in New York City. Puerto Ricans now account for under a third of the Hispanic population, outnumbered by a combination of Dominicans, Mexicans, Ecuadorians, Colombians, and other Latin Americans, the majority of them first-generation immigrants and their second-generation children. In Chicago, Mexican inflows have mainly been responsible for the enormous growth in the Hispanic population, which went from a bit over 7 percent of the city in 1970 to 29 percent in 2019, when those of Mexican ancestry were the vast majority of all Hispanics. Chicago's Hispanics now rival African Americans and nearly equal non-Hispanic Whites in size.[28] Houston, currently the nation's fourth-largest city, went from 18 percent Hispanic in 1980 to 44 percent in 2010, while the non-Hispanic White population shrank from 52 percent to 26 percent in the same period. Demographer William Frey predicts that the rise of Hispanics as the "major city minority" in recent decades foreshadows tomorrow's urban America.[29]

Already the phrase Latinization accurately describes what has happened in a number of cities where Hispanics have grown to around half of the population, and sometimes significantly more, with much of the gain triggered by immigrant and domestic migrant inflows as well as natural increase.[30] We are not just talking about cities on or close to the US-Mexican border. A striking case is Miami-Dade County, which was only about 5 percent Hispanic in 1960 (and 80 percent non-Hispanic White) and is now a Latino global metropolitan giant, with a whopping 69 percent of its population Hispanic in 2019; the city of Miami, on its own, was 73 percent Hispanic in that year.[31] The mass exodus of Cubans after the 1959 revolution on the island provided the roots for a huge Cuban community that came to dominate the city economically and politically, later joined by large numbers from countries in Central and South America. The city of Los Angeles once may have been in Mexico— it became incorporated as a US city in 1850 after the Mexican-American War—but in 1960 it was less than 10 percent Hispanic (and overwhelmingly non-Hispanic White); by 2019, Hispanics, mostly of Mexican origin, were nearly half (49 percent) of the population.[32] As of 2010, more than two dozen US cities over a hundred thousand were majority Hispanic, nearly all in Southern California and Texas, but also among them were two northern New Jersey cities that have attracted a mix of Caribbean, and South and Central American newcomers: Elizabeth, nearly two-thirds Hispanic, and Paterson, nearly three-fifths in 2017, with the latter also home to large numbers of Turks and Arab Americans.[33]

The metropolitan areas with the fastest-growing Hispanic populations are predominantly in the nation's southeast. Among the areas with at least a hundred thousand Hispanics, Charlotte and Raleigh, North Carolina, and Nashville, Tennessee, led the list, each of which experienced more than a 1000 percent increase in its Hispanic population in the twenty-year period between 1990 and 2010.[34] The old Black-White binary that dominated the South is being altered by these growing Hispanic (as well as Asian) inflows. In 1970, virtually all the residents of Charlotte and Raleigh were either Black or White; by 2010, Hispanics were slightly more than 10 percent of the population in both cities. Latinos, as geographer Jamie Winders writes, have brought a new *sonido* (sound) and beat to Nashville, another Black-White city until the 1990s. Already by 1996, Nashville had almost thirty Hispanic-owned restaurants, twenty-two Hispanic soccer teams, two Spanish-language newspapers, two Spanish radio stations, and thirteen churches with Spanish-language services.[35]

Asian immigrants and their children have also changed the racial and ethnic landscape in the nation's metropolitan areas. Of course, East Asian groups, most notably Chinese, have been a presence in many cities for over a century and a half—New York, San Francisco, and Los Angeles among them, each with a famous old Chinatown. But the number of Chinese and other Asian Americans increased there by leaps and bounds in the post-1965 years after the severe restrictions on Asian immigration were lifted. And national origin groups that barely existed before 1970 are now part of the Asian mix. In New York City, the number of Asian Americans increased more than twentyfold between 1960 and 2015, now 14 percent (over 1 million) of the total population up from less than 1 percent (about 43,000) in 1960. Asian in New York City no longer means only Chinese, but also Indian, Korean, Filipino, Bangladeshi, and Pakistani to name the largest non-Chinese groups in the city today. Los Angeles County, with around 1.5 million Asian Americans in 2019, has the largest Asian American population of any county in the

United States, with the Chinese, Filipinos, Koreans, Japanese, and Vietnamese the most sizable groups. In the city of San Francisco, Asian Americans are about a third of the population, or roughly 300,000 people; the Chinese and Filipinos are the two biggest groups.

Asian Americans also have spread out to and grown in number in areas where they were hardly present half a century ago, such as Houston, Las Vegas, Minneapolis, and Philadelphia.[36] The Asian American (mostly Indian and Chinese) population of Raleigh, North Carolina, which was slightly over 17,000 in 2010, may be tiny by New York, Los Angeles, and San Francisco standards, but it is a huge increase from the less than 400 Asian Americans in 1970. This is just one of many examples all around the country.

As for the impact of Black immigrants, they may represent only about 10 percent of all immigrants in the United States, but Caribbean and African immigrants, too, have added ethnic diversity to the Black populations of a number of metropolitan areas where they are substantial in number, most notably New York–Newark–Jersey City and Miami–Fort Lauderdale–West Palm Beach, where as of 2013, they were 28 and 34 percent, respectively, of the Black population; in the Washington, DC, metropolitan area, 15 percent of Blacks were foreign born.[37] To what extent the descendants of Black immigrants may eventually meld into and become largely indistinguishable from the African American population is hard to predict, but there is no doubt that the first generation has brought African and Caribbean sounds, flavors, and festivals to areas of the cities and suburbs where large numbers have settled, and thus are another component of immigrant-driven diversification.

Changing Neighborhoods

This brings us to neighborhoods, where immigrants—as well as the native born—live out important aspects of their lives, from making family homes and developing friendships to going to school and frequenting houses of worship. Immigrants have transformed neighborhoods all over the United States. In the process, they have re-created old neighborhood patterns with contemporary twists and generated some altogether new arrangements.

The ethnic neighborhood, to mention one of the most familiar types, is a timeworn feature of immigrant America. Looking back in time, Manhattan's Lower East Side has sometimes been called America's most famous immigrant neighborhood, which at the turn of the twentieth century had become a Jewish cosmopolis. The touchstones of the eastern European shtetl were all around: synagogues, burial societies, kosher butchers, and Yiddish-language newspapers. In New York, and many other cities such as Baltimore and Philadelphia, Little Italies flourished where "people speak their own language, trade in stores kept by countrymen, and put their savings in Italian banks. . . . The stores bear Italian names, the special bargains . . . are advertised in Italian, and they offer for sale the wines and olive oils, 'pasta,' and other favorite foods of the people." Little Italies were further subdivided into subnational colonies as villagers from the same province or region clustered in specific locations. In South Philadelphia, migrants from the province of Catanzaro in the Calabria region clustered along Ellsworth Street, while the area around Eighth and Fitzwater Streets was home primarily to people from Abruzzi.[38]

Much of course is familiar about today's immigrant ethnic neighborhoods. Even the terms to describe them sometimes echo those of the past, as the Little Italies have given way to Little Saigons in states like California, Virginia, and Texas along with a well-known (although now gentrifying) Little Haiti in Miami. The social dynamics are similar too. As in earlier immigration eras, many new arrivals from the same country, region, or ethnic group have gravitated to areas with kinfolk and friends, allowing them to find comfort, security, and support in an environment of familiar languages, stores, and cultural institutions, such as churches, synagogues, and mosques, as well as housing that is affordable. They are also better shielded from prejudice and discrimination in finding a place to live and in community life.

But if contemporary ethnic neighborhoods have arisen for the same reasons and function for new arrivals in many of the same ways that they did in previous eras, cultural features and institutions within them reflect the character of today's Latino, Asian, and Caribbean immigrant groups as well as contemporary social realities. In this sense, they represent some genuine changes in the landscape. Or one might say, ethnic neighborhoods have reemerged in the United States in modern-day guise. Among the new features are Islamic mosques, Buddhist and Hindu temples, and Latino Pentecostal churches; cell phone companies and money transfer services; and ethnic restaurants with new cuisines that may cater beyond an ethnic clientele to serve adventurous and educated middle-class patrons searching for authenticity and a foreign culinary experience close to home.[39] Whereas in the late nineteenth and early twentieth centuries, large and dense immigrant ethnic settlements in northern gateway cities typically arose in overcrowded working-class areas with substandard housing, today many have sprouted up in communities that previously had been home to middle- and lower-middle-class natives who had decamped to the suburbs and Sun Belt.[40]

Ethnic neighborhoods created and sustained by new arrivals are also more likely than in the past to be a suburban as well as urban phenomenon. As today's immigrants have moved to suburban areas—which they have done in growing numbers—they have often gone to neighborhoods with those who hail from the same country or region. Langley Park / Adelphi, an inside-the-beltway suburb in Prince George's County near the northern boundary of the District of Columbia, has been described as a Latin American enclave, with Salvadorans accounting for more than a third of the foreign-born residents, Guatemalans another 15 percent, and other Spanish-speaking immigrants an additional 12 percent in 2000: "*Pupusa* trucks and fruit venders line the main streets and serve a steady stream of customers on foot and in cars. Locals refer to it as the Barrio de Langley Park, and many immigrants consider the area a cultural center for the Salvadoran community."[41] Brentwood, a suburban hamlet of around sixty thousand in Suffolk County some forty miles from New York City, has such a large Salvadoran population that El Salvador has a consulate there.

As part of the immigrant suburbanization process, what social scientists label "ethnoburbs" have emerged in many metropolitan areas, especially on the two coasts. Ethnoburbs are concentrations of socioeconomically well-off coethnic immigrant families in advantaged suburbs, where immigrants frequently mix with native families of similar status. They are associated today with Asian American groups.[42] In some ways, contemporary ethnoburbs are reminiscent of a type of earlier suburban community. Think of the heavily "Jewish suburbs" that developed in the mid-twentieth century, peopled by the adult second-generation children of eastern European Jewish immigrants who moved there from nearby cities in search of better housing, in owner-occupied single-family homes, and excellent schools. Affluent Great Neck, located in Nassau County, not far from the New York City border, had become majority Jewish by the 1960s; Shaker Heights and Cleveland Heights, Ohio, outside Cleveland, along with the Skokie and Highland Park suburbs of Chicago, among others, were heavily Jewish and prosperous suburban communities too. Well-to-do Jews sought out these suburbs partly because they did not feel welcome elsewhere, and ethnic- and kinship-based real estate markets led more of them over time to join earlier pioneers. Economically and occupationally successful Jews also sought a sense of being at home—that is, feeling comfortable in areas where they were a majority or substantial presence, and that boasted synagogues, "Jewish" delicatessens, and neighbors with whom they shared a common bond of Jewishness. In a real sense, they were creating an affluent version of the old ethnic urban neighborhood, or as sociologist Herbert Gans put it in his 1950s study of the Chicago suburb of Park Forest, an adaptation of Jewish life to the suburban environment.[43]

Today, well-off Asian Americans are doing something similar, although they are bringing different cultural features with them. Also, Asian Americans in ethnoburbs are more likely to be recent immigrants as compared to the mainly second-generation, post–World War II Jewish suburbanites now that a much larger proportion of today's Asian arrivals are highly educated and high-income earners than were Jewish immigrants of a century ago. On the East Coast, one ethnoburb is Fort Lee, New Jersey, across the George Washington Bridge from Manhattan, where in 2018, Asian Americans (mostly Korean and Chinese) were 40 percent of the residents, while Whites constituted 43 percent (down from 97 percent in 1970).[44] Asian ethnoburbs are especially noteworthy

in California, where they have dramatically altered the suburban land-
scape, transforming communities that used to be predominantly non-
Hispanic White. One account lists a dozen Chinese ethnoburbs in the
Los Angeles and San Francisco Bay areas in 2010 in which Chinese
Americans were a fifth or more of the population; in all but one, Asian
Americans altogether were over 50 percent.[45] The degree to which the
Silicon Valley region is "ethnoburban," sociologist Tomás Jiménez
writes, is palpable in a drive down any of the main thoroughfares, reveal-
ing "ethnically themed strip malls that house restaurants, grocery stores,
bakeries, and tutoring centers."[46]

Perhaps the best-known ethnoburb is Monterey Park, which has
been called the first suburban Chinatown. This small suburban city of
around sixty thousand east of downtown Los Angeles in the San Gabriel
Valley was transformed from an Anglo bedroom town—99.9 percent
non-Hispanic White in 1950—to a community that by the mid-1980s,
had an Asian American majority and visible presence of immigrant Chinese. By 2010, nearly half the population was Chinese American, and
altogether, around two-thirds were Asian American. In addition to a
broad range of upscale restaurants, trendy cafés and coffeehouses, huge
supermarkets, and professional parks, there are a host of Chinese language schools and ethnic institutions offering young children and youth
language and cultural classes, enrichment courses in Chinese music,
folk dance, and calligraphy, and preparation for SAT exams. New religious organizations, including Buddhist houses of worship and Chinese
Protestant churches, have taken root. Political institutions reflect Chinese influence as well; Monterey Park has had a series of Chinese American mayors since 2006, with the first, Lily Lee Chen, born in China and
brought up in Taiwan, elected in 1983.[47]

Also striking is the decline of all-White neighborhoods in metropolitan areas—a development in which immigration has played a significant
role. Looking back in time, immigration inflows in the late nineteenth
and early twentieth centuries gave rise to urban neighborhoods with a
welter of groups from different countries, and in fact ethnically identified neighborhoods then were actually often quite diverse in terms of
residents' national origins. But as far as we know, they did not contain

much of a presence of those from the then-dominant White Protestant group, which one might say were the established native Whites of their time. Today's settlement patterns are different, with the development of many communities that are home to non-Hispanic Whites in addition to people from multiple immigrant groups.[48]

In metropolitan regions that have added significant numbers of immigrants in recent decades, few neighborhoods with many White residents are racially exclusive anymore, which as Alba notes, is a momentous change from the situation prevailing a half century ago.[49] In a study of 24 highly diverse metropolitan regions in the year 2000, three-quarters of the neighborhoods mixed a significant presence of Whites with that of one or more minority groups.[50] In nearly half of all the neighborhoods, Whites lived with substantial numbers of both Asian Americans and Hispanics, reflecting the broad impact of immigration. The change from 1980 was remarkable: of the 1,210 all-White neighborhoods in these metropolitan areas in 1980, only 333 remained all White in 2000.[51]

Admittedly, White flight has occurred in some of these diverse neighborhoods, especially as the proportion of minority residents has risen. Yet for Whites wanting to stay in what are now highly diverse metropolitan regions—if only because of economic opportunities there—it is increasingly hard to avoid racial and ethnic minorities in their communities altogether, even though they may be able to find a mixed neighborhood with a high percentage of Whites.[52]

What does the growth of neighborhood diversity mean for on-the-ground relationships? After all, living near to and seeing members of other ethnic and racial groups on the street and in public places is no guarantee of friendly relations. People in different groups may pass each other by with little recognition or interaction; they may even hunker down, distrusting their neighbors and withdrawing into mutually antagonistic subcommunities.[53] In formerly all-White towns and small cities with no recent memory of immigration, the sudden upsurge in newcomers, especially undocumented and low-skilled Latinos, has given rise to fears among many longtime residents that immigrants are bringing crime and other social problems as well as undermining traditional American ways.[54]

Yet there are also some encouraging signs. Over time, long-established residents tend to become used to new immigrant arrivals as interaction and communication develop; greater familiarity often has a way of leading to accommodation and eventually in some instances meaningful acceptance. In general, evidence from intergroup contact studies indicates that face-to-face interpersonal contact typically reduces intergroup prejudice.[55] Other research suggests that in highly diverse urban neighborhoods, ethnic and racial diversity frequently comes to be seen as a normal and taken-for-granted part of social life, or what anthropologist Susanne Wessendorf calls commonplace diversity in public space. In the super-diverse London community she studied, private relations were fairly parochial, with people's closest ties tending to be with those most like themselves in terms of ethnicity, race, and social class. At the same time, an ethos of mixing emerged in which it came to be expected that people should mingle and interact with residents of other backgrounds in public spaces and associations.[56] No doubt this situation has also developed in many diverse American neighborhoods. Interestingly, the American cities and metropolitan areas with the largest immigrant populations are often those where long-established Whites have the most positive attitudes to ethnoracial diversity; the most negative attitudes are frequently found in places such as heavily White peripheral suburbs, exurbs, and rural areas with few immigrants and low ethnoracial diversity.[57]

New and Changing Institutions

Changing neighborhoods go hand in hand with new or changing institutions. One domain in which this is evident is in the religious sphere. In earlier eras, the inflow of millions of Catholic and Jewish immigrants led to the establishment of a huge network of Catholic churches and hundreds of synagogues along with related institutions, prominent among them Catholic parochial schools, which by 1920, enrolled nearly two million pupils at the elementary level in local parishes around the country. The immigration of the last half century has added another layer of diversity to American religious life, giving rise to new religious institutions in many communities and altering the character of long-established congregations in others.

Given that most immigrants in the United States are Christian—about 70 percent of all the foreign born—it is not surprising that new ethnic or panethnic congregations have developed among them, from Korean American Protestant to Latino evangelical churches featuring services and programs geared to the needs of the first and second generations.[58] Millions of Latino immigrants and their children, with origins in predominantly Catholic Latin America, have put their stamp on the US Catholic Church as a growing number of local churches offer masses in Spanish and some have incorporated customs such as devotional practices dedicated to the Virgin of Guadalupe, the patron saint of Mexico.[59] The non-Christian immigrant groups have brought especially dramatic changes to the religious landscape, with Muslims and Hindus standing out; the overwhelming majority of Muslims (three-quarters) and Hindus (nearly all) in this country are immigrants or children of immigrants.[60] By 2010, according to one estimate, over 2,000 Muslim mosques were scattered around the country, up from 1,200 just ten years before; there were also an estimated 235 private elementary and secondary Islamic schools in the United States.[61] The number of Hindu temples had grown to more than 400 by the second decade of the twenty-first century, with many of them on the East Coast in the greater New York City area.

Admittedly, Muslims and Hindus are small in number; in 2014, each represented just 1 percent of the total US population and around 4 percent of foreign-born residents.[62] Nevertheless, Muslims in particular have had an outsized impact, although this is mostly—and unhappily—owing to negative attitudes toward them. The very presence of new Muslim immigrants has been fraught in the wake of terrorist incidents in the United States and elsewhere, including the September 11, 2001, attacks on the twin towers of the World Trade Center in New York City as well as the widespread framing of Islam as a security threat. Anti-Muslim sentiment received a boost under President Trump, who banned visitors from several Muslim-majority countries, and stoked prejudice and fears with anti-Muslim rhetoric in tweets and speeches. Even before his presidency, a 2002–3 national survey found that about two-fifths of Americans said that they would not welcome a stronger presence of Muslims in the United States (a third said this about Hindus); four in ten Americans said that they would not be happy about a mosque being built in their neighborhood (about a third said that they would be bothered by the idea of a Hindu temple being nearby).[63] In a number of places, the building of mosques has been met by open hostility, attempts to block their construction, and occasionally even violence and arson. Not only do many Americans continue to view Islam as an existential threat, but anti-Muslim sentiment could be intensified by unforeseen political events. That about one in ten adult Muslim immigrants are from sub-Saharan Africa adds further complexity since, as sociologist Tod Hamilton notes, they are likely to face threefold discrimination as Muslims, Blacks, and immigrants.[64]

Yet there is another, more optimistic side to the story. With greater familiarity, many long-established Americans are becoming more accustomed to Muslims and mosques in their midst. That a substantial proportion of foreign-born Muslims are well educated and middle class may also reduce hostility toward them and their institutions, and give their children advantages in getting ahead. Many Muslim immigrants and particularly their US-born children are adopting American customs and ideas, including a pride in being American, even as they have a strong Muslim identity.[65] Whatever the reason, a Pew Research Center survey in 2017 found that Americans expressed more positive feelings toward Muslims (as well as Hindus) than they had in 2014, although it should be said that they remained coolest toward Muslims than any other religious group.[66] As for Muslims themselves, while around two-thirds of the foreign born and 90 percent of the US born in a Pew survey said that there is a lot of discrimination against Muslims, about three-quarters of foreign-born Muslims and a third of the US born said that the American people as a whole are friendly toward Muslim Americans. There are also many instances of cooperation and amicable relations between Muslims and other Americans. In discussing efforts to create an Islamic Center of New England in the Boston area, religious studies scholar Diana Eck describes "a saga of relations with non-Muslim neighbors . . . from the threats and arson attack [in 1990] to the zoning battles and finally the successful effort to build new bridges of relations with other communities of faith." More than a decade later in the small south Texas city of Victoria, after a 2017 arson attack devastated a mosque and Islamic community center, local Jewish and Christian congregations responded by offering to host Muslim services in their buildings, and rallies and prayer vigils were held in the community "to reject hate."[67]

There are some other hopeful developments. Despite pockets of opposition, about 40 percent of the mosques in the United States in 2010 were built in the previous decade, and no doubt more have been constructed since then. A growing number of Muslim Americans with immigrant origins have been running for electoral office; in 2019, Somali-born Ilhan Omar and second-generation Palestinian Rashida Tlaib became the first female Muslims in Congress, representing districts in Minnesota and Detroit, respectively. Surveys show a declining number of Muslims saying that all or most of their close friends are Muslim, indicating a greater branching out beyond the Muslim community.[68] Looking ahead, the future will bring increased intermingling of the children of Muslim immigrants with long-established Americans in neighborhoods, workplaces, and schools, which can increase comfort with people of Muslim background and their institutions, reduce prejudice, and lead to friendships and even intermarriage.

Ultimately, a key question is whether Islam will eventually attain the charter status now occupied by Protestantism, Catholicism, and Judaism, and whether Muslim religious institutions will come to be seen as part of mainstream America. It is too early to tell. It is now commonplace to think of the United States as a Judeo-Christian nation and a tripartite perspective of Protestant, Catholic, and Jew, but this was hardly the case in the nineteenth and early twentieth centuries. At that time, Protestant denominations were more or less "established" in that they dominated the public square, crowding out Catholicism and Judaism; both were the subject of deep-seated and virulent prejudice and discrimination, associated with disparaged immigrants, mainly from Ireland, Italy, and Russia, and seen by nativist observers to be incompatible with mainstream institutions and culture.[69] "Catholicism was depicted not only as the enemy of God," historian Gary Gerstle writes, "but the enemy of republicanism. To Protestant Americans, the Catholic Church stood for monarchy, aristocracy, and other reactionary forces that America was seeking to escape. Where the pope ruled, Protestants charged, the people most certainly did not. And, thus, Catholic influence had to be resisted, contained, and even eradicated."[70] It may have taken more than a century, but the United States was able to overcome its fear of the "Catholic menace." By the mid-twentieth century, both Catholicism and Judaism had been incorporated into the system of American pluralism—a development that may be able to provide a model for the inclusion of new groups.[71] We cannot rule out the possibility that eventually, many decades from now, we will, to cite Gerstle again, be talking about America as an Abrahamic civilization, a phrase joining Muslims with Jews and Christians. The United States is "at present a long way from that formulation of American national identity, but no further than it once was from the Judeo-Christian one."[72]

To return to the here and now, institutional change and innovation are evident outside the religious sphere. Institutions that are less visible or controversial than Muslim mosques, and owe their existence or expansion to the post-1965 immigration, have come on the scene in many cities and local communities.

In the field of education, to give one example, contemporary immigration has spawned a new kind of public school: newcomer schools. A relatively small but growing number of newcomer middle and high schools have been set up around the country in such varied places as New York City and Philadelphia in the Northeast, Indianapolis (Indiana) as well as Columbus and Cleveland (Ohio) in the Midwest, Louisville (Kentucky) and Guilford County (North Carolina) in the Southeast, and Oakland (California) in the West. Specifically designed for recently arrived immigrant students who lack proficiency in English, some of the schools take students through to high school graduation, while others are intended to be transitional so that after a year or so students move to regular schools. In addition to teaching English, newcomer schools aim to help the students make social and emotional adjustments to the United States and learn about American culture. At Oakland International

High, nearly half of the students in 2018 had arrived from El Salvador and Guatemala, many as unaccompanied minors, and nearly two-fifths of the more than four hundred students at the school had missed two or more years of formal education. Many of them attended Students with Interrupted Formal Education classes, where they could work to catch up, with the goal of getting them to grade level in English and math.[73]

Outside the public school system, Chinese and Korean immigrants have added a new dimension to the nation's exam preparation and tutoring industry through the creation of hundreds of ethnic after-school institutions providing supplementary education in their communities. Chinese language schools have a long history in the United States, dating back to the 1880s in San Francisco's Chinatown, but they have greatly expanded in number—enrolling more than a hundred thousand students around the country in 2004—and now go beyond Chinese language and cultural enrichment classes to tutoring in such subjects as math and English as well as offering preparation for college entrance exams. Since the 1970s, centers owned by Chinese Americans solely devoted to children's education have emerged and proliferated; the 2004 Southern California Chinese Consumer Yellow Pages listed 135 academic after-school tutoring establishments. "Driving through the commercial corridor of Chinese ethnoburbs east of Los Angeles," sociologists Min Zhou and Rebecca Kim observe, "one can easily see the . . . bilingual signs of these establishments such as 'Little Harvard,' 'Ivy League School,' 'Stanford-to-Be Prep School,' and 'IQ180.'" *Hagwons*, a South Korean transplant, have sprung up since the 1990s in areas with large Korean populations, offering tutoring in school subjects as well as help with getting into magnet programs and honors classes, and scoring well on standardized tests like Advanced Placement and SAT exams.[74]

Institutional change in education, as in other arenas, is to a large extent about innovative programs, policies, and initiatives that have been incorporated into long-established mainstream community or citywide institutions. Already-existing schools have institutionalized new language programs and policies in the wake of new legal mandates in post–civil rights America and the need to provide for immigrant students who speak an array of languages. This is a clear change from the past.

In the last great wave of immigration more than a hundred years ago, it was basically sink or swim in public schools for the vast majority of non-English-speaking children of European immigrants in the eastern and midwestern cities where they generally settled. True, bilingual instruction was hardly unknown at the time. Some Polish immigrant children in Chicago, to give one example, attended Catholic schools where a small amount of teaching was in the mother tongue. Public schools in several midwestern cities offered bilingual German and English programs in the late nineteenth century, although these were outlawed in many states during the anti-German hysteria of World War I. Some local school systems at the turn of the twentieth century, like those of New York City, Detroit, and Cleveland, initiated special "steamer" or "C" classes, basically structured English-immersion classes meant to allow non-English-speaking children to learn enough English to function, however haltingly, in the regular program. But these classes lasted only a short time, from six weeks to six months, and were available to only a tiny fraction of those who would have benefited. In New York City, where the C classes originated, nearly three-quarters of public school students in the first decade of the twentieth century had foreign-born parents. The C classes, however, "never exceeded 2 percent of the total school enrollment, a result of severe overcrowding, limited resources, and inertia and opposition among teachers and principals."[75] Children in New York City who spoke no English were generally put in the first grade whatever their age. Bilingualism was not an option. Yiddish and Italian were taboo in the classroom, including in the special steamer language classes. On the immigrant Lower East Side, district superintendent Julia Richman even forbade students to speak Yiddish among themselves during recess or in the halls and bathrooms. She told teachers to give demerits to those who used the hated "jargon" and encouraged them to wash out with soap the mouths of students who relapsed.[76]

It's a different story now. For all the problems associated with language programs for immigrants in today's public schools, and debates about the relative merits of different approaches, they are a distinct improvement from the past. They also represent a significant change in the organization of schools in the post-1965 period. The Civil Rights Act of

1964 paved the way for an infusion of government funds for bilingual education programs, which typically use English and the native language in teaching academic content. The 1968 Bilingual Education Act provided financial assistance for innovative bilingual educational programs, although the 2001 No Child Left Behind Act moved away from explicit support of bilingual education; instead it emphasized the attainment of English proficiency in loosely defined "language instruction educational programs," distributing funds to states depending on enrollments of English-language-learner students, and requiring schools to show improvement in these students' test scores.[77]

What this has meant on the ground for actual language programs has varied from school to school. Based on their in-depth study of immigrant students and schools in Boston and San Francisco, Carola and Marcelo Suárez-Orozco and Irina Todorova concluded that "U.S. language policies are literally all over the map. Each state, each district—each school—seemed to have its own set of priorities, rules, and predilections."[78] Some bilingual programs, for example, teach content areas through the native language more than others; some programs labeled English only permit a minimal amount of assistance in a child's native language while others completely immerse students in English. To add to the mix, dual-language immersion programs have become more common in recent years. Beginning in kindergarten or first grade and continuing through elementary school, these programs integrate native English and English second-language speakers, using each of the languages (most often English and Spanish) for various portions of the school day and developing reading skills in both. By 2019, these programs numbered about three thousand in at least forty states and the District of Columbia, up from a few hundred in 2009.[79] Despite the variation in programs and practices, the bottom line is that language instruction programs geared for immigrant children with limited English-language ability have become a regular feature of the educational landscape.

Schools have been affected by immigration in an additional way. While the introduction of multicultural approaches in many of the nation's public schools owes much to the civil rights movement, immigration has played a role as well. In New York City, where the elementary schools often serve students from well over a dozen countries, teachers are encouraged to create classrooms where, among other things, they display pictures, artwork, maps, charts, and flags representing the homelands of students and their families.[80] This kind of educational approach also has been adopted elsewhere in the country as many teacher training programs and schools promote ways for teachers to create classrooms in which students learn about as well as celebrate cultural diversity, and develop respect for each other's cultures and backgrounds.

Hospitals are another established institution in cities and local communities that have undergone changes in the context of large-scale immigration. A notable new feature is the addition of translation programs to hospitals' organizational roster to assist immigrant patients with limited English-language ability. This is not a return to practices at the time of earlier waves of immigration. Certainly, some hospitals a hundred years ago made efforts to assist non-English-speaking immigrants. Beth Israel Hospital, for instance, founded at the turn of the twentieth century on New York City's Lower East Side, made a point of serving kosher food, and doctors and nurses conversed with patients in Yiddish. In Chicago and New York, women's communities of Catholic nuns involved in nursing acted as interpreters between doctors and patients who spoke different languages.[81]

The interpreter services in today's hospitals, in contrast, are legally mandated by federal and state laws, and are much more extensive than in the past. They also involve new approaches that benefit from modern technology, among them interpreter services via phone, teleconference, translation software, and apps, in good part because these are so much less expensive than on-site interpreters. Although hospitals receiving federal funds like Medicaid have been required to provide interpreting services, admittedly what they offer is frequently woefully inadequate, "part of an ad-hoc system that often means if translation is provided at all, it's likely from a bystander, family member, or friend with no idea how to say things like 'mitral valve prolapse' in a foreign language."[82] Still, innovative interpreter programs have become part of the organization of contemporary hospitals and are likely to persist as long as immigration remains substantial.

Quite apart from changes in schools and hospitals, many city governments—twenty-eight as of 2015—have established new immigrant affairs offices under the auspices of the mayor that, among other things, aim to coordinate and streamline city efforts to foster immigrant integration, support immigrant entrepreneurs, and nurture new community organizations serving immigrants.[83] Also, at least a dozen city governments have instituted something else that is new: municipal identification cards. The introduction of municipal IDs is a response to the difficulties confronting undocumented immigrants in obtaining a valid government-issued ID, such as a driver's license, which as of 2020, was not permitted to the undocumented in thirty-five states.

New Haven, Connecticut, led the way as the first city to issue municipal ID cards in 2007; since then a number of other cities have followed suit, among them New York, Chicago, Washington, DC, Los Angeles, and San Francisco. In New York City, which has the largest municipal ID program in the country, nearly 1.2 million people were cardholders in 2016, almost half of them immigrants. To entice nonimmigrant New Yorkers to sign up for the card and reduce any potential stigma they might carry, the card has come with free one-year memberships at or discounts to many of the city's cultural institutions. Valid only in New York City, the cards can be used for identification with the police, public schools, and libraries as well as in stores and some banks, but cannot be used for air travel, or to prove legal age to purchase alcohol or tobacco.[84]

In stark contrast to municipal ID cards, and indeed the changes in local mainstream institutions I have already mentioned, are institutional changes of a different order: those explicitly meant to be punitive and that involve policing undocumented immigrants. For much of the twentieth century, US immigration enforcement was nearly exclusively about border enforcement in the Southwest. In the 1990s, partly owing to the growth and increasing dispersion of the undocumented population, the federal government for the first time "ramped up its efforts to engage states and localities in immigration enforcement on a formal, ongoing basis" deep within the American heartlands, enlisting local police and sheriffs around the country in a drive to detect and remove unauthorized immigrants.[85]

Just how local officials responded to the initiatives to bring them into the enforcement process varied; a series of national surveys of police chiefs and sheriffs found that responses ran the gamut from eagerness to enforce federal law to active resistance, with most falling in between. An especially egregious example of local overenforcement was Arizona's Maricopa County sheriff Joe Arpaio, in office from 1993 to 2016, when he styled himself "America's toughest sheriff." Arpaio engaged over a hundred deputies to conduct raids of workplaces, neighborhood sweeps, and traffic stops of "Latino-looking" drivers, and became famous for setting up a tent city jail, with sweltering temperatures inside that could reach 130 degrees Fahrenheit in the summer, and requiring inmates to wear pink underwear. At the other end of the spectrum, in 2015 over three hundred cities and counties, including Chicago and San Francisco, did not fully cooperate with US Immigration and Customs Enforcement.[86]

Overall, the surveys of police chiefs and sheriffs revealed that a bigger immigrant population was associated with supportive policing practices; in both large and small cities with a heavy immigrant presence, law enforcement leaders were more likely to recognize that officers had to learn to serve as well as communicate with newcomers and gain their trust. When it came to restrictive city policies and harsh practices, the political leanings of the local population were key; on average, the police were more likely to crack down on suspected unauthorized immigrants by reporting or detaining them in localities where the public leaned conservative or Republican. Is this because conservative public opinion and politicians placed more pressure on police to engage in immigration enforcement? Or because law enforcement personnel in conservative localities were themselves more likely to hold conservative views on immigration? It is unclear.[87] Either way, political orientations were involved. Indeed, it is hardly surprising that institutional innovations to assist the undocumented, such as municipal ID cards, have been introduced in liberal, heavily Democratic cities. With regard to local institutional and policy changes aimed at the undocumented, politics obviously matters.

————

In cities, towns, and suburbs all across the country, immigrants have been remaking communities so that they have changed dramatically from five decades ago—a time before the huge post-1965 influx began to take off. This process of remaking is of course an age-old one, part of the nature of immigration's impact on American society since the nation's founding, and so inevitably leads to questions about how the current changes are similar to those that took place in the past. Undeniably, the way immigration has now been reshaping cities and communities often resembles patterns found before. Mass immigration, now as in the nineteenth and early twentieth centuries, has brought new ethnic, racial, and religious diversity to urban areas, for example, and given rise to new ethnic neighborhoods. There is even a strong resemblance of today's ethnoburbs to an earlier version created by the descendants of European immigrants in mid-twentieth-century America. But to resemble is not to be exactly the same. Among other things, today's new ethnic and multiethnic communities involve different national origin groups, cultures, and religions than in past eras of large-scale immigration so that we have been currently witnessing genuine transformations rather than just a replica of old patterns.

There are a slew of other late twentieth- and early twenty-first-century elements that give the community transformations rooted in immigration today a distinctive form and character. Many suburbs that did not even exist at the beginning of the twentieth century have been strongly impacted by the large number of contemporary immigrants and their children who now live in them; the same goes for many of the country's largest metropolitan areas in the South, Southwest, and West, which a hundred years ago were more thinly populated and attracted few immigrants. Schools, hospitals, and local governments—these mainstream institutions have seen the introduction of entirely new programs in the wake of contemporary mass immigration, while new institutions such as Muslim mosques have come on the scene for the first time in many communities.

No matter how much the changes today resemble, or build on, those that occurred in earlier eras or are altogether new developments, one thing is clear. Without the mass immigration of the past half century, cities, towns, and suburbs in the United States would look and feel very different. Much as some Americans would like to go back to the way things were in the 1950s and early 1960s, before large-scale immigration got underway, the fact is that this is impossible. And this, in important ways, is a good thing. Immigration has been a key factor underpinning the expansion of many metropolitan areas that have been growing by leaps and bounds in recent years, and has revitalized urban neighborhoods, and indeed many rural communities, that were losing people and were in decline. This changing demography is closely linked to changes in the economy—a significant part of the account to which I now turn.

CHAPTER 4

The Economy

A huge increase in America's population—more than one-fourth of the people in this country are immigrants and their children—was bound to make huge changes in the nation's economy. Millions of new immigrant workers have not only fueled substantial growth, but have set in motion significant changes and surprising innovations. Our economy would not be the same without them.

Immigrants fill important roles at both the top and bottom of the occupational ladder. From eldercare to office cleaning, to chopping onions at the back of restaurant kitchens, immigrants have become familiar in a wide array of low-skilled jobs. Less well known, they are also working in large numbers in many professional fields. Forty percent of the country's software engineers as well as more than a quarter of physicians and surgeons are foreign born.[1]

As America's economy over the decades shifted away from manufacturing to services, an available pool of hardworking immigrants helped make the evolution possible. They have helped any number of service industries grow and flourish. In some cases they have likely allowed some industries to survive. They have not just filled but also added jobs. As consumers they have expanded the economy, which in turn supports jobs of all kinds.

Immigrants have also been a source of innovation. They have invented new businesses and provided new services. They have played a role in transforming the structure of certain industries—in meatpacking, for example, by supplying low-wage labor for unpleasant jobs. Because of the specialized skills many have brought, they have shaped the development of the remarkable high-tech sector. Indeed, the National Academy of Sciences report on immigration and the economy concluded that high-skilled immigrants "have boosted the nation's capacity for innovation, entrepreneurship, and technological change."[2]

Overwhelmingly, the changes immigrants have brought to the US economy have been highly beneficial, but we should not overlook the potential negative effects. The fact that so many immigrants have been prepared to work hard at jobs with comparatively low wages and difficult working conditions has fueled a debate about whether they are limiting opportunities for native workers—although the evidence shows that overall, the adverse effects on US-born workers' wages and employment have been minimal.

Changes

To begin with, immigrants have changed the composition of the nation's workforce. As their numbers have grown, they have become an increasingly large share of America's workers—17 percent of the civilian labor force in 2019, up from 9 percent in 1990.[3] Immigrant men's employment rate is slightly higher than native-born men's, and among the least educated men, the rate for immigrants is dramatically higher.[4]

Immigrants are also more likely than US-born workers to be employed in lower-skill occupations, for which there has been persistent demand. Partly this is because the younger, less skilled US-born working-age population has substantially shrunk since 1990 given the aging and retirement of baby boomers, and because educational attainment has increased among the native born.[5] Large numbers of immigrants are found in what have often come to be seen as "immigrant jobs"—low-wage and low-status positions in agriculture, construction, manufacturing, and a wide range of services that the native born are either unwilling or unavailable to take.

A look at specific occupations in which workers are most likely to be immigrants makes this clear (table 4.1). In 2014, immigrants in the nation were nearly two-thirds of "miscellaneous personal appearance

TABLE 4.1. Jobs in Which Workers in the US Are Most Likely to Be Foreign Born, 2014

Detailed occupation	Foreign-born share
Misc. personal appearance workers	63%
Graders, and sorters of agricultural products	60%
Plasterers and stucco masons	59%
Sewing machine operators	55%
Misc. agricultural workers	52%
Maids and housekeeping cleaners	50%
Tailors, dressmakers, and sewers	50%
Drywall and ceiling tile installers, and tapers	49%
Taxi drivers and chauffeurs	47%

Source: DeSilver 2017.

workers" (a category including manicurists and pedicurists, makeup artists, shampooers, and skin care specialists), the highest share of any occupation. Immigrants made up about 60 percent of graders and sorters of agricultural products as well as plasterers and stucco masons in construction. They accounted for 55 percent of sewing machine operators, and about half of maids and housekeepers, tailors, and dressmakers.[6] The extent to which immigrants dominate certain manual occupational niches is even more striking in states where they make up a large proportion of the population. In California, for instance, in 2014 more than 70 percent of housekeepers and maids as well as gardeners and groundskeepers were foreign born; so were more than 65 percent of workers in construction occupations (roofers, painters, and drywall installers) in both California and Texas. In states with an important agricultural sector, a high proportion of farmworkers were immigrants—a whopping 81 percent in California, and 70 percent or more in Washington and Florida.[7]

In moving into low-level jobs, immigrants have brought a host of changes. For a start, they helped sustain certain industries that might have had trouble surviving in the absence of lower-cost immigrant labor. Such is the case with the last remnants of garment manufacturing that have stayed in the United States, even while most production has by now moved abroad in search of cheap labor. In my own home city of New York, garment manufacturing, one of the bastions of the economy for much of the twentieth century, may have shrunk beyond recognition, but virtually all those working in the remaining factories and sweatshops—according to a 2016 report, over 90 percent of the sewing machine operators and pressers—are immigrants.[8] Immigrant workers from Latin America and Asia are a mainstay of the Los Angeles apparel manufacturing industry even as it has experienced marked declines too. No doubt some agribusinesses would not have survived if they lacked immigrant workers, or at least had great difficulty making a go of it. Without immigrant labor, journalist Tamar Jacoby opines, labor-intensive agriculture would have taken an enormous hit. Not only would produce be more expensive but "instead of milk from a nearby dairy, the . . . kind available would come from abroad, and it would be irradiated or powdered. Meat would come from Brazil [and] . . . fruits and vegetables from New Zealand—and that's the good expensive stuff. There would be plenty of inferior products, too, and much much less of anything would be fresh."[9]

Why have so many immigrants been willing to take bottom-level jobs? In part, they have no choice but to accept what jobs are on offer. Many enter the labor market without fluent English, legal status, or skills transferable in the United States, and some arrive with extremely low levels of education. If they are unable to get a job, they have few alternatives; federal law limits recent legal immigrants' ability to receive many forms of government assistance in their first five years of residence, and undocumented immigrants have access to hardly any social welfare programs at all. In addition, at least in their early days in the United States, the wages in lower-level jobs look good compared to what immigrants could earn in their home country. They view wages, in other words, with what has been called a dual frame of reference.[10] Many see their stay in the United States and their current jobs as temporary, and those who worked in higher-status occupations back home continue to receive prestige in their own ethnic communities for the positions they used to hold.

Mrs. Thomas (a pseudonym) is a woman I knew in a Jamaican village when I lived there in the late 1960s and, later, when she moved to New York in the 1970s. In Jamaica, she had been an elementary school teacher, a position of great prestige in her local community, but as many other professional immigrants have found, her qualifications were not recognized here. When she came to New York and subsequently relocated to south Florida, she took a series of live-in jobs caring for the elderly, initially to earn money to help finance her daughter's university education in Jamaica. Mrs. Thomas earned considerably more as a live-in companion to the elderly than she did teaching primary school in rural Jamaica. While she soon became aware of wage scales in the United States, she continued to view her earnings in terms of standards in the "old country"—a perspective that was reinforced and renewed by trips to the island along with visits from relatives, Jamaican social networks in New York and Florida, and her definition of her stay in the United States as temporary. Jamaican private household workers usually evaluated their social standing, at least in part, in terms of their position in their home communities, and this evaluation tended to be acknowledged by their former associates. In their Jamaican social world in New York and Florida, their former, rather than their present, occupation or class status was usually the primary basis for their rank. Mrs. Thomas was thought of by her friends and relatives in the United States as a teacher—not as a domestic. As she put it to me, "I'm no scrubber."[11]

Actually, Mrs. Thomas became close to a number of the elderly women she looked after, thus pointing to a positive feature of caregiving jobs for many immigrant workers; another is a sense of pride in providing good care. In work settings generally, the opportunity for sociability and to develop relationships with coworkers is often a plus.[12] And not all lower-level jobs are dead-end positions. A study of Mexican migrants in low-level jobs reveals that some were able to take advantage of chances to learn new skills, advance to better positions, and earn higher wages in construction, auto repair, manufacturing, and the hospitality industry, in the latter case progressing from chambermaids, food preparation workers, or janitors, to waiters and assistant cooks in restaurants, or supervisory positions in hotels.[13]

Regardless of the opportunities on offer, the availability of lower-wage immigrant workers has had an additional economic impact: driving up the demand for labor in some occupations. One example is in-home childcare jobs. To be sure, the call for childcare workers has grown in the post–World War II decades as more middle- and upper-middle-class women entered the workforce, with many looking for someone to care for their children in their own homes.[14] But immigration also has been involved. The dramatic surge in the female immigrant labor supply since the 1970s, coming on the heels of African American women's exodus from private household work as better opportunities opened up in post–civil rights America, was a factor behind the rising number of domestic workers; indeed, the influx of immigrants into the occupation further stimulated a demand for their services, especially in metropolitan areas where many residents are highly paid professionals in affluent households.[15] That the inflow of immigrant women has kept the price of in-home childcare from becoming too costly is critical. With many immigrant women searching for work in cities like New York and Los Angeles, there has been downward pressure on wages for private household workers, and that in turn has made domestic services affordable and available to a large number of families.[16] The result, as studies of Los Angeles and New York show, is that hiring immigrant women, typically from Latin America or the Caribbean, for childcare and housecleaning has become normative, especially among upper-middle-class families. Immigration, as one study puts it for New York City, "altered social norms governing consumption of domestic services in ways that are self-perpetuating."[17]

A similar dynamic has operated in eldercare. With older people living longer, and most developing chronic diseases and disabilities, and more working-age women in the labor force, there has been an increased demand for paid home care—work that native-born Americans would rather not do. In 2018, a striking 38 percent of the home health aides in the country were foreign born, with the proportion even higher in some states, such as a whopping 75 percent in New York, and over 50 percent in New Jersey and Florida.[18] The availability of immigrants to do this work, and for relatively low pay, has itself helped to normalize paid caregiving in private homes as one solution to eldercare, particularly among middle- and upper-middle-class Americans, and in this way, generated additional jobs. The need for workers to care for the elderly, it should be noted, is going to expand further in the future given the aging of the population. The number of those eighty-five and over is expected to more than double from 5.9 million in 2012 to 14.1 million in 2040.[19] In this regard, immigrants have been playing another key role. By keeping the working-age population growing, immigrants and their children help to shore up the finances of our pay-as-you-go social security system, which depends on a large enough workforce to fund the benefits of retirees.

In general, as immigrants have filled lower-level positions, they have reduced the prices of some goods and services, or prevented them from becoming too expensive, in a range of sectors, from childcare and housecleaning to lawn care and house repairs, thus making them more widely available to more Americans. In this way immigrants' lower-paid labor has subsidized the lifestyles of middle-class Americans, affording them some services that only the affluent could have managed to pay for in the past. This of course is another aspect of change.

On top of this, as the National Academy of Sciences report on the economic and fiscal consequences of immigration notes, low-skilled immigrant workers have increased the labor supply of high-skilled natives through providing lower-cost childcare and thus allowing more mothers to work outside the home. To put it somewhat differently, the availability of immigrants for housekeeping and childcare has been a boon for highly educated women with children, enabling them to advance their careers in professions that require long hours and irregular work schedules.[20] And to the extent that low-skilled immigrants have furnished labor that keeps enterprises like restaurants, factories, and hotels operating, they have ended up generating jobs for those higher up the occupational ladder in these sectors, among them accountants, chefs, and managers, who are often native born.

Higher-skilled immigrants have brought a further set of changes. Contrary to popular perceptions, immigrants are well represented at the upper ends of the occupational hierarchy. More than a third of employed foreign-born workers in the nation's civilian labor force in 2019 were in management, professional, and related occupations.[21] At the city level, in New York, immigrants at the end of the first decade of the twenty-first century were not just starkly overrepresented in blue-collar and low-level service jobs but also made up a large share of relatively well-paid and higher-level positions; three out of ten architects, for example, four out of ten real estate brokers and doctors, and a third of financial managers were immigrants.[22]

In the health care professions, immigrants have staved off or shrunk shortages in many areas of the country. Immigrant doctors, many in primary care delivering preventive and routine services, have been a saving grace in rural America as well as underserved communities with poor, less educated, and more minority residents. While in the nation as a whole 28 percent of the nearly 1 million physicians and surgeons in 2018 were immigrants, in the depressed Rust Belt city of Youngstown, Ohio, where the per capita income in 2010 was around $12,000, three-quarters of the physicians were foreign trained (as compared to 17 percent in affluent Westport, Connecticut).[23] The majority of foreign-born physicians and surgeons are from Asia, and Indians are by far the largest nationality group. Immigrants have filled a need for nurses too, especially in hospitals in rural areas and small towns; 16 percent of the country's 3.3 million registered nurses are foreign born, with the largest contingent from the Philippines, which trains English-speaking nurses in an Americanized curriculum.[24]

Immigrants at all occupational levels have strengthened the economy in yet another way. They are not only workers but also consumers and customers of goods and services. When the nation's millions of immigrants purchase even such basic items as food for themselves and their families, they end up supporting many US enterprises and jobs within them. Given the extensive offshoring of so much manufacturing and industrial production to other countries as well as technological advances reducing the need for labor in some sectors, this economic growth dynamic is especially prominent in services that cannot go abroad or be easily automated. Public schools in many cities may be bursting at the seams, for instance, but without large-scale immigration and a substantial second generation, many would have downsized or been closed; the demand for teachers would have been reduced along with the need for lower-level employees, from custodial to kitchen staff.

Indeed, because immigration has significantly expanded the population of so many cities and metropolitan areas, it has sustained and often created jobs for local and state government workers who provide fundamental services in a broad range of jobs at different occupational levels.

Immigrants have also had a role in the expansion of the housing market, another key sector of the economy. The thirty years between 1980 and 2010 saw an added 5.3 million immigrant homeowners in the nation, with the numbers going up each decade. In a number of states, including New York, California, Illinois, and Pennsylvania, immigrants accounted for the major share of growth in homeowner households in the first decade of the twenty-first century.[25] Without growth in the foreign-born population, according to a study of five metropolitan areas, regions with strong housing markets such as San Francisco would not have recovered so quickly after the 2008 recession; regions that continued to struggle in the aftermath of that downturn such as Buffalo would have seen weaker growth.[26] In increasing demand for housing, immigrants have stimulated the real estate industry and other economic activities tied to it, such as real estate agents and workers in construction and building trades, thereby generating jobs for other immigrants as well as the native born.[27] Looking ahead, immigrants as well as their adult second-generation children will no doubt be a key source of demand for new and existing homes in the years to come.

Immigrants create jobs in one more way: through establishing and operating their own businesses.[28] As of 2014, around one in five business owners nationwide were immigrants; they founded about a quarter of new firms in 2012, with the figure around 40 percent in California and New York.[29] Despite the risks, small business ownership offers many newcomers an alternative to less desirable, bottom-level jobs, which otherwise would have been their fate given impediments in the labor market such as poor English facility, inadequate or inappropriate skills, and often discrimination.[30]

Apart from hiring paid workers, many immigrants who start or maintain small businesses have improved and frequently revived neighborhood economies. A Fiscal Policy Institute report, "Bringing Vitality to Main Street," written in the second decade of the twenty-first century, details how immigrants played a major role in revitalizing business corridors in "Main Street" centers in metropolitan areas that had fallen on hard times in a good many cases. They did this by taking over or setting up retail shops as well as food and neighborhood services, from grocery stores and dry cleaners to restaurants, beauty salons, and jewelry and clothing stores. In 2013, immigrants made up 28 percent of Main Street business owners in the country, with the rates much higher in metropolitan areas with large numbers of immigrants—such as fully 64 percent of all Main Street business owners in the Los Angeles metropolitan area, 61 percent in metropolitan San Jose, 56 percent in metropolitan Washington, DC, and 54 percent in metropolitan Miami. Immigrant-owned businesses helped to give new life and character to urban neighborhoods that had previously been in decline (see chapter 3). They also drew a new consumer base to formerly rundown areas, and in general, helped to stimulate overall economic development through "an increased tax base, more local spending, and more local jobs."[31]

Innovations and Structural Transformations

Up to now I have talked mainly about jobs. The section that follows speaks to another dynamic: how immigrants have played a role in structural transformations in the economy, and been an important source of innovation and invention, most notably in technology.

This is not the first time immigration has had a major transformative effect on the economy. Perhaps most striking is its role in the epochal process of industrialization in the late nineteenth and early twentieth centuries as the United States went from a predominantly rural agrarian society to an industrial economy. Immigrant labor, sociologists Charles Hirschman and Elizabeth Mogford conclude, "may well have been a necessary condition for the pace and scale of the rise of the manufacturing sector from 1880 to 1920."[32] Immigrants and their descendants were the primary workforce in the rapidly expanding manufacturing sector in the early twentieth century; in 1920, immigrants and the second generation comprised over half of manufacturing workers, and with the third-generation grandchildren of immigrants more than two-thirds.[33]

Replacing even a fraction of the several million immigrant workers in manufacturing would have required much greater incentives in terms of pay and working conditions than those offered to immigrants. While other factors, such as the evolution of the American system of manufacturing, discovery and development of mineral resources, and lowered costs of transportation, contributed to the rise of industrialization, immigration was, without doubt, of critical significance.

In the contemporary era, immigrants have been crucial in a modern-day economic transformation: the astonishing success of high-tech industries, a vitally important new sector of America's twenty-first-century economy. Immigrants have played an "outsize role in high-tech startup companies as well as their larger and more established Fortune 500 counterparts: as members of the founding teams of roughly one third of all venture-backed companies and more than 40 percent of Silicon Valley high-tech startups."[34] According to a 2018 study of the ninety-one American start-up companies valued at $1 billion or more, over half had at least one immigrant founder; more than 80 percent of these companies employed immigrants in key management or product development roles, commonly as chief technology officers and vice presidents of engineering.[35] Immigration is highly selective, and the US tech sector has pulled in some of the best, brightest, highly educated, and most ambitious from other countries who have helped to make the industry such a success. They have come because US high-tech companies pay well by international standards, and because demand in this country for computer programmers, software developers, and electrical engineers soared after 1980.[36]

The immigrant origins of the iconic companies tell part of the story. One of Google's founders, Sergey Brin, is an immigrant from Russia, and its current chief executive (in 2020), Sundar Pichai, was born in India. An immigrant from Brazil, Eduardo Saverin, is one of Facebook's founders; eBay was started by an immigrant from France (Pierre Omidyar), and Yahoo was cofounded by Jerry Yang, born with the name Yang Chih-Yuan in Taiwan and brought to California by his family at the age of ten. Apple's founder Steve Jobs had immigrant roots too. His adopted mother who raised him was the daughter of Armenian immigrants, while his biological father, Abdulfattah Jandali, grew up in Syria and studied in Lebanon before moving to the United States. Jeff Bezos, the founder of Amazon, was raised from the age of four by his Cuban immigrant stepfather, Miguel "Mike" Bezos. Elon Musk, to give one more example, the founder of Tesla and SpaceX, is from South Africa. Apart from the many immigrant founders, a significant share of the current science and technology workforce in the country—a quarter of all those working in computer and mathematical science occupations in 2014—are immigrants.

Indians have played an especially noteworthy role as entrepreneurs, engineers, and other professionals in the information technology and computer sector, perhaps not surprising because they come from a country with its own high-tech revolution. Indian immigrants are among the tech titans of today, having risen to become chief executive officers of such giants as Microsoft, Adobe Systems, and Micron Technology. Many immigrant information technology workers have been educated abroad, such as at India's well-known Indian Institutes of Technology (as well as at top Chinese universities), with a good number having initially entered under special H-1B visas for skilled foreign labor. High-skilled immigrants, as sociologist Susan Eckstein and economist Giovanni Peri note, have been "fundamental to Silicon Valley's ability to establish and maintain a global competitive edge in information technology."[37]

In line with their high-tech prowess, immigrants stand out as inventors in science and technology. Among college graduates in the United States, according to one study, immigrants are twice as likely to receive patents as native-born Americans owing to their disproportionate share of engineering and science degrees.[38] In raising patenting per capita, they have ultimately contributed to the growth of productivity.[39]

Besides high-tech start-ups, immigrants have created other kinds of new businesses. Miami provides a dramatic example as a city transformed by Cuban immigrants who literally reinvented its economy. Cuban elites in exile, including experienced bankers from the island, established firms and businesses that were pivotal in Miami's emergence as a center of intercontinental trade as well as an important financial and banking hub. A few dozen Cuban enterprises in the 1960s grew to thousands by the 1980s as, in the process, Cuban entrepreneurs reoriented the city's economy away from tourism from northern states and converted Miami into a true global metropolis, or in the words of Alejandro Portes and Ariel Armony, a "strategic center of trade and financial transactions between Europe, the United States, and Latin America."[40]

All over the country, immigrants have developed new types of retail businesses and made significant alterations to old ones so that they are barely recognizable from before. Asian supermarket chains, new on the scene in metropolitan areas around the country, have become big business. Mainly catering to Asian Americans, and typically founded and run by immigrant entrepreneurs and their families, one of the largest is H Mart with over eighty stores across the United States as of 2020, when the company reported $1.5 billion in sales. Founded by a Korean immigrant in New York City in 1982, the *H* stands for *Han Ah Reum*, a Korean phrase that roughly translates to "one arm full of groceries." Another example is 99 Ranch Market, the largest Taiwanese American supermarket chain, with over fifty stores in 2020, mostly in California, but also in Nevada, Oregon, Washington, Texas, New Jersey, Maryland, and Massachusetts.

Immigrants have had a hand, too, in reinvention in the restaurant business (see chapter 5). New "ethnic" restaurants, among them Thai, Turkish, Indian, Vietnamese, Korean, Cuban, and pan-Asian, once rare or nonexistent in many cities, have become a regular feature, often offering relatively inexpensive meals "just when American life style changes [in the post-1965 decades] led to a taste for more exotic foods and greater spending on meals made in restaurants rather than at home."[41] Mexican restaurants, which used to be found mainly in the Southwest, are everywhere. Chinese restaurants have multiplied, with roughly forty thousand across the country as of 2015, or around three times the number of McDonald's outlets. Although Chinese restaurants are still a mainstay of Chinatowns in New York City and San Francisco, they have spread almost everywhere, from Alabama to Alaska, frequently with new all-you-can-eat buffets. Writing a few years ago, journalist Lauren Hilgers noted that there was "one in Pinedale, Wyoming (population 2,043), and one in Old Forge, New York (population 756); Belle Vernon, Pennsylvania (population 1,085) has three." These far-flung Chinese restaurants are staffed by immigrants who often pass through for a few months at a time; many use employment agencies in Manhattan's Chinatown to find restaurant jobs in the Northeast, Midwest, and Deep South, and take long-distance buses based in Chinatown and operated by Chinese immigrants to get to them.[42] Although most Chinese restaurants are small-scale operations, one chain, Panda Express, founded and owned by an immigrant couple, had become a $3 billion business with some two thousand locations by 2019.

Perhaps the most well-known new Main Street immigrant businesses are the nail salons that dot the landscape in metropolitan America. The nail salon as we know it is a post-1965 immigrant invention, associated with the Vietnamese in many parts of the country and Koreans in the New York–New Jersey metropolitan area. Before the advent of new immigrants, getting a manicure was for the well-to-do. Professional nail care was a secondary and expensive service offered in hair salons, typically owned by the native born and catering to better-off clientele.

Enter new immigrants and the modern nail salon. In transforming the nail salon industry, immigrants created a demand for their work—and also expanded it. They did this by what Susan Eckstein and Thanh-Nghi Nguyen call the "McNailing of America," establishing stand-alone nail salons in neighborhoods where people live and work, and offering quick, assembly-line service on a walk-in, no appointment necessary basis. Cost was key. The immigrant-run nail salons offered manicures at a much lower price than upscale beauty salons charged so that nail care came to be within reach for people who previously could not afford it. In the process, standards for nail beauty rose, further expanding the demand for manicurists and pedicurists. Getting a professional manicure has become de rigueur for women of diverse racial, ethnic, and class backgrounds, and important to their presentation of self. Sociologists have called this "niche stretching": immigrants broadened the customer base for professional nail care, and at the same time, diversified the range of nail care offerings to include such services as pedicures and in some cases even fingernail artwork.[43]

The figures are striking: the number of nail salons in the United States more than doubled from a little under thirty thousand in 1991 to close to sixty thousand in 2008, with a large number of them run and operated by immigrants and staffed by mostly female immigrant workers. In the New York–New Jersey metropolitan area alone, the estimated four thousand Korean-owned nail salons in 2006 represented a nearly threefold increase from fourteen hundred in 1991.[44] Nail salons, it should be noted, are a specialized slice of the beauty industry, which is a vibrant part of the US economy; in the early 2000s, beauty salons generated $60 billion in sales and employed more than 1.6 million people. Nail salons at that time accounted for about 10 percent of the revenue and 6 percent of the employment in the sector.[45]

And we should not forget that immigrants have helped make possible major structural transformations in long-established sectors by providing low-skilled and low-wage labor sought by employers. Meat and beef processing is a case in point, which together with poultry production in 2019 was a $213 billion industry employing over 500,000 people.[46] Chicago may be recalled in the poet Carl Sandburg's phrase as the hog butcher of the world, but the city's stockyards are long gone, beginning a decline after the Second World War and closing altogether in 1971. The meatpacking industry has moved elsewhere as it has morphed, or been restructured, into a different form—a development that has heavily relied on immigrant labor.

During the 1980s and 1990s, the meatpacking industry was increasingly dominated by vertically integrated companies that sought to remain competitive by decentralizing production to large plants in rural areas of the Midwest and Southeast.[47] One account describes the key role of geographic location in the industrial transformation in meat processing: "To reduce transportation costs, ensure constant supplies of animals, and maintain high year-round plant utilization, beef and hog processing plants relocated to nontraditional rural regions . . . taking advantage of lower land and labor costs [in states like Iowa and Nebraska]. . . . Relocation to rural areas also weakened the bargaining power of many urban-based unions, resulting in a decline in wages and working conditions that decreased the attractiveness of meat-processing jobs to native-born workers."[48] Indeed, employers' desire to cut costs and weaken or eliminate unions were major factors behind the industry's restructuring.[49]

Finding themselves shorthanded, hog- and cattle-processing firms began to recruit Hispanic migrants to new rural destinations to what were physically demanding, hazardous, and low-paying jobs that native workers, especially younger ones who had better employment alternatives elsewhere, shunned. Immigrants drawn to the industry had fewer options, especially if they lacked documents, and were more willing to tolerate the dirty and dangerous working conditions. For many Hispanic workers, it was a step up from employment in agriculture; cutting meat in a Colorado or Nebraska slaughterhouse paid more than picking strawberries in California.[50] By 2014–18, roughly one-third of the workforce in the meat-processing industry in the United States was foreign born, more than four times the proportion in 1980.[51] Immigrants, in short, facilitated the restructuring of meat processing from a relatively high-wage unionized industry in mid-twentieth-century urban centers providing workers with a middle-class income and generous benefits to one that, by the early twenty-first century, was notorious for low wages, degraded working conditions, and deunionization or waning union power in the midst of rural America.[52]

A different development concerning immigrants and labor organizations is worth noting: the emergence of worker centers. Given that the traditional union movement's share of the labor force (10.5 percent) in 2018, as sociologist Ruth Milkman points out, has shrunk to a level comparable to that of the 1920s, it is not surprising that the vast majority of immigrant workers are outside the union orbit. Despite some successful unionizing efforts among immigrant workers, such as the Justice for Janitors campaign in Los Angeles, the two million immigrant union members in 2018 were mostly hired into jobs already covered by union contracts rather than through unionization drives. In this context, worker centers, a new type of immigrant worker organization, have proliferated. Described as "alt-labor" groups because they rarely engage in traditional collective bargaining, worker centers are grassroots organizations with loose membership structures that, among other things, have mounted campaigns against workplace injustice through media outreach and direct appeals to consumers; offer legal services to workers subjected to workplace violations; and provide basic information to immigrant workers about their rights under US labor and immigration law. By 2018, some 226 worker centers were operating in the United States, up from 5 in 1985, with many of them focused on low-wage, mostly foreign-born workers in industries with weak unions or none at all. The centers are typically led by educated elites, many of whom are veterans of political and labor movements in their home countries, and they operate on extremely limited budgets. Several have morphed from local into national organizations such as the National Domestic Workers Association and National Taxi Workers Alliance.[53]

A Downside?

Immigration has contributed to economic growth and technological innovation in many significant ways, but has it brought any problems? Certainly from the perspective of immigrants themselves it has, especially for those in low-skilled and low-wage jobs, and even more for the most vulnerable of all, the undocumented, who in 2017 made up nearly 5 percent of the US civilian workforce or 7.6 million people.[54]

Low-skilled immigrants may earn more money than in their home countries, but by US standards their pay is often low, the hours long, and the benefits few or absent. There are also perils on the job. Immigrants work in more dangerous industries and occupations than natives, and in riskier jobs in terms of injuries and fatalities.[55] Workers in agriculture, and meat and poultry processing, for example, are exposed to toxic pesticides, hazardous equipment, crush injuries, repetitive motion, and falls; construction workers are subject to hazards involving high elevations, large cutting tools, and heavy lifting.[56] During the coronavirus epidemic, meatpacking workers (as well as the large share of immigrant frontline health care workers) suffered notably high rates of infection and death. As one account of meatpacking plant hot spots observed, "The chief risks [came from] being in close proximity to other workers. A thousand people might work a single eight-hour shift, standing shoulder to shoulder as carcasses whiz by on hooks or conveyor belts. Often, workers get only a second or two to complete their task before the next hunk of meat arrives. The frenzied pace and grueling physical demands of breaking down so many dead animals can make people breathe hard and have difficulty keeping masks properly positioned on their faces."[57]

In the 2020 COVID-19 recession, millions of immigrants were especially vulnerable to losing their jobs given their overrepresentation in many of the hardest-hit sectors of the economy: hotels and restaurants, cleaning services for office buildings, and personal services such as hair and nail salons, in which large numbers of immigrant business owners as well as workers faced financial devastation. According to an analysis by the Migration Policy Institute during the pandemic, 20 percent of the US workers in vulnerable industries facing massive layoffs were immigrants. For a substantial number of them, including undocumented immigrants and those who obtained green cards in the past five years, this situation was worsened by their inability to receive federal means-tested benefits that were available to other workers in times of need.[58]

But what about the impact for native-born workers? Has large-scale, post-1965 immigration caused difficulties for them? Much of the academic and policy literature on immigrants and the US economy centers around the question of whether immigrants compete with established Americans in the workforce, taking their jobs and depressing their wages. Not surprisingly, politicians have entered the fray, with Trump putting his viewpoint in no uncertain terms. "They're taking our jobs," he proclaimed on the campaign trail in 2016. "They're taking our money. They're killing us."[59] Academic commentators don't use this language, but some of them, too, worry that immigrants may be hurting native workers.

The general consensus among economists, however, is that such fears are greatly exaggerated. This is the conclusion of the 2017 National Academy of Sciences report assessing the empirical literature on the economic impact of US immigration as measured over a period of more than ten years, including its effects on the employment and wages of native-born workers. For one thing, the impact of immigrants on the wages of the native-born overall has been very small. To the extent that studies found negative wage effects, they were most likely to occur among earlier immigrants and native-born high school dropouts with job qualifications similar to those of the large share of low-skilled workers among immigrants.[60] Peri's analysis of the period between 1970 and 2014 comes to even more positive conclusions: immigrants were not responsible for the stagnating or declining wages of noncollege workers, either nationally or in regions with high immigration. Among the possible reasons he puts forward are that highly educated immigrants boost local productivity, and immigrant small firms and start-ups may generate local opportunities for native-born workers, further increasing demand for them that offsets any increase in labor supply.[61]

In line with this analysis, the National Academy of Sciences report refers to several studies revealing positive effects of skilled immigration on the wages and employment of both college- and noncollege-educated natives. Such findings "are consistent with the view that skilled immigrants are often complementary to native-born workers, especially those who are skilled; that spillovers of wage-enhancing knowledge and skills occur as a result of interactions among workers; and that skilled immigrants innovate sufficiently to raise overall productivity."[62]

As for employment, fears about competition from immigrants are also overblown. There is little evidence that immigration significantly affects the overall employment levels of native-born workers according to the National Academy of Sciences report. One caveat the report mentions is research suggesting that immigration reduces the number of hours worked by native-born teenagers (but not their employment rate); another is some evidence that recent immigrants reduce the employment rate of prior immigrants. Although the job prospects of native-born workers in particular skill groups may be hurt by immigrant competition, as might happen, for instance, among construction and kitchen workers, immigrants may enhance opportunities for complementary native-born workers in the same fields in other skill groups, such as first-line building supervisors or restaurant waitstaff.[63] The case of African Americans illustrates a similar dynamic. Some scholars have asked whether immigrants are making it at the expense of native minorities, or as has been said, on the "back of Blacks."[64] Tackling this question in a study of Los Angeles, sociologists Roger Waldinger and

Michael Lichter argue that immigration may harm the most vulnerable, most poorly schooled, least skilled African Americans who lack access, through social networks, to fields in which immigrants have become concentrated; employers also generally prefer foreign over native-born lower-level workers. Even so, Waldinger and Lichter maintain that immigration may have had a net positive effect on Los Angeles's African Americans as a whole given its role in swelling demand for the types of public service jobs in which better skilled African Americans have clustered and specialized, such as work in the postal service or public administration.[65]

In general, immigrants, as I have said, create jobs for US-born workers (and other immigrants) by increasing demand for goods and services as well as through their entrepreneurial activities and innovation. Native workers, in addition, may respond to immigration by switching into other jobs, often for the better. Some research indicates that American-born workers have reacted to the inflow of immigrants by moving into occupations that are better shielded from the newcomers and even upgrading their own skills. A comparison of the labor markets of states that received many low-skilled immigrants between 1960 and 2000 and those that received few showed that in the states receiving many such immigrants, less-educated American-born workers tended to shift out of lower-skilled jobs and into work requiring more communication skills.[66]

Overall, then, the fallout for US-born workers in terms of immigrants taking jobs and hurting their earnings has been minimal. And when it comes to the larger picture—and the economy as a whole—immigrants, as we have seen, have been beneficial in a great many ways.

———

Immigrants have been a force for change and innovation as they have helped to build and strengthen America's economy. In an earlier time, immigrants helped to lay the railroads and build our cities; they provided labor for steel mills, auto plants, and textile factories in the rising industrial economy. The sheer pace and scale of manufacturing's growth in turn-of-the-twentieth-century America, it has been argued, may well have depended on the labor of European immigrants and their children.[67]

In the contemporary era, immigrants have been pioneering new industries and fueling our information age, from Google to Amazon, serving as a linchpin of the high-tech sector, now one of the national economy's largest components. High-tech industries employed nearly fifteen million workers in 2016 according to the Bureau of Labor Statistics, accounting for about one-tenth of all employment in the country while contributing 18.2 percent of the economy's total output, or a remarkable $5.3 trillion.[68] Immigrants have played a major role in starting, running, and developing new tech companies, and spearheading innovations in them, so that it is not an exaggeration to say that the success of much of the tech sector has depended to a large degree on immigrant talent.

Immigrants have created new types of businesses in other sectors too, while reinvigorating, expanding, or sustaining many existing enterprises. In filling service industry jobs at every level, immigrants have also introduced changes, from reducing shortages in medical and health care professions to stimulating job growth in an array of lower-level occupations. Because the tens of millions of immigrants use services and consume goods for themselves and their families, they have boosted the economy and job growth here.

A final set of questions remain that have arisen in the wake of the coronavirus epidemic that ravaged the country in 2020. At the time of this writing, it is too early to tell how severe and lasting the scars will be for immigrants and the economy. Among the many unknowns is the degree to which immigrant businesses, including hard-hit nail salons and restaurants, will fail or eventually bounce back, or be replaced by new ones. Or the extent to which service jobs in such devastated industries as hotels, for which there was strong demand for immigrants before the pandemic, will revive afterward. While the economy was badly hurt during the coronavirus recession, immigrants, it is safe to say, will continue to play a significant role in America's economy in the foreseeable future, including renewing and revitalizing it when the pandemic ends—one of the topics I take up in the concluding chapter.

CHAPTER 5

The Territory of Culture

IMMIGRATION, POPULAR CULTURE,
AND THE ARTS

In her book *The Fortune Cookie Chronicles*, journalist Jennifer 8. Lee tells the story of a White American foreign service officer stationed in Iraq in the early 2000s who explained the popularity of the two improvised Chinese restaurants in the Baghdad Green Zone. "It's a taste of home," he said. "What could be more American than take-out Chinese?"[1]

Lee's story makes two points about American culture. First, it shows just how significantly immigration changes the way we live. As of 2015, Chinese restaurants in the United States outnumbered all the McDonald's, Burger Kings, and Kentucky Fried Chickens combined, and they are spread nearly everywhere across the country. Our benchmark for Americanness, Lee notes, is apple pie, but how frequently, she asks, "do you eat apple pie? How often do you eat Chinese food?"[2]

The second point is that the customs immigrants bring with them change when they get here. And here, too, Chinese food is an example— because the "Chinese" food most Americans eat is not the same as what was eaten in China. Many cultural elements from the home country— be they foods, music, or festivals—become "Americanized" in some ways. Often they turn into things that, like chop suey, are neither fully American nor fully Chinese. They turn into mixtures, blending aspects of immigrant and American cultures. Indeed, what is conspicuous about the cultural changes that immigration creates is that they are frequently new, often different, and sometimes wonderfully unique.

There is hardly any part of American popular culture and the arts that hasn't been influenced by immigration. Immigrants along with their children have had an impact on the foods we eat, altered the music we listen and dance to, and shaped the novels we read. Films and television programs reflect the country's greater ethnic diversity. In cities and towns around the country, new ethnic celebrations have become part of public life. These cultural shifts and innovations are an inherent part of how immigration has been remaking and in many ways revitalizing the United States today. It is an age-old American pattern. The very culture we now think of as uniquely American reflects numerous innovations by earlier immigrants, and the changes immigrants are introducing today build on their predecessors' achievements.

We Are What We Eat

The phrase "we are what we eat" generally refers to how food affects our health, but it also relates to immigrant influences on American diets. Immigration has transformed Americans' palates and reconfigured the culinary canon.[3] This pattern is as old as the country itself. Hot dogs and Cracker Jacks may seem quintessentially American, but they were introduced by German immigrants in the nineteenth century; those same immigrants also gave us lager beer. The impact of the turn-of-the-twentieth-century Italian immigrants is legendary. They brought pasta and marinara sauce with them, and, so it is said, invented the spaghetti and meatballs dish in this country; the American staple, pizza, also owes its origins to Italian arrivals over a century ago. By 2014, the United States had over seventy-two thousand pizza restaurants (including four major pizza chains). On any given day, an estimated one in eight Americans had eaten pizza.

When it comes to food, becoming American in the modern era, as historian Donna Gabaccia has argued, has required mass production and mass marketing—go corporate and become American, as she puts it.[4] As foods associated with particular ethnic groups have become mass market products, they have sometimes lost their ethnic identities and along the way become "Americanized" to adapt to popular tastes, and in some versions, added other ethnic or regional ingredients and flavors.

Consider the bagel, a classic immigrant food from the past that has become a standard American product. Eastern European Jews brought bagels to the United States from Poland in the late nineteenth century, although these "humble, hard rolls purchased from the immigrant baker" were not a central culinary icon for Jewish immigrants at the time. The original New York bagels a hundred years ago were smaller than they are today—two to three ounces, and almost always plain, with no sesame seeds or onions. They got their crust from being boiled in water, and then were baked in a gas oven until their chewy interiors were cooked through.[5] By the 1940s and 1950s, the bagel had become a symbol of Jewishness among second-generation Jews even while they were leaving many other aspects of their parents' homeland cultures behind. Joan Nathan, a cookbook author, relates how when her family moved to the New York City suburb of Larchmont in 1946, her father devised a plan to discover whether his new neighbors were, like him, Jewish: he went to the Bronx and brought back some bagels, figuring that if the neighbors knew what the rolls were, they were Jewish. (They were; as soon as the neighbors saw the bagels, they recognized them.) Nathan also describes the Jewish Sunday morning ritual of lox, bagels, and cream cheese with her parents—something that I too, as a third-generation New Yorker, recall from my childhood in the 1950s, although I did not know at the time that cream cheese was not a Jewish product but rather introduced and developed by English Quakers in eighteenth-century America.[6]

Bagels did not make it to the national market until the 1960s, when the Lender family in New Haven, Connecticut, reorganized their bagel business, buying new machines that could produce more bagels more quickly, eliminating hand rolling and substituting steaming for boiling, and adding flash freezing and plastic bag packaging for distribution around the country. Two decades later Lender's was purchased by Kraft, which produced a softer bagel that was now, like most American breads, sweetened with sugar. The new standardized mass-produced bagel also now came in a variety of flavors, including cinnamon and blueberry.[7] Other food conglomerates got into the act as well, with corporate food giants like Thomas, Pepperidge Farm, and Sara Lee producing bagels. No longer a specifically Jewish food, bagels have truly become mainstream, going from the Jewish bun to the American breakfast bread.[8] Nearly two out of three Americans—a whopping 205 million people— consumed bagels in 2019.[9]

Chinese and Mexican foods have also become ubiquitous, although interestingly, unlike bagels and spaghetti, they are often still seen as foreign, despite the long history of many Chinese and Mexican dishes in the United States.[10] No doubt one reason for this perception is that a high proportion of Chinese and Mexican Americans are of recent immigrant origin, in the first or second generation, whereas by now Jews and Italians are overwhelmingly in the third and higher generations. Moreover, Jews and Italians are seen as White, while in the popular imagination the Chinese and Mexicans are generally viewed as non-White and outside the dominant racial majority population.

Chinese restaurants date back to the mid-nineteenth century when the large numbers of male sojourners created both a high demand for eating places and willingness to work in them.[11] It was earlier Chinese immigrants who first invented made-in-America Chinese food, with Chinese-origin dishes in Americanized forms, like chop suey and chow mein becoming standard fare in Chinese restaurants. It may be surprising to learn that in 1942, chop suey and chow mein were added to the US Army cookbook—an indication of how widespread these foods had become by that time.[12] Since the 1970s, Chinese cuisine has been redefined to include dishes from a much broader array of regions in China. Before 1975, Chinese restaurants in the United States were almost always Cantonese, but immigrants in the past few decades have brought a wide variety of cuisines with them, including Sichuan, Hunan, and Shanghai.[13] And there are new American-style dishes. General Tso's chicken, a popular Chinese chef's special in America, was inspired by a dish created in Taipei in the 1950s and named for a Qing dynasty military leader to whom there is no recorded connection; the American version, developed in New York in the 1970s, not only features broccoli, but to the shock of its original Taiwanese inventor, tastes sweet. Interestingly, American Chinese food has developed its own identity "so much so that it is sold in Korea, Singapore, and the Dominican Republic as its own distinct cuisine."[14]

Whereas Chinese restaurants were once associated with Chinatowns or gateway cities with large Chinese populations, in recent decades they have spread all over the country, including to towns far from a sizable Chinese immigrant community, and that may have hardly any Chinese or Asian American residents. Arriving in large numbers in recent years, Chinese immigrants from Fujian Province are key figures behind this dispersion, creating new restaurants or converting older ones into all-you-can-eat-buffets in the South and Midwest.[15] Most of the roughly forty thousand Chinese restaurants in the United States in the second decade of the twenty-first century were small-scale operations, but there are also a number of fast-food chains. The biggest is Panda Express, a Chinese restaurant chain established in the 1980s by an immigrant couple from Taiwan and Hong Kong.[16] By 2019, it had roughly two thousand eateries around the country that, in the words of one newspaper account, dish up a "stir-fry empire."[17] And while many Americans find comfort in old Chinese American classics like chop suey or sweet and sour chicken, and many others savor Hunan and Sichuan dishes tweaked to suit American tastes, new inventions have come on the scene that merge food customs like Panda Express's cream cheese rangoons, wonton wrappers filled with cream cheese and served with sweet and sour sauce. Or to the delight of cosmopolitan foodies, there are such creations as the chili fried chicken conceived by Eric Huang, the "impressively pedigreed Taiwanese American chef" described in the New Yorker's review of Pecking House, a takeout and delivery operation he opened in New York City in 2020. "Inspired as much by the American South as it is by his heritage," the New Yorker's food critic Hannah Goldfield wrote, "the finishing seasoning" for the brined and battered chicken is "a tantalizing medley of crushed Tianjin chilies, Szechuan peppercorn, salt, and sugar."[18]

The Hispanic impact on the American diet and menu is even more pronounced than that of Chinese Americans, which is not surprising given that Hispanics are nearly a fifth of the country's population, with Mexican Americans the largest group. Tex-Mex is an old regional cuisine of the Southwest, but Mexican food was invisible to many, probably most, Americans until the 1970s; it has gone, as one journalist puts it, from Mexican curio to regional American treat, to assimilation into the country as a whole—from barrios to restaurants to supermarkets to school cafeterias.[19]

Salsa has overtaken ketchup in sales since the 1990s, and sales of corn snacks and tortilla chips, a Mexican American variant of fried tortillas born in Texas, were not far behind those of potato chips at last count.[20] It could be argued that salsa as well as tortilla chips have become so popular in recent decades that many or perhaps even most Americans no longer consider them "ethnic." Burritos and tacos (tortillas wrapped around a stuffing), however, are still identified with Mexicans even as they have become pervasive in fast-food restaurants and the frozen food aisles of supermarkets throughout the country.

Fast-food chains have popularized Mexican-origin dishes all across the United States, with Taco Bell the largest chain of all. Taco Bell may have been started by an Anglo named Glen Bell, but the chain took advantage of a growing taste for Mexican food, selling it "fast and cheap" in Americanized versions, and as food historian Jeffrey Pilcher observes, allowing Americans in other racial and ethnic groups to sample it without actually going into Mexican neighborhoods.[21] Beginning with a single location in southern California in 1962, by 2021 Taco Bell had expanded to around seven thousand US branches under the ownership of the global fast-food corporation Yum! Brands. Chipotle, founded in 1993 by a non-Mexican in Colorado, had more than twenty-five hundred restaurants in the United States by 2020, and according to one food writer, set off an American love affair for Mission-style burritos (large sized, and filled with extra rice and other ingredients), which reportedly first became popular among Mexicans in California in the 1960s.[22] The author of a book on the history of Mexican food in the United States (subtitled *How Mexican Food Conquered America*) puts it well when he writes that today, "Mexican food is . . . in our school cafeterias [and] . . . in convenience stores heating on rolling racks. . . . [It] fills our grocery aisles, feeds underclassmen, becomes tween trends or front-page news—and if you don't know what I'm talking about, ask your kid about spaghetti tacos." On space missions, NASA has even used flour tortillas for astronauts' sustenance.[23]

In general, American supermarkets have become sites of multicultural mixing. Walk into virtually any large supermarket in America and the impact of recent immigration is striking. The popular frozen TV dinners of the post–World War II period, with their roast turkey or fried chicken, mashed potatoes, and soft vegetables, are still with us, but they have been joined by an array of new products, including many that owe their origin to immigrants of the post-1965 period. In our era of mass production of ethnic foods by large corporations and in today's fast-food nation, Mexican origin foods as well as those from a wide range of other countries are now part of everyday eating. Tacos, tortilla wraps, pita bread, wantons, and sushi—you name it, immigrants have been a source of innovation in modern American cuisine.[24]

In many ways of course it's a case of business as usual, as entrepreneurs and big companies seek to capitalize on new ethnic products, although it has been easier for new ethnic foods and ethnic-inspired dishes to gain acceptance in contemporary America than in earlier eras now that ordinary Americans, as Gabaccia comments, "are much more eager than in 1900 to entertain themselves with the cultural gifts of new immigrants," and when new foods are picked up and produced by corporate giants, and promoted by modern mass marketing and communications.[25] Also, the growing number of well-off, young, highly educated professionals in major metropolitan areas are an enthusiastic clientele for high-end restaurants whose immigrant-origin owners and chefs offer new tastes along with intricate inventions that draw on home-country cuisines. Of the ten chefs on *Food & Wine* magazine's list of the best new chefs in 2020, six were immigrants or children of immigrants. Among them were Niven Patel, a Gujarati American who supplied his farm-to-table Miami restaurants with produce from his small farm south of the city, including ingredients for "bowls of Rancho Patel eggplant and potatoes simmered in a spiced tomato gravy . . . a riff on a staple found in most Gujarati kitchens." Tavel Bristol-Joseph, a

Guyanese immigrant pastry chef in Austin, Texas, created a sophisti-
cated bread pudding made from a monthslong fermenting process. In
an expensive Manhattan restaurant, Korean-born Eunjo Park served up
panfried rice cakes dunked in chili jam made with "plenty of raw garlic,
mirin, and gochujang, and topped with a translucent layer of Benton's
ham with a flourish of rice pearls for crunch."[26]

Whether Americans are dining at a pricey restaurant, getting a bite
at a fast-food chain, or buying groceries at the supermarket, the fact is
that the immigration of recent decades has been one of the prime mov-
ers in changing American tastes and food-consumption patterns. Eating the cuisines of different ethnic groups, indeed a multiethnic mix of
foods, has become the American way.[27] Many highly popular and
widely consumed foods that immigrants brought with them or created
here still retain strong ethnic associations, but some connected with
recent immigrant groups that are mass produced for a national market,
like salsa and tortilla chips, seem to be in the process of losing their
ethnic ties, and may have lost them already for many Americans.[28]
Either way, what Americans eat is not the same today as it was before
the 1960s, and to no small degree, the massive immigration of the last
half century is responsible.

The Arts and Popular Culture:
New Faces in Old Places

If, as some scholars say, immigration is about new faces in old places,
then this is part of the story in the arts. A growing number of post-1965
immigrants and their US-born children are making a mark in a range of
established arenas, from films and television to symphony orchestras
and literature. To name just a few leading popular actresses and actors,
Hispanics include Salma Hayek, who began her career starring in tele-
novelas (television soap operas) in her native Mexico and whose US
breakthrough role was in the film *Frida* as the Mexican painter Frida
Kahlo; Cuban-born Andy Garcia, whose many starring roles include
the 2001 remake of *Ocean's Eleven*; and Edward James Olmos, a

second-generation Mexican star of the hit television series *Miami Vice* and Academy Award nominee for his portrayal of a Los Angeles math teacher in the film *Stand and Deliver*. Among the Asian American stars who stand out are Aziz Ansari, the son of Indian immigrants and first Asian American man to win a Golden Globe for acting in television, in the comedy series *Masters of None*, which he also co-created; Lucy Liu, a second-generation Chinese American, perhaps best known for her award-winning acting in the television comedy *Ally McBeal* and two *Charlie's Angels* films; and Filipina immigrant Lea Salonga, who broke into American musical theater at the age of nineteen when she origi-nated the lead role in Broadway's *Miss Saigon*, becoming the first Asian woman to win a Tony award.

In classical music, Asian Americans have become an important pres-ence. Between 2002 and 2014, the proportion of Asian American musi-cians in American orchestras went from 5 to 9 percent, and at some top orchestras the figure was even higher, such as around 20 percent at the New York Philharmonic, whose past music director (2009–17) was the mixed-race native New Yorker Alan Gilbert, the son of a Japanese Amer-ican mother and White father.[29]

In literature, too, there has been some changing of the guard. Whereas in the 1950s and 1960s, Philip Roth and Saul Bellow brought the angst and aspirations of the Jewish immigrant and second generation to a wider public in books like *Goodbye, Columbus* and *The Adventures of Augie March*, now a host of award-winning first- and second-generation novelists have been writing of the struggles of children of immigrants with roots in Africa, Asia, the Caribbean, and Latin America to become American, from Gish Jen's *Typical American* (Chinese American), and Junot Díaz's *The Brief Wondrous Life of Oscar Wao* (Dominican Ameri-can) to Jhumpa Lahiri's (Indian American) *The Namesake*.[30]

It is important of course not to exaggerate the ease of ethnic succes-sion as contemporary immigrants and their children follow in the foot-steps of those who came before in the arts; the process is not as seamless or simple as it may at first appear. Although Latinos, Asian Americans, and Blacks of immigrant origin are a growing presence in Hollywood, on Broadway, and in television, they are still underrepresented relative to their proportion of the US population, especially in prominent roles. In 2017, for example, Latinos had 5.2 percent of top film roles and Asian Americans had 3.4 percent, while Whites, with 77 percent, remained overrepresented.[31] The way ethnic and racial characters are portrayed in movies and on television is also, unhappily, in many cases reminiscent of the past, reinforcing views of immigrant-origin ethnic or racial groups as low in status, and bolstering negative stereotypes such as Latino drug dealers and sexpots as well as Asian nerds and exoticized women.[32] Indeed, a hundred years after the mass immigration from Italy ended and when most Italian Americans have become solidly middle class, they are still often stereotyped in television and film as criminals and violent mobsters.[33]

Nor should we overlook tensions or at least ambivalence that may result from another kind of cultural change that has taken place. The calendar of parades and ethnic festivals in traditional gateway cities all around the country has been updated as Caribbean, Latino, and Asian American celebrations have joined old staples like the Irish American Saint Patrick's Day and Italian American Columbus Day parades. On the one hand, many places have been welcoming or accepting of these additions. New York City, for example, has had no trouble integrating more than two dozen new ethnic festivals into the city's event calendar; the Hispanic Day parade, to mention one, now marches up Fifth Avenue on the Sunday before or after Columbus Day. The West Indian American Day parade, another made-in-the-US innovation, is the city's largest ethnic festival of all, attracting hundreds of thousands on Brooklyn's Eastern Parkway, and has become a mandatory campaign stop for politicians seeking citywide office. While modeled after Trinidad's Carnival, it has undergone significant changes in New York, as it has turned into, among other things, a pan–West Indian event drawing West Indians from nations without Carnival traditions and takes place on a US holiday in September, Labor Day, rather than right before Lent.[34] On the West Coast, in the Silicon Valley city of San Jose, California, which boasts a large Cinco de Mayo celebration and Chinese New Year parade as well as a Tet (Vietnamese New Year) festival, residents have grown accustomed to the ethnic celebrations, and see them as part of the regular array of public events in their city and region.[35] On the other hand, research conducted in Kennett Square, a town about thirty miles from Philadelphia, indicates that the welcome, at least initially, may be less warm. In the space of just a decade, this affluent White English-speaking community had by 2000 become home to a significant Latino, mainly Mexican, population drawn to work in the mushroom industry. After three years of celebrating Cinco de Mayo, the festival had been moved in 2004 from the main street to back alleys and parking lots, reflecting, as folklorist Debra Lattanzi Shutika observes, the growing ambivalence of the English-speaking residents toward their Mexican neighbors. By 2015, however, the festival was back on the main street, suggesting that the Mexican community had by then gained enough clout to return it to the town center, although how much discomfort with the celebration remained among White residents is unclear.[36] In Silicon Valley cities, even when long-established residents became used to the growing number of ethnically themed events, some remained ambivalent, complaining in interviews that these events had come at the expense of "American" celebrations.[37]

New Themes, Forms, Styles, and Sounds

Changes in popular culture and the arts are not only about the addition of new celebrations to the existing event roster or immigrants in new groups succeeding those in earlier cohorts. Contemporary newcomers and their second-generation children have also been injecting energy and vitality into popular culture and public rituals. In the process, they have brought new (or in some cases dormant) themes to a wider public and often created new cultural forms that are becoming, or already have become, important parts of mainstream culture. The bottom line is that the changes are evidence of genuine transformations and a significant way that immigrants and their children have been redefining America.

If the Irish gave us Saint Patrick's Day parades and Italians Columbus Day celebrations, Mexicans are already leaving a mark through the institutionalization of Cinco de Mayo festivities. Cinco de Mayo festivals are in truth a made-in-the-US creation, morphing from a Mexican holiday commemorating the victory of Mexican forces over the French in the Battle of Puebla in 1862, into a public celebration emphasizing Mexican cuisine, culture, and music, replete with commercial tie-ins for food and drinks. Cinco de Mayo events have been held all around the country, from San Francisco, Denver, Chicago, and Phoenix, to Boston and New York City; one of the largest is in Los Angeles, where about half the population is Hispanic, mostly of Mexican origin. The White House, too, officially began celebrating Cinco de Mayo in 2001 under George W. Bush, inviting Mexican dignitaries, artists, politicians, and prominent figures in the Mexican community to festivities on the White House lawn. The tradition was continued by President Obama who, in his last year in office, hosted an elaborate party in the East Room complete with a celebrity chef and Latin Grammy–winning band.

In film and television, the immigrant impact is about more than the number of ethnic minorities in leading roles, important as this is. Interestingly, ethnic minorities are more visible than they were in an earlier era when movie stars with Jewish and Italian immigrant origins typically changed their names to hide their ethnicity, and the themes of the films they starred in rarely had anything to do with their ethnic roots. Think, for example, of Lauren Bacall (born Betty Joan Perske), Tony Curtis (Bernard Schwartz), or Kirk Douglas (Issur Danielovitch Demsky), and Dean Martin (Dino Paul Crocetti) and Anne Bancroft (Anna Maria Louisa Italiano). Bancroft actually changed her name twice; initially she appeared in a number of live television dramas as Anne Marno, but was later told to change her surname as it was too ethnic for movies. It was "all right in those days [in 1952] for an Italian [actress] to be called Anna Magnani but not for an Italian American."[38] This pattern of name changing has not altogether disappeared; Natalie Portman was born Natalie Hershlag, Charlie Sheen was Carlos Irwin Estévez, and Nicolas Cage was Nicolas Coppola.[39] But the practice is certainly less common today, when American audiences are well aware of, and have become accustomed to, Hispanic, Asian American, and increasingly African stars on-screen along with hearing names that indicate their ethnicity.

And while Latino and Asian American actors and actresses are still often typecast in "ethnic roles" that reinforce demeaning stereotypical images, this is not always case. Even when they star in ethnic roles on the big and small screen, these roles are in a growing number of mainstream productions that frequently present the problems confronting immigrants and people of color in a realistic and fresh way. This development is partly a product of the greater sensitivity in contemporary America to how racial and ethnic minorities are portrayed on-screen, but also other factors: the large and expanding Latino, Asian American, and African American market; efforts by Latinos, Asians Americans, and Blacks themselves to carve out a larger role in the entertainment industry; and a sincere desire by those of immigrant origin in the industry as well as, it must be added, by others to highlight themes that are close to the heart of and reflect concerns in immigrant communities. A number of recent films and television productions have drawn attention to the prejudice and discrimination experienced by immigrants and their children, reviving a concern depicted in some films of earlier eras, although with a modern sensibility. Topics of specific importance to today's immigrant groups have been featured in the mainstream entertainment industry, such as undocumented immigration and, especially among South Asians, arranged or semi-arranged marriages. A major theme of the 2017 romantic comedy *The Big Sick*, to mention one film, is about pressure from the male lead's Pakistani immigrant parents to marry one of the Pakistani American women they introduce him to, while secretly he is involved with a White American graduate student, whom he ultimately marries. The film was inspired by the real-life love story of the male star and cowriter, Pakistani-born Kumail Nanjiani, who has spoken of how he "really thought I would get disowned by my parents" for marrying someone from outside the culture "because that is the narrative that you're sort of raised with. . . . But . . . now they've been in America a little more than a decade I see them changing as people." The film's lesson for other cultures, according to Nanjiani, is that "when two representatives from two different cultures come together, it can be beautiful, but it is also quite challenging."[40]

Or consider two award-winning situation comedies that occupied prime-time slots and were cited by critics for adding freshness to network television. *Ugly Betty*, which won, among others, two Golden

Globe and three Emmy awards, broke new ground in that it was produced by Latinos, had a Latino cast with a Latino story line, and was adapted from a Latin American telenovela. America Ferrara, herself the daughter of Honduran immigrants, played a Mexican American assistant from Queens who, despite sorely lacking in fashion sense, was determined to make it in fashion-magazine publishing. Running for four seasons on ABC, from 2006 to 2010, *Ugly Betty*, one reviewer noted, was one of the rare network shows to tackle such controversial issues as undocumented immigration, gay teens, and body image—doing so as part of the story lines, with humor and without adopting a didactic tone.[41]

Fresh Off the Boat, inspired by the memoir of chef and food personality Eddie Huang (the son of immigrants from Taiwan), ran for six seasons on ABC beginning in 2015. Its focus was a Taiwanese American family that moves from Washington, DC's Chinatown to a mostly White neighborhood in Orlando, Florida, to open a cowboy-themed steak restaurant; the children struggle with adjusting to and fitting in at school, the mother wrestles with the cultural clash between her Taiwanese heritage and the Florida community where the family now lives, and the father embraces all things American. As the *New Yorker*'s television critic put it reviewing the first season, "The show has a radical quality, simply because it arrives in a television landscape with few Asian characters, almost none of them protagonists. . . . Simply watching people of color having a private conversation, one that's not primarily about white people, is a huge deal. It changes who the joke is on."[42] Among innovations in later seasons, about half of one episode in 2018 was in Mandarin. A writer on the show explained, "I never thought there would be a primetime network sitcom centered on an Asian family. The fact that I get to work on it and pull so directly from my childhood, being a half-Chinese kid raised in a Mandarin-speaking household, is still hard to wrap my head around. . . . Why did we do an episode that features an entire storyline spoken in Mandarin? Because on a TV show about a Chinese family, we can. And hopefully people will enjoy it."[43]

To mention one more example, Ramy Youssef, the New York–born son of Egyptian immigrants, won a 2020 Golden Globe award for his role in the semi-autobiographical Hulu series *Ramy*, the first scripted television comedy about the Muslim American experience, drawing its humor from Ramy's being caught between the world of his Egyptian Muslim parents and that of the American millennial generation. "You sit in contradiction," Youssef said, "and that has been the space that I'm trying to navigate. And that's the kind of space that I bring to the work."[44]

In the world of television, another change stimulated by immigration is the striking success of two Spanish-language television networks, Univision and Telemundo, catering to the huge Latino market, with more than 37 million Latinos in the United States speaking Spanish at home. Launched in the 1980s, the two networks have become media powerhouses, frequently beating their English counterparts in television ratings and featuring programs imported from Latin America as well as made in the United States, including news and talk shows as well as soap operas. Univision proclaimed itself the undisputed leader in Spanish-language news in the United States in 2019, when it was home to the number one evening news program on broadcast television with a Hispanic audience, *Noticiero Univision*, which averaged some 1.6 million viewers. The program's ten-time Emmy-winning coanchor, Mexican-born and Miami-based Jorge Ramos, was listed by *Time* magazine as one of the 25 most influential Hispanics in the United States.[45]

Fewer Americans may read novels than watch television news shows or situation comedies, but they are an important part of American culture—and today's immigrants have had a profound impact on them. The early twentieth-century immigration stands out for giving rise to many first- and second-generation Jewish American writers who shaped the development of the American novel, won important awards, and sold hundreds of thousands, or often millions, of copies of their books. Among the most notable are, as already mentioned, Bellow and Roth along with Joseph Heller, Norman Mailer, Bernard Malamud, and Isaac Bashevis Singer, all considered American literary "greats." Indeed, Bellow and Singer won the Nobel Prize for Literature (as did Eugene O'Neill, the son of an Irish immigrant), and many think that Roth should have received that honor as well.[46]

Today, American literature is once again being influenced, and enriched, by a spate of recent immigrant and second-generation novelists, this time with origins in countries all over the world—Africa, Latin America, Asia, and the Caribbean as well as Europe. As before, these writers are garnering major awards and authoring books that reach a wide readership. Between 2000 and 2020, three immigrant novelists (Jhumpa Lahiri, Junot Díaz, and Viet Thanh Nguyen) won the Pulitzer Prize for fiction, and Chimamanda Ngozi Adichie (*Americanah*) as well as Díaz (*The Brief Wondrous Life of Oscar Wao*) won the National Book Circle Critics Award; books by all four authors have been *New York Times* best sellers.[47] Noteworthy, too, is the second-generation Chinese American playwright David Henry Hwang, best known for his Tony Award–winning and Pulitzer Prize–finalist play *M. Butterfly*, based on the true story of a French diplomat who had a long affair with a singer in the Beijing opera who turned out to be a man and a spy. Hwang's work was honored by New York's Signature Theater, which devoted an entire season (2012–13) to mounting plays from his more than thirty-year career.[48]

Although many contemporary immigrant and second-generation novelists draw on perennial immigrant themes—ethnic and racial prejudice, for example, and adjusting to new cultural values and norms, and in many cases, low-paid and demeaning jobs—they do so with new interpretations and concerns that reflect the particular cultures and regions they come from as well as late twentieth- and early twentieth-century American realities. Indeed, one way they are having an impact on the literary landscape is through accounts of migrants' lives both before and after the move to the United States. American readers are being exposed to gripping accounts of experiences in the countries immigrants left behind, including war-ravaged African and Asian countries, and China under Communist rule.[49] Once in the United States, a new theme in a number of recent novels is the all-too-common contemporary problem of undocumented status. To mention just three examples, there is Reyna Grande's *Across a Hundred Mountains*, a tale of a Mexican girl's journey across the border to California in search of her father; Imbolo Mbue's *Behold the Dreamers*, on the struggles of a Cameroonian family without papers in New York; and Lisa Ko's *The Leavers*, about a US-born boy's loss of and eventual reconciliation with his undocumented Chinese immigrant mother.[50]

While most fictional narratives dealing with race in the United States are about African Americans, immigrant novels are adding a new dimension to the literature, giving a deep, personal sense of what it means for the growing number of Africans and West Indians to be Black in America.[51] In this regard, it is interesting that Paule Marshall's critically acclaimed semi-autobiographical novel *Brown Girl, Brownstones*, a coming-of-age story of the daughter of Barbadian immigrants growing up in Brooklyn with her parents during the Depression and World War II, was out of print for years. Originally published in 1959, it did not attract much attention until after 1981, when it was reissued by the Feminist Press in post–civil rights America at a time when massive immigration was again underway, including from the West Indies. With growing interest in the Black diaspora in the academy, the book was now recognized in many newly established Black and African American studies programs as a pioneering novel in contemporary African American women's writing, and became a staple of many college courses.[52]

Contemporary immigrant novels (about and by those of recent immigrant origin) are enriching American literary culture in additional ways. Because the leading characters in many of them are the US-born or US-raised children of immigrants, the novels often focus on the struggles to become American while maintaining an ethnic identity in an era when ethnic affiliations are more accepted than they were in earlier times. Many of the novels also capture the nuances of relations with immigrant parents today—including conflicts over dating and sexual relations as well as career and marriage choices—in an America that has experienced radically changed attitudes about gender, sexuality, and women's roles in recent decades.[53]

In another domain in the arts, contemporary immigrants and the second generation have been pioneers in transforming popular music and musical theater. In some ways this is a reprise from the past, although as sociologist Philip Kasinitz observes, some of the best-known immigrant-origin popular music innovators in mid-twentieth-century America drew self-consciously on American themes at a time when the second generation felt intense pressure from mainstream institutions to reject old country ways and show that they were truly "American."

Irving Berlin (born Israel Beilin in Russia and emigrated as a child) gave us the now-classic songs "God Bless America" and "Easter Parade," George Gershwin (born Jacob Gershowitz to Russian Jewish immigrants) wrote the folk opera *Porgy and Bess*, and composer Richard Rodgers and lyricist Oscar Hammerstein (grandsons of European Jewish immigrants) portrayed an imaginary rural American heartland in their Broadway musicals *Oklahoma* and *Carousel*.[54] Today's immigrant and second-generation musical pioneers, living in a climate in which they are frequently encouraged to retain and indeed celebrate their cultural roots, often fuse sounds and styles from their countries or regions of origin with those they encounter in the United States. In some notable cases, they have created remarkably successful innovations.

Immigrants from the Caribbean have had an outsized influence on American popular music, from introducing the sounds of Jamaican reggae to Cuban salsa and Dominican merengue. Hip-hop, created out of a blend of cultural influences, is a genre that revolutionized the American music scene and includes (and sometimes is used synonymously with) rap, in which rhythmic or rhyming speech is performed or chanted, usually over a backing beat or musical accompaniment. According to one statistical analysis, hip-hop/rap was the defining genre on the US Billboard Hot 100 charts from 1991 and for the next two decades.[55] Although hip-hop is commonly thought to be an African American invention, it was originally as much a creation of Afro-Caribbean and Latino youths in New York City as an African American form. In fact, "toasting," a form of reggae in which artists speak words over a soundtrack, helped set the stage in the Bronx of the 1970s for a format that became hip-hop. Many of the early stars of that genre had Caribbean origins, including Biggie Smalls (born Christopher Wallace in Brooklyn to Jamaican immigrant parents), rapper Wyclef Jean (whose work celebrates his Haitian origins while also mixing African American, Latin American, and other elements), and DJ Kool Herc (born Clive Campbell in Jamaica and moving to the Bronx at the age of twelve).[56] Among more recent rap celebrities are two immigrant young women from the West Indies: Nicki Minaj (born Onika Tanya Miraj in Trinidad), said to be the best-selling female rapper of all time, and Rihanna (born Robyn Rihanna Fenty in Barbados), who incorporated a wide range of genres, among them hip-hop, pop, and rhythm and blues, into her many hits, including thirty-one top-ten singles in the United States.

A host of other superstars with roots in Latin America as well as the Caribbean have had a transformative effect on popular music. One of the best known is Cuban-born and Miami-based Gloria Estefan, a multiple Grammy Award winner listed on *Billboard's* Top 100 Greatest Artists of All Time and recipient of Kennedy Center Honors in 2017 for her contributions to American culture. Called one of the most successful crossover artists in Latin music history, she brought Latin rhythms, fused with American popular music, to a mainstream American audience. At the beginning of her career she was told that her sound was "too American for the Latins, too Latin for the Americans." She ignored the advice to change her name and lose her band's percussion and horns: "We were trying to do music that we felt could do something new, and was fresh and different."[57] Ricky Martin (born Enrique Martin Morales in Puerto Rico) is perhaps most famous for his hit and signature song "Livin' La Vida Loca," which drew on the tradition of a swing song, but with horns and rhythms giving it a Latin base; Martin was at the forefront of what is called the Latin pop explosion of 1999, injecting Latin sounds and Spanish into mainstream popular music hits, and making it easier for other Latino performers to cross into the English-language market.[58] A ten-time Grammy Award winner and Kennedy Center honoree, Mexican-born and US-raised Carlos Santana pioneered a fusion of rock, blues, jazz, and Afro-Caribbean and Latin influences with his band Santana. Rising to fame in the late 1960s and 1970s, he became a guitar legend in popular music, and was known for his distinctive tone that has been described as crystalline, clean, and recognizable in just one note.[59]

Migration has also been transforming musical theater. Lin-Manuel Miranda's *Hamilton*, it has been said, is as radical and innovative as *Oklahoma* was in its day.[60] To go back some eighty years, *Oklahoma* was first performed in 1943. Written by Rodgers and Hammerstein, it revolutionized musical theater: "It seamlessly blended story, song, and dance in the service of realistic character development, in ways that made the typical froth of 1940s Broadway musical comedy seem puny by comparison. The American musical theater would never be the same, and neither would Rodgers and Hammerstein, who would go on to resounding successes with 'Carousel,' 'South Pacific,' 'The King and I' and 'The Sound of Music.'"[61]

Miranda's *Hamilton* is taking musical theater in new directions. A native New Yorker and son of Puerto Rican migrants, Miranda had already broken new ground in 2008 with his first Tony Award–winning musical, *In the Heights*, which was about immigrants and their children in an upper Manhattan Dominican neighborhood, and drew on hip-hop, Latin music, and Broadway show tunes.[62] *In the Heights* was a hit, but *Hamilton's* impact on the theater scene was nothing short of revolutionary. A largely hip-hop-based retelling of the story of Alexander Hamilton, it seamlessly integrates rap and storytelling, although as Kasinitz notes, "The rapping founding fathers never come across as a gimmick, nor does the multi-racial cast."[63] Most of the major parts have been played by people of color from diverse ethnic backgrounds and have included Miranda himself, who was the lead in the original production—and also wrote the book, music, and lyrics. *Hamilton* stands out as one of the biggest critical and commercial hits in Broadway history, garnering eleven Tony Awards as well as the Pulitzer Prize for drama and a Grammy Award for best musical theater album.[64] "I am loath to tell people to mortgage their houses and lease their children to acquire tickets to a hit Broadway show," a *New York Times* theater critic wrote when the show opened in 2015. "But *Hamilton* . . . might just about be worth it—at least to anyone who wants proof that the American musical is not only surviving but also evolving in ways that should allow it to thrive and transmogrify in years to come."[65] That is, if you were able to get a ticket. The Broadway show set all-time box office records, with an average ticket price in 2017 of over $300, and a top premium price of over $1,000 for the week between Christmas and New Year's.

———

The innovations in *Hamilton* are unlikely to raise the hackles of most Americans—though to be sure, the show's stress on ethnic and racial diversity might concern some. To the extent that popular culture champions ethnic and racial diversity—and Asian Americans, Latinos, and Blacks are seen as making significant headway in various popular culture arenas—this may add to resentments among those, particularly less well-off Whites, who believe that people of color are gaining advantages at the expense of Whites and that the America they remember, of taken-for-granted White hegemony, is no more (see chapter 6).

And yet these same people generally are happy to eat Chinese or Mexican food; may eagerly watch movies or television programs that star Latinos or Asian Americans; and often delight in listening and dancing to melodies of Afro-Caribbean and Latin singers. Their college-educated children may enjoy novels by immigrant-origin authors. Few, I imagine, would have turned down a ticket to *Hamilton*.

By and large, the changes in popular culture and the arts I have discussed have not upset most Americans, or been points of bitter contention or conflict. In her analysis of food, Gabaccia puts forward one reason: the pursuit of pleasure with minimal obligation encourages Americans to cross cultural boundaries and incorporate parts of other cultures into their intimate lives. Americans, she observes, have not been as tolerant of and curious about their neighbors as they have about their neighbors' foods: "Consumers need not convert to Judaism or have Jewish friends to relish lox and bagels; they don't need to understand Islam or its faithful to enjoy babaganoush."[66] Beyond food, long-established Americans don't need to have Cuban American friends to enjoy the music of Estefan, African friends to be drawn to Adichie's novel *Americanah*, or Pakistani friends to appreciate movies with a South Asian lead like *The Big Sick*. The same goes for attending a host of immigrant celebrations in cities all over the country, from Caribbean carnivals to Cinco de Mayo festivals.

The Cinco de Mayo festivals are a good example of an aspect of cultural change that has come up throughout this account: how customs from immigrants' home countries become the basis for new mixtures in the American context. What was a relatively minor holiday in most of Mexico commemorating a military victory has become more important in this country among Mexican Americans as a celebration of their

Mexican heritage—not only involving Mexican food and music, but in the American way of many public festivals, frequently carnival rides as well. In at least one city, Portland, Oregon, the celebration has included a naturalization ceremony for new citizens.[67]

Popular music is full of new cultural combinations pioneered by immigrants and their offspring, from rap to Latin sounds and genres. Foods with origins in homeland cuisines, as they have developed in the United States, have often Americanized to some degree, in the case of General Tso's chicken, sweetened and with added broccoli to appeal to American tastes, or to mention salsa, the addition of new types with different degrees of spiciness (or mildness) and sweet versions to serve with dessert. Many new mixtures bring together different ethnic flavors, from nacho bagel bites to the pastrami egg rolls I have sampled at the upscale Red Farm restaurant on New York's Upper West Side.

There are two additional points. One concerns changes produced by immigrants whose culinary and artistic activities are, to a large degree, confined within their own communities. Even when many foods with origins in homeland cuisines are only or mainly eaten by immigrants and coethnics, and many ethnic festivals are just celebrated by those in immigrant communities, they often have an impact in expanding the cultural horizons of long-established Americans. Being an onlooker at an ethnic parade, or learning about it through a newspaper or television report—and becoming aware of foods in local markets or restaurants that mostly cater to coethnics—may make what initially seems strange more familiar and a normal part of the landscape. In this way, change is likely to take place as well.

Finally, there is the question of why immigrants and the second generation are frequently a source of innovation in a wide variety of the arts, introducing new forms and addressing new themes, or reviving old ones in light of their own cultural backgrounds and experiences. Being an immigrant or member of the second generation, it has been argued, is itself partly responsible for this talent for innovation. "Because immigrants have to work to learn the system," sociologist Charles Hirschman writes, "they are intensely curious about American culture. For the most talented, this tendency leads to a rich and expansive creativity that has left its imprint on American music, theater, dance, film, and many other realms of artistic endeavor."[68] Those in the US-born second-generation may have an advantage, too, in their ability to combine elements from their parents' and the receiving society's cultures in new and often original ways. And their position of being slightly outside the dominant culture may also spark creativity and insight.[69]

Ultimately, I come back to my main theme: whether looking at what we see on the screen or in the theater, hear on streaming platforms, or eat at restaurants and at home, immigrants and their children have been adding vitality, dynamism, and new features to popular culture and the arts in this country. This is yet another and important way that they are transforming America.

CHAPTER 6

Electoral Politics

In the winter of 2019, President Trump partially shut down the federal government for thirty-five days over his demand for nearly $6 billion to build a wall with Mexico—a dramatic example of Trump using immigration to rally support from his political base. Immigration, or should we say anti-immigration, was a central theme of his entire 2016 campaign and much of his presidency. Trump repeatedly and falsely portrayed undocumented immigrants as dangerous, violent criminals who must be kept out of the country at all costs. During his first full week in office, he placed a travel ban on several Muslim-majority countries. Among his many other actions, he canceled the Deferred Action for Childhood Arrivals (DACA) program, instituted by President Obama's executive order in 2012, that in the absence of court intervention, would have left hundreds of thousands of undocumented youths and young adults who grew up in the United States without the legal right to work and vulnerable to deportation; Trump also largely dismantled the country's asylum system. In a White House meeting, he was widely reported to refer to immigrants from Haiti and Africa as coming from "shithole" countries.[1] And this is just a partial list.

Trump's rhetoric and policies are a dramatic example of immigration's role in changing American electoral politics in the early twenty-first century. As Trump's public speeches, tweets, and policies suggest, one change is the degree to which the massive immigration, and especially undocumented immigration, of recent years has become a subject of national political debates and campaigns. The remarkable centrality of anti-immigration policies in national Republican political campaigns and strategies in the Trump presidency along with the legitimation of anti-immigrant speech at the highest levels of government constituted a modern-day transformation in presidential politics.

That anti-immigrant politics became a central feature of Republican Party support speaks to another political change related to the growing ethnic, racial, and religious diversity created by the post-1965 immigration: the realignment of politically engaged Americans into partisan camps. Although changing national partisan coalitions are as American a tradition as can be found, each shifting realignment, in the past as well as present, has its own particular features and consequences.[2] What happened in recent years is a reshaping of the Democratic and Republican Party coalitions, with a movement of Whites, especially those with low levels of education, and who hold less favorable views of racial and ethnic minorities, from the Democratic to Republican Party, while the increasing number of minority voters have become a more critical part of the Democratic Party electorate.[3] In the first two decades of the twenty-first century, to a large and growing degree, the Democrats had become the party of minorities and White liberals, while the Republicans had become the party of White conservatives.[4] These changes were in no small part a product of, and response to, the ongoing transformation of the country by contemporary immigrants and their children.[5]

A third political change involves ethnic succession, another longtime feature of US politics as politicians in new ethnic and racial groups are elected to office and replace those who came before, often using their ethnic community as a base of support to build on or begin the climb to electoral success. Ethnic succession, whether at the city, state, or national level, is not just about new faces in established positions. Elected politicians from recent immigrant groups have spoken for new interests, and in some instances, developed new coalitions and institutional arrangements in legislative bodies in ways that represent innovations in the political arena.

Looking ahead, the effects of immigration are likely to result in additional political transformations in the years to come, if only because of further shifts in the racial and ethnic composition of the electorate.

Will the growing number of eligible voters descended from post-1965 immigrants, for example, lead to a new Democratic majority in the nation, and turn some purple swing states and perhaps even some currently red (predominantly Republican) states blue (predominantly Democratic)? Can we expect the Republican Party to adjust its positions on immigration to attract voters, including a greater proportion of those in ethnic minority groups, or continue on a more nativist path? In short, does the analysis of immigration's role in the political arena in recent years provide any clues about the shape of the future?

Party Realignment and Coalitions

Perhaps no change in US electoral politics in the last few decades has been as consequential as the remaking of electoral coalitions and partisan allegiances. Large-scale immigration has been an important element in this transformation and so is a good place to begin.

This is not the first time that immigration has played a role in a major political realignment. Immigrants and their children were key players in the 1930s New Deal realignment, which reconfigured the party system as Democrats went from being a minority to majority party at the national level. Much of the base of support for the New Deal and Franklin Delano Roosevelt's electoral coalition was the eastern, southern, and central Europeans who had arrived between the 1880s and 1920s in combination with their second-generation children. By the 1930s, large numbers of the US-born second generation were of voting age; more immigrants themselves could vote, and "more had good reason to vote and . . . a sense that their votes mattered."[6]

They heavily backed Roosevelt. Like other Americans, immigrants were deeply affected by the crisis of the Great Depression; the Democratic Party and labor unions, in the steel and auto towns of Pennsylvania and the Midwest as well as the garment factories of New York City, took the lead in incorporating new Americans into electoral politics in support of Roosevelt's measures to combat the Depression and create new social welfare programs. Northern White ethnics with recent immigrant origins together with the heavily unionized northern White working class and White South formed the three major pillars of the New Deal coalition that put FDR in the White House and Democrats in the majority in Congress. This coalition, although it began to fracture after World War II, continued to underpin Democrats' control of the nation almost without interruption through 1968.[7]

The fracturing of the New Deal coalition stemmed in part from the civil rights movement and subsequent legislation in the 1960s, leading to a growing African American electorate and the end of the solidly Democratic South. Indeed, the civil rights–era changes provided a major impetus for what some refer to as a second realignment of the twentieth century: the massive movement of southern Whites from the Democratic to Republican Party in the 1970s and 1980s.[8] The willingness of Democratic leaders to support the civil rights movement's demands to guarantee the vote to southern Blacks not only fueled growing African American support for the Democratic Party but also, and critically, a counterreaction that opened the White South to Republicans. (Remember that in the Deep South, a combination of poll taxes, literacy tests, economic pressure, and physical intimidation had long kept almost all Black citizens out of the voting booth so that as late as the 1950s, the electorate in the Deep South states of Alabama, Mississippi, Georgia, South Carolina, and Louisiana was nearly all White. In these five states, where Blacks made up a third of the voting-age population, only 4 percent of African Americans reported voting in presidential elections in the 1950s, and Blacks made up just 3 percent of voters.) By 1980, the once reliably Democratic South had become a Republican stronghold at the presidential level—1976 was the last year a Democratic presidential candidate won a majority of southern electoral votes—and later in state elections too.[9]

And so we come to the more recent changes and new partisan divisions. The trend toward what political scientist John Sides and his colleagues call the racialization of partisanship that began after the mid-1960s, when President Johnson aligned the Democratic Party with civil rights for African Americans, intensified after the 1980s. By the early twenty-first century, the national-level Democratic Party's core electoral base had become dominated by minorities as well as

Whites with more formal education identifying as liberal, while the Republican Party now drew the great majority of its support from Whites, especially Whites with less formal education and conservative views on major social issues.[10]

As late as 1980, more Whites identified as Democrats than as Republicans. By 2010, it was the reverse: White Republicans substantially outnumbered White Democrats.[11] At the same time, the Democratic Party has increasingly become a party supported by non-Whites. In 1980, a little more than a fifth of Democratic voters in the presidential election were non-Whites. By 2019, according to a Pew Research Center national survey, they made up 40 percent of registered voters who identified with or leaned toward the Democratic Party; in contrast, the non-White share of Republican and Republican-leaning voters was much smaller (17 percent), although an increase from just 6 percent in 1994.[12] Minority voters, to put it another way, have become an essential part of the Democratic coalition.

In addition to the racial gap, a remarkable diploma divide in party identification stands out among Whites. During the Obama presidency, White flight from the Democratic Party became heavily concentrated among those with less education—and turned into a broad national trend. From 1992 to 2008, according to Pew surveys, Whites who did not attend college were about evenly split between the two parties. Since then, the GOP has made decisive gains among Whites without a college degree, with much of the movement among those with the lowest levels of education. By 2019, White registered voters who had a high school diploma or less were 31 percentage points more likely to identify with or lean toward the Republican than Democratic Party (62 versus 31 percent); White voters with some college education but no four-year degree were 18 points more Republican (56 versus 38 percent). Meanwhile, many better-educated White voters have shifted toward the Democrats. In 1994, Whites with a college degree were significantly more Republican than Democratic, but in the last several years Democrats gained a substantial advantage among these better-educated voters, with a 12 percentage point edge in 2019.[13]

The Republican Party thus now not only draws its strongest support from Whites but also certain sectors of the White population, including those without a college degree as well as evangelical Protestants and other religious conservatives.[14] Republicans get some support from minorities, of course. In the last four presidential elections, according to various polls, roughly 20 to 35 percent of Asian American and Hispanic voters went for the Republican candidate (John McCain, Mitt Romney, or Trump). Still, the lion's share of Asian Americans and Hispanics voted for Obama, Hillary Clinton, or Joe Biden, who also got the overwhelming support (about 90 percent) of Black voters.

A number of factors have shaped the new partisan coalitions. Civil rights legislation, as I already noted, added huge numbers of African American voters in the South to the electorate, and affected Black and White support for the Democratic Party. If many Whites gravitated to the Republican Party because they found the expansion of rights to African Americans troubling and threatening, other social changes had a similar effect. These included changes in gender roles and family patterns stimulated by the women's movement, the expansion of LGBTQ rights, and the development of a more religiously diverse and secular American society. On the other side, the Democratic Party, with its more liberal policies on social issues, drew support from those who benefited from or welcomed these social changes, among them racial minorities, the LGBTQ community, religious moderates and skeptics, and the better educated.[15] Economic transformations in postindustrial America are also part of the picture; such trends as the globalization of economic markets, decline of manufacturing, technological change, erosion of organized labor, and rise in income and wealth inequality have heightened economic insecurity among many less educated Whites, and translated into greater support for a GOP that, among other things, promised a return to a pre-1960s and Whiter America. There is a geographic aspect to political polarization too. Whites living in rural areas that have suffered economic and demographic declines or stagnation, and who are relatively isolated from racial and ethnic minorities, seem to have been especially favorable to Republican anti-diversity messages.[16]

And of course, and of concern here, there is immigration, which has played an important role in remaking the two national party coalitions. In the last twenty-five years, the American electorate has become increasingly diverse as the share of ethnic and racial minority registered voters rose from 15 to 30 percent between 1996 and 2019.[17] Immigration is to a significant degree responsible for this trend. The massive inflows from Latin America, Asia, and the Caribbean have added large numbers of new minority voters as a growing number of immigrants have become naturalized citizens, and along with their second-generation children (US citizens by birth), are eligible to cast ballots—which they do, in especially large numbers, for Democrats. Just considering the foreign born on their own, in 2020, 23 million immigrants—nearly double the number since 2000—or about 10 percent of the nation's overall electorate, were eligible to vote, having gained US citizenship through naturalization; about two-thirds were Asian American or Hispanic.[18]

Immigration has also affected party coalitions through its impact on Whites. This has been particularly consequential in national elections since Whites make up a large majority of the electorate—nearly seven out of ten eligible voters at the time of the 2016 and 2020 presidential elections.[19] Immigration has contributed to a backlash among working-class Whites or those without a college degree that helps to explain why so many defected to the Republican Party, which in a time of growing racial and ethnic diversity has remained a White bastion.

The very presence of millions of immigrants from the Global South, who have moved all over the United States in recent decades, has stimulated fears and anxieties among a significant segment of White America about whether the newcomers will undermine the basic foundations and identity of the nation. Latino immigrants are a special focus of these anxieties partly because of their sheer number: 44 percent of all immigrants in 2019, or almost twenty million people, reported having Hispanic or Latino origins.[20] Also, Latinos are associated with undocumented immigrants, whose numbers have soared since 1990, and who are a target of so much unease and hostility. Although the majority of Latin American immigrants are authorized to live and work in the United States, a large proportion of the roughly eleven million undocumented, more

America's economy and society at their expense, receiving preferential treatment from the government and getting ahead while they are being left behind.[29]

For Whites worried or alarmed by the changes wrought by immigration and racial change, the Republican Party has provided "a natural home."[30] They find the more pro-immigrant stance of the Democratic Party, and its celebration of ethnic and racial diversity along with immigration, disturbing, and are distressed by the growing number of high-ranking Democratic ethnic and racial minority elected officials, the most prominent, of course, being Obama, the nation's first Black president, who represented a powerful symbolic threat to Whites' political power.[31] To many conservative and noncollege-educated Whites, the Republican Party is a kind of safe haven. Whereas many working-class White voters have felt abandoned by a Democratic Party that seems to them to favor African Americans and immigrants, many Republican candidates for office in recent years—who are overwhelmingly White— have stood against affirmative action and a path to citizenship for the undocumented, and have used appeals to White resentment of ethnic and racial minorities to win over sympathetic voters and lure Democrats into their camp.[32] In this regard, it should not come as a surprise that only a minority of Republicans (38 percent) in a 2019 Pew survey agreed that immigrants strengthen the country compared to the great majority of Democrats (83 percent), and that half of the Republicans saw immigrants as burdening the country by taking jobs, housing, and health care.[33]

Trump took the appeal to White resentment to a new—explicit and overt—level, whipping up fears about immigration and alleged White victimization, initially to win over Republicans in the 2016 primary campaign to become the party nominee, then to broaden his appeal in the general election against Clinton, and still later, throughout his presidency, when his popularity remained low with the general public, to solidify support from his core constituency, a base of religiously and socially conservative and less educated Whites. Trump's slogan, "Make America Great Again" (MAGA), emblazoned on red hats worn by his supporters, was a not-so-subtle reference to an America before large-scale

than seven in ten, are from Latin America, and about half are Mex
In the imagination of many Americans, Mexican or Latino has b
synonymous with unauthorized immigrants, whom they see as
serving criminals.[22] They often make invidious comparisons be
today's undocumented and their own "legal" European ancestors
nineteenth and early twentieth centuries, forgetting or unaware th
ropeans at that time faced few restrictions on immigration.[23]

A Latino threat narrative, promulgated by a substantial sector
media as well as many politicians, falsely portrays Latino immigra
prone to violence, and unwilling or incapable of integrating and b
ing part of the national community.[24] To note just one analysis, of
than forty-two hundred stories in newspapers in four southern
between 2002 and 2013, immigrants were characterized negativ
about a third of the stories on immigration, with the perceived cri
tendencies of Mexican and Latino immigrants frequently mentior

The economic and cultural threat many Whites feel from immig
reflects their sense of marginalization in an increasingly ethnicall
racially diverse country, and their racial fears about the loss of W
dominant status. Many Whites who supported Trump, as politica
entist Ashley Jardina observes, feel that the benefits they have enj
because of their race and status atop the racial hierarchy are in j
ardy.[26] Something else seems to be involved too, as sociologist
Hochschild's research in the archconservative Louisiana bayou cou
suggests. The working-class Whites she met expressed resentment
immigrants, refugees, and beneficiaries of affirmative action were
ting in line"—"sailing past the Statue of Liberty into a diminis
supply of good jobs" at the expense of White men and their wiv
Racialized economics is what Sides and his colleagues call it:
'I might lose my job' but, in essence, 'People in my group are losing
to that other group.'"[28] Instead of pure economic anxiety in the fac
the loss of "good"—well-paid and secure—blue-collar jobs in the w
of technological change, globalization, and economic restructur
working-class White Trump supporters commonly express their e
nomic anxiety, at least in part, through racial grievances: the belief
other, non-White and often immigrant groups are making gain

immigration that was Whiter and less racially and ethnically diverse than it is today—as well as a promise to protect and restore Whites' status, power, and resources.[34] He followed through with a host of measures to reduce immigration, and mandate harsher treatment of asylees and the undocumented. Although immigration was less central in Trump's 2020 campaign, in which he focused more on "law-and-order" issues and opposing racial-justice protests, he continued to use anti-immigrant rhetoric to fire up his base in rallies, social media ads, and tweets. As before, he twisted facts and told outright lies about immigrants as well as native minorities to tap into and further stir up fears of White voters and capture their support. Immigration, in short, became a key element of Trump's electoral and governing strategy, and in the process, an even more powerful basis for and symbol of the country's partisan divide.

Anti-Immigrant Politics and Public
Discourse in the Trump Era

Closely intertwined with the new partisan alignments in national party politics is another set of changes that are directly connected to the post-1965 immigration: the increased focus in mainstream politics on anti-immigrant themes and policies, and the ramping up and indeed legitimation of anti-immigrant discourse at the presidential level during the Trump era.

The United States of course has a long history of nativism. Whenever the country has experienced sharply rising and sustained large-scale immigration, an anti-foreigner reaction against newcomers has ensued based on perceptions of economic, cultural, political, racial, and religious threats. Xenophobia, writes historian Erika Lee in her book *America for Americans*, is a defining feature of American life: we are not just a nation of immigrants, but a nation of xenophobia in which fear, hatred, and hostility toward immigrants are long-standing elements.[35] Throughout American history, writes historian A. K. Sandoval-Strausz, "alarmists have tried to stir up hostility against immigrants whom they warned would destroy our traditions, radicalize our body politic, mongrelize our population, wreck our economy, or balkanize our culture."[36]

Since the mid-nineteenth century, such sentiments have periodically underpinned and bolstered concerted efforts in the mainstream political arena to limit immigration and restrict immigrants' rights. In the antebellum decades in the 1800s, the huge Irish Catholic immigration triggered virulent anti-Catholicism that found political expression in the Know Nothing movement (formally known as the American Party), whose national agenda included a twenty-one-year residence requirement for naturalization and the exclusion of foreign-born Americans from holding public office. This agenda was not achieved, but in the 1850s, the party at its peak achieved astonishing electoral success, including more than a hundred members of Congress, eight governors, mayors of Boston, Philadelphia, and Chicago, and dozens of other local elected officials.[37]

Only a few decades later, the Chinese, who had begun to immigrate in significant numbers to California and the American West in the 1850s, were specifically targeted by restrictive immigration legislation. The 1882 Chinese Exclusion Act barred the entry of Chinese laborers and prohibited Chinese immigrants from becoming naturalized citizens. By 1917, Congress had banned the immigration of many other Asian groups as well, and the naturalization rule was extended through a series of court decisions to other immigrants from East and South Asia.[38]

Another triumph of nativist politics was the passage of the 1924 Johnson-Reed Immigration Act, which was designed to drastically cut immigration from southern and eastern Europe. The act established a national origins quota system, with each nation assigned a quota equal to 2 percent of the number of its nationals in the United States based on the 1890 Census—or what some called the "Anglo-Saxon" census because it came before the period of heaviest eastern and southern European immigration.[39] The legislation fulfilled the aims of those who fashioned it, playing a critical role, in combination with the Great Depression and World War II, in ending the massive influx from eastern and southern Europe that had brought millions of eastern European Jews and southern Italians to the United States in the late nineteenth and early twentieth centuries.

In the Trump era, xenophobia once more became a feature of national politics, shaping political agendas and policy decisions by the Republican Party at the highest levels of government. In many ways it is a case of new wine in old bottles. Even Trump's xenophobic focus on the undocumented and Mexican immigrants has strong echoes from the past. Animosity to Mexicans is nothing new, going back to the Mexican-American War of the 1840s, when after defeating Mexico, the United States annexed its northern portion; during the campaign in the mid-1950s known as Operation Wetback to remove undocumented Mexicans (pejoratively referred to as "wetbacks"), border patrol agents and local officials used military-style tactics to round up and send back to Mexico several hundred thousand Mexican immigrants.[40] We also should not forget that the late twentieth and early twenty-first centuries, under presidents George W. Bush and Bill Clinton, witnessed the increased militarization of the US-Mexico border to deter undocumented immigration, and that the Obama administration dramatically raised the number of deportations.[41] The rise of Trump and his ascendancy to the country's highest office, however, intensified anti-immigrant politics, and made them more central in the Republican Party's campaigns and appeals for voter support to a degree not seen in national politics in recent memory. This represented a real change.

This change developed in the context of the new political party alignment that encouraged Trump to focus on appeals to his base through White identity politics and fear of foreigners to the virtual exclusion of bipartisan approaches. In a kind of feedback loop, the positive and indeed enthusiastic response of his core supporters to campaign promises for a more restrictive as well as punitive immigration system—including most famously building a "giant wall" with Mexico—led to further emphasis on these policies to energize and mobilize his following. No sooner had Trump taken office then he placed a travel ban on individuals from several Muslim-majority countries. Within the same year, he ended the DACA program established by Obama's executive order, which enabled around eight hundred thousand eligible undocumented young adults who had arrived in the United States as children to receive work permits and protection from deportation. The program was only kept alive by court rulings during

Trump's presidency. His administration's "zero tolerance" policy that involved separating Central American parents and children seeking asylum at the southern border was part of a goal to reduce Latino immigration, and show his strongest supporters that he was being tough in pursuing it even as the policy was harshly criticized by much of the public and media.

The centrality of Trump's anti-immigrant policies during his administration—publicly backed by virtually the entire Republican congressional delegation—was heightened by his norm-shattering governing style and use of the media, which put immigration in the spotlight in a way that did not happen with his predecessors. Before Trump, politicians generally hewed to a basic rule: wanting as much positive and as little negative news coverage as possible. Trump was not immune to this approach, but to a significant degree he upended it. As political commentator Ezra Klein put it, "His realization is that you want as much coverage as possible, full stop. If it's positive coverage, great. If it's negative coverage, so be it. The point is that it's coverage—that you're the story, that you're squeezing out your competitors, that you're on people's minds." Trump dominated news cycle after news cycle, in a reality-show style, with outrageous, offensive, and often false statements, frequently about immigration. His tweets—of course a modern invention—came to be considered official statements of the president. In his first three years in office, according to *Washington Post* fact-checkers, Trump made an incredible twenty-four hundred false or misleading claims about immigration—more than on any other issue. In his attention-creates-value approach, he set the tone and terms of many debates, and kept immigration, or more accurately anti-immigration, in the news.[42]

What Trump said about immigration upended existing norms. His openly xenophobic and racist statements in his widely covered campaign rallies, presidential speeches, and tweets were far more explicit than the racial and ethnic appeals of Republican presidential candidates in modern times. In the early twentieth century, to be sure, openly racist statements were not unheard of from leading national politicians, including those elected president. In his 1902 *A History of the American People*, Woodrow Wilson referred to Blacks as an ignorant and inferior race; in a 1925 column, Franklin Roosevelt wrote that "the mingling of Asiatic blood with European or American blood produces, in nine cases out of ten, the most unfortunate results."[43] Nearly a century later, Trump, overtly and in fact proudly, defied an etiquette about race and ethnicity that had prevailed in public discourse in post–civil rights America. In challenging what he called a culture of political correctness that made it impossible to "tell it like it is," he legitimated blatant anti-immigrant and racist appeals at the highest level of American politics and society.

Trump's overt xenophobia and ethnic slurs took on a particular tone and meaning precisely because they followed several decades after the civil rights movement, which had ushered in a new climate and under-standing about what was acceptable to say in public about race and ethnicity. By the 1970s and 1980s, as historian Lawrence Fuchs wrote, candidates for high office and public officials could not disparage or even tolerate the disparagement of any ethnic, racial, or religious group without suffering severe and widespread condemnation.[44] In an atmo-sphere of greater public tolerance, more subtle means were used to cast aspersion on racial and ethnic groups. Instead of egregious racial epi-thets or slurs, code words were used to refer to negative characteristics of minorities as well as dog whistle politics—that is, sending messages about racial minorities in coded language that might appear to mean one thing to some in the general public but had a different resonance for a target audience.[45] In his 1980 campaign for president, Ronald Rea-gan told stories about Cadillac-driving "welfare queens" and "strapping young bucks" buying T-bone steaks with food stamps; Reagan did not need to mention race because he was blowing a dog whistle. The Willie Horton ad used in the 1988 presidential campaign of George Bush Sr. is another example. In attacking Democratic opponent Michael Duka-kis as soft on crime for supporting his state's "weekend pass program," the ad played into racial stereotypes. It linked crime to Black men and stoked fears about Black crime by featuring the mug shot of convicted African American murderer Horton, who had been able to escape dur-ing a weekend furlough, and then later raped a woman and stabbed her fiancé.[46]

Dog whistle politics hardly disappeared under Trump. What was different was his use of unambiguous insults and smears not only against African Americans—he essentially launched his political career by promoting the racist "birther" myth that Obama was not born in the United States—but also a virtual drumbeat of attacks against immigrants. His three presidential predecessors waxed eloquent about America as a nation of immigrants, drawing on a narrative that by the 1960s had become widely and popularly used as a celebration of the United States. In speeches, George W. Bush referred to "immigration [as] . . . not just a link to America's past; it's also a bridge to America's future"; President Clinton spoke of how "more than any other nation on Earth, America has constantly drawn strength and spirit from wave after wave of immigrants"; and Obama stressed that "we are and always will be a nation of immigrants."[47] Trump painted a different, dystopian image.[48]

In framing immigrants as a threat to the United States, Trump changed the national conversation about immigration, and stood out, as journalist Thomas Edsall comments, for his "willingness—indeed his eagerness—to openly and aggressively unleash the forces of ethnic and racial hostility that Republican elites had quietly capitalized upon for decades."[49] During the 2016 campaign and afterward, including State of the Union addresses, he raised the specter of an immigrant crime rampage and repeated grisly stories of violent crimes committed by undocumented immigrants, even though statistics show immigrants having lower crime rates than the native born. Among his better-known statements, Trump said that a Hispanic judge could not be fair in the fraud case against Trump University because "he's a Mexican." In summer 2019, he attacked four minority members of Congress—American citizens all, with three born in the United States—by saying they should "go back" to the countries they came from. Trump, in short, went where other politicians and certainly previous presidents in the modern era dared not go in their rhetoric, shifting the bounds of acceptable public discourse about immigration in the process, and giving nativist and racist demagoguery the presidential seal of approval.[50] Whether or not leading Republican politicians who follow Trump will retire this rhetoric is a major question for the future.

Ethnic Succession

Yet another way that immigration has changed electoral politics is through ethnic succession as politicians of recent immigrant origin have begun to win contests for political office. This is the "new faces in old places" phenomenon that I noted in the last chapter. Whether in popular culture or politics, ethnic succession is not just a matter of new personnel in familiar roles; it may lead to deeper and sometimes even quite dramatic changes. In the political sphere, new ethnic politicians and officials often represent different interests than those who came before them; may give rise to new coalitions; and may support, and sometimes help create or implement, new measures, policies, and institutional arrangements.

This is a timeworn story in urban America, perhaps nowhere more striking than in New York City, where the history of ethnic politics and succession has been recounted in scholarly studies as well as become the stuff of city lore.[51] The Irish, arriving in massive numbers in the mid-1800s, were "masters of the art" of ethnic politics, able to infiltrate and take over the helm of New York City's Democratic politics by mobilizing the ethnic vote and turning Tammany Hall into a powerful political machine. Under Celtic tutelage, as political scientist Steven Erie puts it, Tammany, a now-defunct New York political organization, ran the city, with minor exceptions, from 1874 to 1933.[52] It naturalized and registered immigrants, and got them out to vote. In its formative stage from the 1840s to the 1880s (and before more restrictive naturalization laws), Tammany churned out new voters through running "its naturalization mill full blast"—and rewarded the faithful with patronage jobs and social services.[53] "Tammany is for the spoils system," explained George Washington Plunkett, Irish American Tammany ward chieftain in 1905, "and when we go in we fire every anti-Tammany man from office that can be fired under the law. It's an elastic sort of law and you can bet it will be stretched to the limit."[54]

Many turn-of-the-twentieth-century Jewish and Italian politicians, too, initially won local office in New York in large part by wooing coethnic voters, thereby reinforcing the legitimacy of ethnic politics. Whether it was the late nineteenth- and early twentieth-century Irish politicians, whose political priorities were patronage and prestige, or mid-twentieth-century Jews, who aimed for protection from discrimination and reforms to provide more equal access to jobs and power, shared ethnicity was a way for aspiring leaders to mobilize their base, attain political representation, and contend to be part of the governing coalition, all the while shifting old alliances and creating new ones.[55] And it still is. The era of strong political machines is over, and much else has changed about the structure of urban politics facing ethnic minorities today, yet ethnic politics is still very much part of the political scene.

Typically, ethnic succession in New York City has begun with efforts to displace incumbents in local districts where the new populations have been rapidly growing, and later—usually considerably later—winning power at the mayoral level. Although Jews and Italians had become a huge part of the city's population by the first decade of the twentieth century, New York did not elect its first mayor of Italian heritage until 1933 (La Guardia) nor have another until 1950.[56] La Guardia, an anti-Tammany machine reformer who served three mayoral terms until 1945, "was the son of Italian immigrants, but raised Episcopalian, born of a Jewish mother, and married to an American of German-Lutheran descent. . . . He was a balanced ticket all by himself and he campaigned in the city's polyglot neighborhoods in a half-dozen languages," actively working to win the votes of Italians and Jews.[57] New York City's first full-fledged Jewish mayor, Abraham Beame, was elected in 1973, and African Americans, who arrived in large numbers from the South between World War I and the 1960s, did not elect their first mayor, David Dinkins, until 1989.[58] So far, New York has had no mayor with roots in the post-1965 immigration, although by 2019, the fifty-one-seat city council had fourteen elected members of recent immigrant origin. In that year, three of the city's US congressional representatives were from new immigrant communities: a Dominican immigrant and two members of the second generation, one with parents from Jamaica, and the other's parents from Taiwan. In 2021, a fourth, the daughter of Greek and Cuban immigrants as well as the lone Republican in the city's congressional delegation, joined this list.

Throughout the country, Hispanics and Asian Americans have made headway at the polls, with Hispanics especially successful given their large numbers, heavy concentration in certain regions and cities, and significant proportion with a long history in the United States. Altogether in 2019, there were a little over 6,800 Hispanic elected officials in the nation as a whole, including 85 state senators and 245 state representatives.[59] In the same year, two central cities in the ten-top metropolitan immigrant gateways, Los Angeles and Miami, had Latino mayors. Miami, a heavily Cuban city, has morphed from having a power structure dominated by an Anglo elite to a political order governed by Cuban émigrés and their offspring.[60] Since 1985, Miami has had a string of Cuban American mayors, with the most recent being Francis X. Suarez, elected in 2017 with a whopping 86 percent of the vote; he followed in the footsteps of his Cuban-born father and namesake, who was a several-term mayor of the city, first elected in 1985. On the West Coast, in Los Angeles, where Mexicans far outnumber other immigrants, in 2005 the city elected its first modern Latino mayor, Antonio Villaraigosa, whose father was a Mexican immigrant. The paternal grandfather of his successor, Eric Garcetti, was born in Mexico (his maternal grandparents were from Russian Jewish immigrant families). By 2010, 4 of the 15 city councillors in Los Angeles were Latinos, whereas there were none in 1980.[61]

The composition of the US Congress reflects recent immigration as well, even though Hispanics and Asian Americans are still underrepresented compared to their proportion of the total population.[62] As of January 2020, the 116th Congress (2019–21) included forty-three Hispanic representatives in the House and four Senators; fourteen Asian Americans were US representatives along with three senators.[63] After the 2018 midterm elections, the first Muslim women were sworn into Congress, Somali-born Ilhan Omar representing a district in Minnesota and Rashida Tlaib, a second-generation Palestinian from Detroit. Among the other firsts are Stephanie Murphy, the first Vietnamese American woman to win a seat in Congress (from central Florida) in 2016, and in 2020, the first Korean American women—three in all—elected to Congress, two from California (Young Kim and Michelle Steel), and one from the state of Washington (Marilyn Strickland).

While the great majority of Asian American and Hispanic congressional representatives and senators are Democrats, the Republican delegation has been diversifying too. In fact, two of the female Korean American representatives elected in 2020 are Republicans. Some of the leading lights of the GOP are of immigrant origin. Ted Cruz and Marco Rubio, both second-generation Cubans and among the best-known senators, sought the Republican presidential nomination in 2016, and are talked about as future contenders. Nikki Haley and Bobby Jindal, former governors of South Carolina and Louisiana, respectively, are children of Indian immigrants who have risen to national prominence, with Haley often mentioned as a possible future presidential candidate.

Certainly, the changing of the guard in many elected offices has brought benefits to new immigrant groups. The ability to attain highly esteemed and powerful positions as a mayor, city councillor, or member of Congress is in itself a significant achievement. Seeing people like themselves voted into office can be a source of great pride for those in immigrant communities as well as for elected officials themselves. And electoral success can bring tangible rewards since elected politicians, for example, often can influence hiring for public offices that are exempt from civil service regulations—patronage, in other words, or the spoils of electoral victory.

Ethnic succession has also played a role in institutional change: the growing number of Hispanics and Asian Americans in Congress has led to the formation there as well as in many state legislatures of new officially organized coalitions linked to ethnoracial groups. The Congressional Hispanic Caucus was founded in 1976 to advocate for issues important to Hispanics through the legislative process; in 2019, after the midterm elections, it had grown to thirty-nine Democratic members. The Congressional Asian Pacific American Caucus, founded in 1994, had twenty members in the 116th Congress. By that time, the so-called Tri-Caucus, which also included the fifty-five-member Congressional Black Caucus, had over a hundred members and worked together on many issues.

A critical question is whether ethnic succession, involving the replacement of former elected officials with those from newer immigrant

groups, leads to substantive changes in political debates and official policies. To put it in political science terms, does descriptive representation—
the degree to which a group's representation in political positions reflects its population share—pave the way for substantive representation,
or the reflection of a group's interests and concerns in political decision-
making? Or to pose the question somewhat differently, does ethnic succession produce genuine policy and legislative change?

This is not inevitable. For one, we cannot simply assume that politicians from a particular background will represent the interests of their
group of origin; indeed, their electoral success may depend on distancing themselves from their roots. By the same token, progressive nonimmigrant White politicians may at times better represent the interests
of minority and immigrant origin groups than coethnics.[64] Indeed, even
White politicians who are not themselves immigrants or especially liberal may adopt a pro-immigrant stance, or avoid taking anti-immigrant
positions, if they represent districts and cities where the immigrant vote
is substantial, and obtaining it is important for election. When Rudolph
Giuliani was Republican mayor of New York City, he praised immigrants and supported policies to reduce the difficulties facing the undocumented; this is not surprising given, among other things, the city's
large and growing immigrant population at the time, and rising number
of voting-eligible citizens with recent immigrant origins.[65]

That said, the election of politicians of recent immigrant origin can
have positive policy impacts for immigrant communities. It is not just
that they bring experiences and perspectives into legislative bodies and
political offices that might not otherwise be represented there. In giving
officials from longer-established groups insights into the concerns of
immigrant minorities, they also may be able to have some influence on
them. More directly, newly elected ethnic politicians often advocate as
well as vote for policies that will help members of their group, or ward
off those with potentially negative consequences; they may be able to
influence the allocation of public resources such as public contracts;
and they may serve as spokespeople for their group's concerns.[66] To
come back to New York City, immigrant-origin politicians have been
especially likely to champion pro-immigrant measures, partly for pure

political reasons—they are usually dependent on the immigrant vote, or parts of it, to gain and maintain office—and also because they tend to closely identify with immigrants and their problems. Although immigration has not been a top priority for New York's city council, the presence of a growing number of immigrant-origin councillors has played a role in the adoption of such immigrant-friendly measures as a language access law requiring city agencies to provide direct services for the translation of commonly distributed documents in the top-ten citywide languages and the creation of a municipal identification card that undocumented immigrants can receive.[67]

On the national stage, the Congressional Hispanic and Asian Pacific American Caucuses have been active in promoting legislation directly affecting their communities, ranging from pro-immigration measures to health care and education policies in support of working-class and minority families that tend to help immigrants. In early 2019, for example, the Hispanic Caucus led two oversight trips to the Mexican border, and introduced a resolution to reaffirm that US Customs and Border Protection must provide basic standard humanitarian and medical care to all individuals in custody. Studies of the workings of Congress show the impact of Latino legislators too. According to an analysis of all bills sponsored during the 109th Congress (2005–7), individual Latino representatives sponsored significantly more Latino-interest bills than their non-Latino counterparts. Moreover, Latino representatives were particularly devoted to the concerns of Latino constituencies, and especially willing to advocate openly and actively on their behalf. In the 111th Congress (2009–11), Latino House members were more active in cosponsoring bills on the high-salience issues of immigration, education, and labor than were non-Latino members.[68]

A poignant illustration of the impact of substantive representation for immigrant-origin groups takes us back to the late 1980s and passage of a bill granting compensation to Japanese Americans sent to internment camps during World War II. The bill's principal advocate in the Senate was Spark Matsunaga, a Japanese American from Hawaii who "almost wept as, recalling the suffering of internees, he related the story of an elderly man who crossed a fence to retrieve a ball for his grandchild and was machine-gunned to death." Matsunaga, it should be noted, was elected to the US Senate in 1976, which did not have any Asian American member until 1959.[69]

The Shape of the Future

Looking ahead, we can expect ethnic succession in electoral politics to proceed apace. More elected officials will trace their origins to the post-1965 immigration as additional immigration and naturalizations augment the number of immigrant citizens, and as the adult second and third generations grow. Not only will they be able to vote and thus provide a potential base for coethnic politicians, but some will seek influence, prestige, and power through winning elected office as they climb the social and occupational ladder.

But how will ethnic succession, and much more important, the growing number of eligible voters descended from post-1965 immigrants, affect party alignments and schisms as well as electoral strategies and outcomes in the years ahead? Is it inevitable that the Democratic Party will emerge as the new majority in the US Congress and White House? Will the forces producing the current divisions into partisan camps, including increasing ethnic and racial diversity in American society, persist over the short and perhaps medium term?[70] Will Trump's impact on the Republican Party's immigrant politics and political rhetoric outlast his presidency? Or will Republicans shift their strategies to capture more of the immigrant minority vote?

As these questions suggest, predicting the future is not an exact science. We need look no further than fifteen or twenty years ago when some policy analysts were forecasting that "the rising Latino tide" of voters swelled by the enormous immigrant inflows would help to realign the nation in a decisively Democratic direction, leading to the dawn of a new progressive era.[71]

This has not yet happened. It is the Republican Party that gained the presidency and control of the Senate in 2016, and despite losing the 2020 election, Trump expanded his support among Hispanics by nearly 10 percentage points, according to Latino Decisions election eve polls.[72]

Still, the increasing number of Hispanic voters in particular has benefited the Democratic Party given that Hispanics as well as Asian Americans have been leaning strongly Democratic in recent years, with about
two-thirds or more supporting the Democratic presidential candidate.
This development has helped turn several states that had often voted
Republican in presidential elections, such as Nevada and Arizona, into
swing or battleground states. Both went for Biden in 2020 and may become more securely Democratic in the future. And there are the lessons
of now blue state California, which gave us Reagan and voted Republican in presidential elections in all but one year between 1952 and 1988.
Since then the state has consistently supported the Democratic presidential candidate; after the 2018 midterm election, all but seven of the
fifty-three members of the House of Representatives from California
were Democrats—the first time the state had a single-digit Republican
representation in Congress since the 1940s. The growing Latino population helped make California a Democratic stronghold, with some assist
from the backlash against the 1994 passage of Proposition 187, which
had it not been ruled unconstitutional by the courts, would have denied
public services, including education, to undocumented immigrants.
Republican support for the anti-immigrant ballot initiative turned many
Latinos away from the Republican Party, which was tainted by association with Proposition 187 and the GOP governor, Pete Wilson, who
championed it. The Brookings Institution's Elaine Kamarck has mused
about the possibility of Texas becoming more California-like in the next
decade given the growing Hispanic population—40 percent of the state
in 2019, up from 26 percent in 1990—and Hispanics' increasing share of the
state's electorate.[73]

Changing demographics may help Democrats in other ways too. If
the nation is becoming more racially diverse, it may also be poised to
become more socially liberal as the rapidly aging White population declines and the base of the Republican Party shrinks. Not only are
younger Americans increasingly racial and ethnic minorities—by 2018,
45 percent of the nation's population under age fifteen was Black, Hispanic, or Asian American—but according to a Pew Research Center
survey in the same year, Generation Z young people aged thirteen to

twenty-one and millennials aged twenty-two to thirty-seven had more liberal views than older generations on a range of issues. Among other things, those in the two younger generations were more accepting of racial and ethnic diversity; even the Republicans in Generation Z were much more likely than their older GOP counterparts to say that increased racial and ethnic diversity is a good thing for the country.[74] How much these attitudes will persist as the millennials and Gen Zers age is unclear, but the opinions formed in their younger days will likely continue to play a role in shaping the views of many of them as they move into or further along in adulthood.

Some commentators predict that Republicans will moderate their tactics, scaling back hard-edged racial appeals and stands on immigration in attempting to attract a younger, more diverse audience, and make greater inroads into the racial and ethnic minority population, whose share of the electorate continues to grow. Former president George W. Bush, after all, tried to garner greater support from Latinos, and received 40 percent of their votes in 2004, when he advocated for comprehensive immigration reform legislation, although in the end, the bill died in the Senate when it came up three years later. Whatever Bush's positions in the past, Trump's hard-core base, as opinion writer Greg Sargent observes, will not have outsized political influence forever.[75]

Forever is of course a long time, but at least in the near future there is a quite different set of countervailing possibilities. One issue is that the percentage of non-Hispanic Whites may not be shrinking as fast as recent Census projections have suggested because many people with one White parent sometimes identify, and are identified by others, as White or partly White, have friends who are White, and live among Whites. It is possible that many will vote like Whites as well, including some as relatively conservative Whites.[76]

Even using existing Census classifications, non-Hispanic Whites will still have considerable voter clout for some time to come. According to one projection, 59 percent of eligible voters in the 2036 national election will be Whites, and 34 percent will be noncollege-educated Whites.[77] There is also the issue of relatively low voter turnout among Latinos and Asian Americans; in the 2016 presidential election, 48 percent of eligible

Latino voters and 49 percent of their Asian American counterparts voted, compared to 65 percent of non-Hispanic Whites and 60 percent of Blacks.[78]

Moreover, Hispanic support for the Democratic Party, while hardly likely to disappear, could weaken so that the slippage reported between the 2016 and 2020 presidential elections might be a sign of things to come. Republicans could increasingly appeal to many Hispanics on the basis of conservative cultural, religious, or social values on such questions as abortion and gay marriage as well as an ideology of pulling yourself up by your bootstraps and a small-business orientation that many Hispanic men in particular may identify with. Republicans are bound to run more Hispanic as well as Asian American candidates, and many Hispanics and Asian Americans might become more conservative as they advance economically.[79]

At the same time, the structure of the American political system gives Republicans built-in advantages. The US Senate is a less than entirely democratic institution, giving residents of small states a lift because every state, regardless of population, has two senators. This has been a benefit to Republicans, who are dominant in many states with small populations; four of the five smallest states—Alaska, Wyoming, and the Dakotas—strongly tilt Republican. In terms of Senate representation, Wyoming, the least populous state with fewer than six hundred thousand residents, has the same representation as the nearly forty million people in California.[80] Klein puts it bluntly: "As a Californian, I think the fact that my state gets exactly as much representation as Wyoming is insane."[81] Senatorial inequality is not going away. In 2040, according to one prediction, about 70 percent of Americans will live in the fifteen-largest states; they will have only thirty senators representing them, while the remaining 30 percent will be represented by seventy senators.[82]

Republicans have also benefited from the electoral college system, which can overturn the popular vote in presidential elections, as it did in 2000 when Al Gore lost despite more than a half-million popular vote lead over Bush and in 2016 when Trump won with three million fewer votes than Clinton. The electoral college skews elections by giving a structural advantage to small states. Each state receives a number of electoral votes equal to the number of US House of Representatives members, apportioned by population, from that state plus two for its number of senators. These additional two votes effectively triple the voting power of the smallest states that have only one congressional representative. Reliably Republican Wyoming has one-sixty-sixth of California's population, but with its three electoral votes, it has one-eighteenth of California's fifty-five electoral votes.[83]

Also important is that many Republican-controlled states have used various types of voter suppression to reduce the Black and ethnic minority vote through such measures as restrictive voter identification laws and laws making it harder to register and stay registered. In some states, for example, voters must present a government- or college-issued photo ID in order to vote, and a few states have canceled registrations of voters because they have not voted recently and failed to return a mailed notice.[84] Gerrymandering has helped Republicans, too, because of their greater control in recent years over state legislatures, which oversee redistricting after the decennial Census. The resulting drawing of congressional district maps with pronounced partisan slants has significantly improved Republican chances of winning seats in the House of Representatives. Although Republicans in Texas, to mention a particularly egregious case, were half of the votes in the state's 2020 congressional elections, they ended up controlling twenty-three of the state's thirty-six seats, and underrepresenting Hispanics and African Americans in the political process.

Nor is it a sure thing that Republicans will significantly alter their anti-immigration strategies and racial appeals, at least in the short run, to improve their standing with minorities. The forces producing polarization in the American electorate, political scientist Alan Abramowitz argues, are far from spent. Republicans risk deeply offending large segments of their base if they take steps to expand the party's appeal to ethnic and racial minorities and socially liberal Americans—something that few Republican elected officials may be willing to do. It is not hard to see many Republican candidates in the near future exploiting the politics of White racial resentment and White racial identity as a winning strategy.[85] In one worrisome scenario put forward by political scientists Marisa Abrajano and Zoltan Hajnal, the Republican Party "continues to fuel a white backlash against immigrants and minorities, an increasingly anxious and aggrieved white population fights against the rising tide of minority voters, they in turn flock in ever larger numbers to the Democratic Party, the racial divide in US party politics expands to a racial chasm, and the prospects for racial conflict swell."[86]

Ultimately, however, the choices that future political leaders make will be shaped by a broad range of social, political, and economic circumstances that are hard to predict. On one side, the choices have the potential to sustain or even increase political polarization along racial and ethnic lines, but on the other, they could reduce it. Whether future Republican presidents will follow Trump's path and style, making issues of race and immigration central in their appeals, and continuing to exacerbate and legitimate anti-immigrant and racist sentiments to the degree that he has done—or alternatively, seek to welcome others, find common ground, and even heal the country—remains an open question.[87] So too is much about the course a Democratic president will take, although it is a safe bet that a Democrat in the White House will not follow Trump's lead and will be much more supportive of immigration. As the election of Biden has already shown, a Democratic president is virtually certain to be more open to diversity than a Republican; avoid, and indeed condemn, inflammatory anti-immigrant and racist rhetoric; and give more support to humanitarian protections and legal permanent immigration.

In looking to the future, one thing is guaranteed: as more immigrants arrive and naturalize, and especially as more members of the second and third generation reach adulthood and can vote, the effects of immigration on the country's electoral politics will continue to be felt in the years to come. The result is likely to be additional and often unexpected political changes.

CHAPTER 7

Conclusion

A NATION IN FLUX

"The interaction of disparate cultures, the vehemence of the ideals that led the immigrants here, the opportunity offered by a new life, all gave America a flavor and a character that make it as unmistakable and as remarkable to people today as it was to Alexis de Tocqueville in the early part of the nineteenth century." So wrote John F. Kennedy in *A Nation of Immigrants* about the influence of newcomers from abroad in the peopling and foundation of the United States.[1]

Kennedy was writing in 1958, at a time of extremely low immigration, and he had in mind European arrivals when he celebrated immigrants for creating the nation in remarkable and unmistakable ways. In fact, the groups he singled out for special attention were the Irish, Germans, and Scandinavians, who dominated immigrant inflows for much of the nineteenth century.

Today as we enter the third decade of the twenty-first century, the tens of millions of immigrants who have come to live in the United States in the past five decades have been giving the country a new flavor and character that would no doubt have been remarkable, and indeed unrecognizable, to Kennedy, who was assassinated in 1963, two years before the passage of a landmark law that ushered in a new era of mass immigration that has helped to redefine the nation and brought newcomers from all over the world.

The United States is in essence a nation in flux, and an essential ele-ment has long been the continuous inflows of immigrants who have helped to make and remake American culture and society since the days of the country's founding. It is no exaggeration to say that immigrants are a source of transformation in American society; this was true in the past, with the arrival of earlier waves of European newcomers, and it has been true in recent times when most immigrants have come from Asia and Latin America.

In detailing many of the changes in which the post-1965 immigration has played a key role, the preceding chapters have covered a wide ter-rain; they have ranged from transformations in the racial order and cit-ies, towns, and suburbs, to popular culture, the economy, and electoral politics, focusing on the contemporary period while also sensitive to similar changes generated by immigration in the past. In this final chap-ter, I reflect on some additional questions: What are the implications of the analysis for our general understanding of immigration and change in American society? Is the United States unique in its experience with immigration-driven change as compared to western Europe? And to return to this country, what further changes may be in store in the years ahead, particularly in a post-pandemic America?

Immigration and Change: What Have We Learned?

Immigrants and their descendants have been a driving force behind consequential and profound institutional as well as cultural changes in American society. From the beginning, in colonial days and the early years of the republic, Americans with roots in England gave us the basic foundations of government, common law, and language, defining many of the fundamental institutional pillars of the country that persist to this day. As we know, many far-reaching changes occurred in the decades and indeed centuries that followed, with each new wave of immigration having a part in important transformations. The nineteenth-century Irish, to give one example, built an extensive network of parochial schools to protect their children from the overtly Protestant character of the state-supported school system, and were central in the creation of political machines that dominated politics in many large cities in the late nineteenth and early twentieth centuries.

As millions of Italian and Jewish immigrants and their children assimilated and became recognized as full-fledged Americans in the mid-twentieth century, they became part of an all-inclusive White community; the United States also left behind the idea that it was a Protestant nation, turning into one premised on the notion that it was composed of three equally American faiths—Protestants, Catholics, and Jews.[2] Moreover, immigrants of the 1880–1924 era and their second-generation children had a prominent role in the development of the modern industrial economy as well as the reorienting of the Democratic Party that led to the New Deal under Roosevelt and Great Society under Johnson.[3]

The post-1965 inflows have been a source of equally momentous changes, transforming, among other things, the nation's racial composition as well as perceptions of racial and ethnic groups, playing an important role in reshaping the substance and form of party politics, and serving as central players in the development and enormous success of a key sector (high tech) of the economy. They have brought new religions, most prominently Islam, into the heart of many American towns and cities.

Changes that may seem less dramatic represent noteworthy transformations too, as examples from earlier chapters indicate. Immigrants have not only created tens of thousands of small businesses but also given many a new character and pioneered new types of enterprises. They have introduced new foods and cuisines as well as innovative sounds, artistic styles, and themes. Local institutions and organizations such as schools and hospitals have developed new programs to adapt to immigrants' needs.

In propelling change, immigration of course often operates in tandem with other forces. Or to put it somewhat differently, time and again immigration has played a major role in significant transformations that involve other factors as well. Immigrant talent has been vital in the creation and evolution of high-tech companies, but other features of America's society and economy have helped to nurture this sector, among them the presence of world-class research universities and a financial system that supports entrepreneurial activities.[4] To offer another illustration, in the world of politics, immigration has had a part in shaping the new alignment or remaking of national political party coalitions, but it is not alone. The civil rights movement and legislation began the process of large numbers of Whites gravitating to the Republican Party so that the "Solid Democratic South" became a relic of the past; later on the growing defection of working-class Whites to the Republican Party was a response not only to fears, anxieties, and resentments owing to immigration-driven racial and ethnic diversity but also a slew of other changes, including the expansion of rights to women and LGBTQ people, development of a more secular America, and economic challenges posed by technological change, deindustrialization, and globalization.

Then there is the question of what is new today. Needless to say, there are similarities between immigration-driven changes in the past and present, but history does not repeat itself in exactly the same way. The changes stimulated by immigration in the current era are not timeless replays of institutional and cultural patterns from the past but involve new features that represent modern-day shifts or transformations. This should not be surprising. The changes take place in an America with a broad range of distinctive social, economic, political, and cultural elements, and immigrants who differ in significant ways from those in earlier inflows.

There is no better illustration than the creation of ethnic neighborhoods and businesses that, although a perennial feature of immigrant life in the United States, have taken on new qualities in the contemporary context, if only because of the cultural backgrounds of post-1965 immigrants and the character of the modern-day America they come to. Unlike the old ethnic neighborhood of years gone by, contemporary ethnic enclaves are often located in areas formerly the domain of middle- and lower-middle-class Whites. They are now more likely to be in the suburbs, and have an array of new cultural features and institutions, from Hindu temples and Muslim mosques to branches of cell phone companies. Ethnic businesses still cater to the needs and tastes of newcomers, but it is no longer just the corner store that sells ethnic products;

today there may be a large ethnic supermarket as well. Ethnically themed restaurants offer a wide variety of new dishes and flavors appealing to coethnics, but also beyond this, middle-class educated foodies and, especially in the case of Chinese eateries around the country, a broad American public. Many new kinds of businesses are immigrant creations. In New York City, which is home to more than three million immigrants, Korean-owned nail salons can be found in practically every neighborhood, and immigrants have invented new types of transportation services as well. West Indians brought the concept of a privatized network of passenger vans to the city as their jitneys ply the streets of Queens and Brooklyn, offering lower prices along with more frequent and convenient services than city buses. The Chinese created relatively inexpensive shuttles from Manhattan's Chinatown to Chinese communities in Queens and Brooklyn, and developed intercity buses, originally to transport workers to and from jobs in Chinese restaurants in such cities as Boston, Philadelphia, and Washington, DC, at low cost, but later extending them to further destinations and attracting non-Chinese customers too.[5]

In taking up established roles in mainstream institutional arenas, today's immigrants and their children in the process have often introduced distinctive changes—another way the present can differ from the past. In the arts, writers with origins in Latin America, Asia, and Africa have been leaving their own stamp on the American novel just as musical performers have been taking popular music in new directions. Recently elected immigrant and second-generation politicians frequently have much in common with their predecessors, yet at the same time they may advocate different and new policy measures to reflect the interests of their electoral base, and initiate, shore up, or utilize new minority coalitions.

Lastly, in analyzing immigration and change, this book provides a corrective to the one-sided picture found in much of the academic literature, which heavily focuses on how post-1965 immigrants have been changed in this country, but often neglects how they have been remaking it as well. A copious literature exists on the integration of immigrants. Indeed, an exhaustive review of the large body of research on this topic by a National Academy of Sciences panel demonstrates that integration increases over time across all measurable outcomes, "with immigrants becoming more like the native-born with more time in the country, and with the second and third generations becoming more like other native-born Americans than their parents were."[6] Language is a prime example. Immigrants who arrive as adults without English make some progress, but are usually more comfortable and fluent in their native language; the vast majority of US-born children are proficient in English (though often bilingual); and the third generation is to a large extent monolingual in English. The second generation shows strong intergenerational progress in educational and occupational attainments; in most contemporary immigrant groups, this generation equals or surpasses the schooling level of typical native-born Americans in the third generation and higher. Over time, most immigrants and their descendants gradually become less residentially segregated from the general population of native-born Whites, and more dispersed across regions, cities, communities, and neighborhoods. And if immigrants rarely abandon distinctive ethnic identities, beliefs, and cultural practices altogether, homeland customs and values begin to shift in the US context; by the second and especially third generation, ethnic cultural patterns are often symbolic aspects of the remembered old country culture—such as celebrating particular holidays or enjoying ethnic dishes—and even these are frequently Americanized to a considerable degree.[7]

Important as it is to appreciate the changes immigrants experience in the United States, the fact is that we know far less about how they have been reshaping American society and culture, though understanding these processes of change is equally crucial and calls for further systematic research. This, too, is a lesson of this book.

Is the United States Unique?

The United States is not the only wealthy country to be deeply affected by mass immigration in the last half century. So have western European nations, where the foreign born are generally around a tenth to a fifth of the residents.[8] A comparison with western European societies is particularly apt because they are rich democracies that have also undergone significant social, political, and cultural changes in response to the enormous growth of their immigrant-origin populations. The comparison makes it clear that despite many similarities, the American experience with immigration and change is distinctive, or unique, in many respects. It also puts into sharp relief that a nation's particular institutional history can determine whether and how immigration leads to change.

What, to begin with, are some of the similarities? One broad parallel is that immigration has reshaped the racial order, which in the case of many European countries has led for the first time to sizable Black populations with origins in Africa and the Caribbean; another is immigration's alteration of the religious landscape, which in Europe has introduced a large and highly stigmatized Muslim minority. Large urban centers in western Europe, as in the United States, have experienced new immigration-driven diversity as the percentage of foreign born has soared; about one out of three residents in Amsterdam, London, and New York City were foreign born by the second decade of the twenty-first century.[9] New ethnic neighborhoods have sprung up all over Europe along with highly diverse communities that include a welter of groups from different sending countries. Also echoing the pattern across the Atlantic, immigration in Europe has given rise to a wide range of small businesses that added vitality to urban economies, and provided an array of goods and services on which those in immigrant communities as well as outside them have come to depend—from Turkish bakeries and kebab outlets in the Netherlands and Germany, to North African small retail stores in France and South Asian newsagent's shops in Britain.[10]

There are many other examples, including the influence of the huge immigrant inflows on popular culture. If more salsa than ketchup is sold in the United States, the Turkish *doner kebab* has become the most popular fast food in Germany, and "going out for a curry" at a South Asian restaurant is now a regular part of English social and cultural life. In Europe as in the United States, immigrants and the second generation have drawn on their own experiences and concerns as they have enriched the artistic scene in novels, plays, and films, and brought new sounds and forms to popular music. *Brick Lane* by Bangladeshi-born

Monica Ali and *White Teeth* by Zadie Smith, daughter of a Jamaican mother and English father, are just two of the widely celebrated novels about immigrants and the second generation in Britain; the development of British hip-hop music has been heavily influenced by Afro-Caribbean migrants and their children in the same way that Dutch hip-hop has been shaped by youths of Surinamese and Moroccan background, and the French version by those with origins in Africa and the French Antilles.[11] There are transatlantic parallels in the world of politics too, as immigrant-origin politicians have begun to make a mark at the local and national levels, with one of the best known in Europe being London's second-generation Pakistani mayor, Sadiq Khan.[12] Less happily, anti-immigrant rhetoric has become a staple of right-wing populist European parties that have gained electoral clout just as it has been a tactic used by President Trump to rally his Republican Party base. On both sides of the Atlantic, anti-immigrant appeals have particular resonance with less educated voters of lower socioeconomic status.[13]

If these and other changes have much in common in western Europe and the United States, the differences are prominent as well. Of special interest are a number of significant institutional changes and innovations that only developed in European countries in the wake of the huge contemporary immigration. Three examples show how much institutional histories related to race and religion matter in understanding these contrasts.

Take citizenship. In many continental western Europe countries, basic principles of citizenship law have undergone a fundamental change owing in large part to postwar immigration. In making it easier for the second generation to acquire citizenship, these countries have moved closer to a central principle of the US citizenship regime, jus soli or birthright citizenship, which was guaranteed to almost everyone born in the United States more than 150 years ago in an automatic and unqualified form by the Fourteenth Amendment, designed to ensure legal rights to formerly enslaved Black people.[14] Three decades later, in 1898, in a case involving the US-born child of Chinese immigrants, who themselves were ineligible for citizenship, the Supreme Court reaffirmed that no matter where their parents were born or what their parents' status, US-born children are US citizens.[15] Post-1965 immigrants, in other words, have come to an American society with an entrenched legal tradition of jus soli. This was not the case for most immigrants who arrived in continental western Europe in the last six or seven decades. Before the Second World War in much of mainland Europe, jus sanguinis, the principle that citizenship is inherited from parents, was prevalent so that many children of immigrants remained foreign even if they were born and had spent all their lives in the European country.[16]

By now, however, the majority of western European countries provide some form of jus soli citizenship to the second generation, although unlike in the United States, it is granted only if certain conditions are met, such as if your parents have lived in the country for a certain number of years or one of your parents was born there.[17] Among the explanations for the widespread shift to some form of birthright citizenship in mainland western Europe is the internal logic of liberal democracies in the context of mass immigration, including the need to integrate immigrants and their children; the old rules have been recognized as incompatible with modern democratic norms and impediments to the integration of the second generation.[18]

A second example draws attention to the role of this country's particular racial history in understanding why immigration was not an engine for the development of significant anti-racism legislative initiatives here the way it was in western Europe. Unlike European countries, the United States has long had a large and stigmatized Black population on its soil, subject first to centuries of slavery and then, after official abolition, to a harsh regime of legal segregation in the South that lasted until the mid-twentieth century. It was African Americans' struggle for civil rights in the 1950s and 1960s, another distinctive feature of the United States, that led to the passage of a series of federal legislative acts that attempted to redress the injuries incurred by centuries of legal oppression. The legislation created new institutional arrangements along with monitoring and enforcement mechanisms that while hardly eliminating all-too-persistent racial barriers and discrimination, opened up new educational and occupational opportunities for racial minorities, including many children of immigrants. The Voting Rights Act of 1965, a hallmark civil rights era law, led to a huge growth in voter registration among Black people in many southern states; it also helped minorities achieve political representation in a number of places by allowing the creation of voting districts where they had a better opportunity to elect their own representatives, although in 2013 the law was severely weakened when the Supreme Court struck down a key provision designed to combat racial discrimination in voting.[19]

In western Europe, it was not a civil rights movement among a long-established racial minority group to ameliorate the enduring damages of slavery and segregation that led to legislation and policies to combat racial discrimination; it was the response to the influx of non-European immigrants.[20] The move in western Europe to pass laws to reduce and prevent racial discrimination was especially notable—and early—in Britain, where it occurred in reaction to the huge Afro-Caribbean and South Asian immigration that began in the 1950s. The first legislation in the United Kingdom to address racial discrimination, the 1965 Race Relations Act, prohibited, among other things, discrimination on the grounds of race in public places; it was supplemented by legislation in 1968 extending protection against discrimination beyond public places to employment and housing, and broadened again in 1976, when the definition of discrimination now also included indirect discrimination. At the level of the European Union, an anti-discrimination directive ("the racial equality directive") was adopted in 2000 requiring member states to prohibit discrimination on the basis of racial or ethnic origin in many aspects of everyday life such as employment, education, health care, and housing.[21]

By and large, the legislation and policies to reduce racial discrimination have been more extensive in the United States, but whatever their exact nature or effectiveness, the main point here is that the introduction of such legislation and policies in Europe occurred in the context of large-scale immigration. This was not the case in the United States, where as a consequence of the civil rights movement, they predated the massive post-1965 inflows.

The third example has to do with historically based relations between the state and religion. In the United States, the way relations between the state and religious bodies have been institutionalized precluded the creation of government-organized councils like those established in a number of western European countries to negotiate relations between the growing Muslim migrant-origin population and the state on religious matters of public concern.

These councils, in a state-brokered arrangement, gather Muslim federations together under one umbrella to address religious issues of a public nature. The French Council of the Muslim Faith, created in 2003, has a mandate to negotiate with the French state over issues affecting Islamic religious practice such as the training of imams and regulation of ritual slaughter. As political scientist Jonathan Laurence and historian Justin Vaisse note, it represents an attempt by the state to establish an Islam of France rather than simply tolerate Islam in France. In 2006, the German federal government, too, established an Islam Council, the Deutsche Islam Konferenz, drawing on a core of representatives of Germany's Muslims and the government to engage in exchanges as a way to try to resolve the practical challenges of religious observance facing Muslims, with initial discussions on, among other topics, the future of mosque construction and Islamic burials in Germany.[22]

The creation of these councils, to be sure, reflects the greater political and public focus in Europe on integrating Muslims, which in turn has a lot to do with demographic features of the Muslim immigrant population there. A much larger proportion of immigrants and their children in western Europe are Muslim—or about 40 percent of all immigrants from outside the European Union.[23] In the United States, Muslims are an estimated 4 to 5 percent of all immigrants, and only about 1 percent of the total population.[24] By comparison, in France and Germany, which have the largest Muslim populations in western Europe, 8 percent of the French population in 2016 was Muslim and 6 percent in Germany. Muslim immigrants in western Europe also have a much lower socioeconomic profile than those in the United States, where a substantial proportion are well educated and middle class.[25]

But the development of Muslim councils in Europe is not just a reflection of demographic characteristics of the Muslim population. Relations between church and state, which are rooted in institutional history, are important in understanding why European countries like France and Germany developed state-supported councils that have no equivalent in the United States for Islam or indeed any religion.

In this country, the principles of religious freedom and prohibition of an established state religion enshrined in the Constitution's First Amendment have provided the framework for church-state relations since the nation's founding. These constitutional principles were fashioned because of the religious diversity among the original colonies and resulting impossibility of institutionalizing a single state church in the new republic.[26] Religious entities in the United States are loosely governed by laws on nonprofit organizations, whereas religion in "continental Europe is nearly everywhere a government affair. National ministers of the interior oversee orderly religious practice, for example, by regulating religious facilities (mosques, temples, churches, and so forth), and ministers of education may supplement clerical training through the national university system. . . . Other matters of religious practice also require state oversight: ritual animal slaughter, establishment of cemeteries, and appointment of state-paid chaplains in the military, hospitals, and prisons."[27]

In France, laïcité, the exclusion of religion from the affairs of state, is the official ideology, yet the state owns and maintains most Christian churches, and allows them to be used for regular religious services—although the 1905 law giving the state most church property and committing it to maintaining already-standing religious buildings has prevented the government from providing the same support to places of worship built after that year, including mosques.[28] The establishment of the French Council of the Muslim Faith puts Islam on the same plane as other major non-Catholic religions in relationship to the French state in at least one way, for they are represented by a similar kind of body: the Jewish Consistoire Central dates to the emancipation of Jews in the Napoleonic era and the Protestant Federation of France to 1905. In Germany, the Deutsche Islam Konferenz is of a piece with other linkages between church and state, in which long-established Catholics and Protestants as well as Jews—though not, so far, Islam—are recognized as public corporations, entitled to federally collected church taxes, and have the right to run state-subsidized religious social services and hospitals. Clearly, such linkages between church and state are strikingly different from institutionalized patterns in this country.

In sum, whether looking at government-brokered Muslim councils, race relations legislation, or principles of citizenship law, particular historically based institutional arrangements on the two sides of the Atlantic help explain why certain institutional changes occurred in western Europe, but not the United States, in response to contemporary immigration. No two countries of course are exactly alike, and I have not gone into the many marked differences among western European nations themselves—something I have explored elsewhere.[29] From an American perspective, though, this broad transatlantic comparison underscores the importance of this country's racial and religious history in understanding what has changed—or indeed not changed—in reaction to the massive immigration of recent years.

Where Are We Going?

And this brings us squarely back to the United States, with an eye to the future. If understanding immigration-propelled changes is difficult because we are in the midst of them, it is even more challenging to speculate about what will happen in the years ahead. This is especially true in light of the earth-shattering coronavirus pandemic and economic recession, which by mid-2021 had caused more than six hundred thousand deaths in this country and unemployment for millions of Americans.

Still, some developments are highly likely in a post-pandemic era. For one thing, and critical to immigration's role in future change, there is the prospect of continued substantial inflows of lawful permanent immigrants from abroad. This is a virtual certainty when Democrats are in the White House given their commitment to humanitarian and legal immigration and a wide range of pro-immigrant policies, many of which can be implemented through administrative actions without congressional legislation. If Republicans regain the presidency, lower levels of legal immigration are a definite possibility. Trump, after all, slashed refugee admissions and aimed to severely cut the number of green cards issued annually through various administrative measures. Whichever party is in power, however, we can expect at the very least the admission of several hundred thousand lawful permanent residents per year and many temporary workers too.

Pressures for immigration in a post-pandemic America will come from many quarters, including employers seeking high- and low-skilled workers, from top talent in science, engineering, and research development in the high-tech sector to farm laborers in agriculture. On the Democratic Party side, many immigrant minorities and liberal college-educated Whites, key elements in its coalition, will push for sustained and sizable legal immigration.

The demand for immigrant workers will continue and likely go up in the context of demographic changes. Our country is aging. By 2030, all of the baby boomers will be older than sixty-five, expanding the size of the older population so that one in five US residents will be retirement age.[30] More people will be required to fill jobs that retiring baby boomers are vacating at all levels of the occupational hierarchy, and to meet expanding needs in health care and other services. The US Bureau of Labor Statistics predicts, for example, that in the third decade of the twenty-first century, 176,000 registered nurse positions will need to be filled every year through 2029 as aging baby boomers create more patients requiring care while a large number of nurses are slated to retire. Even more home health and personal care aides will be called for in that decade—with 568,000 openings projected on average each year—to meet the increasing demand for elder home care and replace aides who transfer to other occupations or retire.[31] Moreover, immigrants and their children are an important source of tax revenues for the social security system, which will be facing fiscal strains in the context of the growing number of elderly. And to add to this, US fertility rates have been falling. Already in 2018, the total fertility rate had dipped to a record low, with the expected number of births per American woman dropping to 1.73, well below the replacement rate needed to sustain the existing population.[32] Fewer immigrant residents ultimately would mean the birth of fewer future American citizens, especially given higher birth rates among foreign- versus US-born women, thereby portending slower growth of the workforce in the years to come. As one demographer puts it, "Any appreciable lowering of immigration levels will lead to tepid population growth, potentially negative growth in the youth population, and extreme age dependency."[33]

Two important questions are how much the pandemic and recession will undo changes in the economy that immigrants spearheaded earlier, and what role immigrants will play in facilitating economic recovery. Certainly, the epidemic had disastrous effects for untold thousands of immigrants and their families. Because large numbers work in essential frontline services such as health care—caring for patients in hospitals, for instance, and cleaning hospital rooms—and support jobs—such as stocking shelves and checking out customers in grocery stores and supermarkets—they were vulnerable to illness, and many, in the end, lost their lives.[34]

Especially devastating was the rate of infection and death in two major COVID-19 hot spots: meat-processing plants, where about half of the frontline meatpacking workers are immigrants, and nursing homes, where they make up about a quarter of the direct-care staff.[35] Immigrants also suffered massive layoffs and high rates of unemployment given their heavy concentration in a number of industries that were particularly hard hit, including hotels, restaurants, and retail businesses. In food services alone, 38 percent of the nation's chefs and head cooks and 22 percent of food preparation workers in 2018 were foreign born.[36] Many of the Main Streets that immigrants helped to revive endured damaging slumps; many of the innovative businesses that they founded, from nail salons to eateries with new ethnic cuisines, did not survive, and those that did faced extended shutdowns, thinner margins, and risky futures in the era of social distancing. Sociologist Zai Liang, who has studied Chinese restaurant owners and workers around the country, reports that while some restaurants held on through takeout business, others closed with no plans to reopen. "The impact of Covid-19 on my business is really catastrophic," said one owner, who planned to shut down his restaurant while discussing renting the property to a chain drugstore.[37]

It will take time in a post-pandemic America for many immigrants to get back on their feet again, and some will never regain their losses. Nevertheless, as they recoup, and as new arrivals enter, we can expect immigrants once more to play a role in reviving troubled parts of the economy, revitalizing weakened urban communities, and stimulating growth in the housing market in many metropolitan areas. This is what happened in numerous places after previous economic downturns, such as the slowdown of the 1970s and the 2008–9 recession, and earlier disasters, such as Hurricane Katrina, when migrant workers converged on Louisiana to assist in cleanup and reconstruction.[38] Recent immigrants are among the readiest to move for work, and many will undoubtedly do so in response to opportunities that reappear.

As immigrants open new businesses and revive dormant ones, they can be counted on to introduce changes, pioneering new types of enterprises, including in specialized services, and expanding businesses that have the potential for success in a post-pandemic environment, giving them new shapes and sizes as well as orienting them more to an online world.[39] Already during the pandemic, many first- and second-generation restaurant owners not only adapted by turning to outdoor dining and meeting an increased demand for takeout; some experimented with new dishes and projects. In the southern Louisiana city of Lafayette, in the heart of Cajun country, for example, two Jamaican immigrants made the leap in spring 2021 to move their restaurant, Di Jerk Stop, which started as a barbecue shack, to its first stand-alone brick-and-mortar location. Along with a menu with such dishes as jerk chicken pasta and curried goat, Merick Chambers and Bobby Marshall planned to sell Jamaican condiments, establish a bar serving rum punch and imported island beverages, open a gaming area with a pool table, and host a karaoke night.[40] Just as immigrants like these will help restore the economy, they will also continue to influence what Americans eat and, along with their children, go on enriching other aspects of American culture. Indeed, one of the most critically acclaimed films released during the pandemic in winter 2021, the semi-autobiographical *Minari*, was written and directed by second-generation Korean American Lee Isaac Chung about the challenges facing a Korean immigrant family who move to an Arkansas farm.

In another domain, the pandemic will not put an end to the polarized national politics we have seen in recent decades or xenophobic appeals of many Republican politicians, at least in the near term. Indeed, many working-class White Trump voters who suffered economic devastation will no doubt continue to blame immigrants for their troubles—resentments that some Republican candidates will exploit and intensify in their election strategies. Trump's legitimation of anti-immigrant rhetoric and policies will be hard to expunge. Or as *New York Times* columnist Frank Bruni opined in 2019, he is in the nation's bloodstream, and his impact may linger long after his presidency is over.[41] Support from White, noncollege-educated voters (especially men) in combination with structural inequities in the electoral system and voter-suppression measures may continue to work for a time for many hard-right Republicans seeking national office, and encourage them to appeal to anti-foreigner and racist voter sentiments.

Yet demographic forces rooted in immigration will operate in another direction, especially in the longer run. According to one projection, Hispanics alone will increase to 19 percent of eligible voters by 2036, up from 12 percent in 2016. Demographic realities are bound to move some Republican office seekers in a more pro-immigrant or pro-diversity direction in a bid to capture a greater share of the ethnic and racial minority vote, particularly in places where it is becoming more significant, and also in a post-Trump era when possibilities emerge for new alignments and leaders within the Republican Party.[42] For Democrats, the increasing share of racial and ethnic minority voters in the electorate will no doubt boost their future prospects in many local and state elections, and despite some defections to Republicans, should make Democratic candidates more competitive in national contests as well. The pandemic and inequalities it laid bare may also enhance Democratic support from parts of the minority population by contributing to strengthening center-left economic policies among influential sections of the Democratic Party leadership.

When it comes to race, the pandemic exposed racial disparities in America like few other events in recent US history. The COVID-19 outbreak hit Blacks and Hispanics especially hard. They suffered disproportionately high rates of death and unemployment, which both reflected and reinforced racial inequalities in this country. As for Asian Americans, the rise in verbal abuse and physical attacks against them, involving being blamed for the spread of COVID-19, Jennifer Lee and Monika Yadav argue, should be a "reckoning for Asian Americans that . . . native-born status, US citizenship, elite degrees, and professional jobs are no shields against hate, xenophobia, racism, and scapegoating."[43]

Still, as we look ahead to a changing racial order, it is hard to imagine the pandemic reversing the overall trend toward increasing inclusiveness for many who are currently seen as minorities or people of color. The signs are that in the decades to come, Americans will be more comfortable with and accepting of ethnic and racial diversity. As one journalist wryly put it, we cannot turn back the clock to a time when Americans never heard someone speaking Spanish behind them at the supermarket.[44] The country will continue to have many immigrants in it as well as a rising number of their children and children's children.[45] For more and more Americans, interacting with people of different races and ethnicities in schools, workplaces, religious congregations, and local communities will be a normal, commonplace feature of everyday life. This does not mean that racial prejudice and discrimination—and race-based inequalities—will disappear. They will not. But there is every indication that increased social contacts among those of similar social status from different racial and ethnic backgrounds will reduce prejudice as well as foster less conflict-ridden, indeed often amicable, and sometimes even intimate relations.

As changes in the racial hierarchy and meaning of racial categories evolve in the coming years, immigrants, and even more their children and grandchildren, will play an important role in shaping them. It is a safe bet that altered conceptions of race and ethnicity will provide more scope for many Americans with origins in Asia, Latin America, and Africa as well. The ability of more children and grandchildren of post-1965 immigrants to move into positions in the upper ranges of the occupational hierarchy and the growth in the proportion of mixed marriages and multiracial children—these developments are bound to lead to greater inclusion for many now routinely categorized as racial minorities or non-White, and may eventually result in the emergence of new terms to talk about racial divisions. In the end, changes in the racial order will be one of the most important transformations and legacies of the post-1965 immigration for American society.

———

It is now more than half a century since the inflows of millions of immigrants from across the globe began to transform the United States. In thinking of the years to come, cohorts of new arrivals, along with their children and grandchildren, will inevitably leave their own mark. This in truth is the story of America. "Our growth as a nation," historian Oscar Handlin wrote more than sixty years ago, "has been achieved in large measure through the genius and industry of immigrants of every race and from every quarter of the world. The story of their pursuit of happiness is the saga of America. Their brains and their brawn helped to settle our land, to advance our agriculture, to build our industries, to develop our commerce, to produce new inventions and, in general, to make us the . . . nation that we now are."[46] Certainly, there will be new twists and turns as we move further into the twenty-first century, but immigration has always been part of the evolution of American society, and there is every reason to expect that this will continue to be so in the years ahead.

ACKNOWLEDGMENTS

In the course of writing this book, I have acquired a great many debts. They start with my debt to the institutions that provided the time and support to work on it. I began working on the book when I had a year off from teaching as a fellow at the CUNY Graduate Center's Advanced Research Collaborative, then directed by Donald Robotham. A few years later, I benefited from a semester as a fellow at the American Academy in Berlin, and a Guggenheim fellowship allowed me to take additional time off from teaching to complete several chapters. In addition, Jan Willem Duyvendak, Francesca Decimo, and Patrick Simon made possible shorter stints for concentrated writing at, respectively, the Netherlands Institute for Advanced Study in the Humanities and Social Sciences, the University of Trento, and INED (the French National Institute for Demographic Studies), where I also profited from conversations with them and their colleagues.

Over the years, I have had the good fortune to be part of a large community of immigration scholars who have enhanced my understanding of international migration and influenced my ideas on its impact on the United States. It's not possible to name them all, for there are so many, and I wouldn't want to leave anyone off the list. I do, however, want to acknowledge my debt to several people who had a direct role in the development and writing of this book. Many thanks to Richard Alba, Kay Deaux, Mary Waters, and an anonymous reviewer for Princeton University Press for their helpful comments on the manuscript. I gained insights and ideas while writing the book from my collaborations with Richard and Kay as well as Christophe Bertossi, Maurice Crul, Katharine Donato, Jan Willem Duyvendak, Philip Kasinitz, Leo Lucassen, John Mollenkopf, and Patrick Simon. I learned a great deal as well from my social science colleagues on the National Academy of Sciences panel on the integration of immigrants into American society (chaired by Mary Waters), and the historians I worked with on the Statue of Liberty / Ellis Island history advisory committee (chaired by Alan Kraut) and the Tenement Museum's scholarly advisory group (organized by Annie Polland, now the museum's president).

My own institution, the City University of New York, has been a wonderful place to be an immigration scholar, not least because my undergraduate students at Hunter College, nearly all immigrants or children of immigrants, have helped me to better understand the experiences of immigrants and their impact on this country. In the doctoral program at the Graduate Center, I have greatly benefited from my many exchanges with colleagues as well as students, the latter including, most recently, Brenda Gambol, Rebecca Karam, Abby Kolker, and Karen Okigbo.

At Princeton University Press, executive editor Meagan Levinson was an enthusiastic backer of the book project from its early days, made enormously helpful and detailed comments on the manuscript, and guided it through the publication process. I feel fortunate to have had the opportunity to work with her. Thanks as well to the rest of the Princeton University Press team, including assistant editor Jacqueline Delaney, senior production editor Kathleen Cioffi, and copyeditor Cindy Milstein.

Finally, I want to thank members of my family. My husband, Peter Swerdloff, spent hours talking over ideas with me, helped me sharpen many of the arguments, and provided critical insights and expert editorial advice. My daughter, Alexis, her husband, Byron, and their young son, Sam, have been a source of joy and delight. This is my first book in which my mother, Anne Foner—professor emerita of sociology at Rutgers University, and nearing the age of a hundred as I finished the manuscript—was unable to read drafts of chapters and offer suggestions. As usual, however, she provided encouragement and support at every step of the way. I dedicate this book to her.

NOTES

Chapter 1. Introduction: Immigration and the Transformation of America

1. According to the 2020 Current Population Survey, immigrants and their US-born children numbered approximately 85.7 million people or 26 percent of the US population (Batalova, Hanna, and Levesque 2021). This figure includes about 44.9 million immigrants (Jeanne Batalova, personal communication).

2. Alba and Foner 2015; Alba 2020.

3. Gabaccia 2010; Jacobson 2006, 9.

4. According to Portes (2012, 566–67), the phrase "immigrants are transforming the American mainstream" is merely a rhetorical device and immigration has a limited transformative capacity: in the United States, "there have been adaptations responding to the needs and demands posed by a large foreign population in organizations like schools, the legal system, and the labor market but, by and large, the fundamental pillars of society, including its value-normative system and its class structure, have remained intact."

5. Alba and Nee 2003.

6. Waters and Pineau 2015.

7. On immigration and the changing construction of race, see, for example, Alba 2009, 2020; Lee and Bean 2010. On immigration's impact on the economy and the labor market, see, for example, Borjas 1999; Waldinger and Lichter 2003. On immigration and the changing religious landscape, see, for example, Eck 2001; Wuthnow 2005.

8. On New York, see for example, Foner 2013b, 2013c. On Miami, see, for example, Portes and Armony 2018. On Los Angeles, see, for example, Waldinger and Bozorgmehr 1996. On Nashville, see, for example, Winders 2013. On California's Silicon Valley, see, for example, Jiménez 2017. A few edited collections examine how immigration has affected new immigrant destinations, or reshaped urban and metropolitan America more generally: Jones-Correa 2001; Massey 2008; Mollenkopf and Pastor 2016; Singer, Hardwick, and Brettell 2008; Vitiello and Sugrue 2017a; Waldinger 2001; Zúñiga and Hernandez-León 2005.

9. Huntington 2004; Brimelow 1995.

10. Foner 2000, 2005, 2006, 2013a, 2014, 2019; Foner and Lucassen 2012. This book looks broadly at the post-1965 period rather than a step-by-step chronicle of shifts during these years.

11. Chishti, Hipsman, and Ball 2015.

12. Chishti, Hipsman, and Ball 2015. An interplay of factors led to the 1965 act, including foreign policy pressures, ethnic lobbying, and concerns about the racial and ethnic biases of

existing immigration law in the context of the civil rights movement (Alba and Foner 2015, 109; for a recent analysis, see Fitzgerald and Cook-Martin 2014).

13. Railton 2017. The number of Italians who entered annually between 1925 and 1930 was somewhat higher—for example, eight thousand in 1924—since wives and unmarried minor children of US citizens were exempt from the quota (Daniels 2004, 56–57; Ngai 2004, 66–67).

14. Bean and Stevens 2003, 17.

15. Batalova and Terrazas 2010. Following common scholarly practice, I use foreign born and immigrant interchangeably in this book. The official US census definition of the foreign born, all persons who are not US citizens at birth, includes lawful permanent residents, naturalized US citizens, refugees and asylees, people on certain temporary visas, and unauthorized immigrants (Batalova, Hanna, and Levesque 2021; Waters and Pineau 2015, 21).

16. Gelatt 2019. Lawful permanent residents are noncitizens who are lawfully authorized to live permanently in the United States; they can apply for US citizenship after five years, or three if they are married to a US citizen. The diversity visa program allocates up to fifty thousand visas annually through a virtual lottery of qualified applicants from underrepresented countries. Africans have been major beneficiaries, making up 40 percent of the lottery "winners" from 1995 through 2017, while Asians were 25 percent (Congressional Research Service 2019).

17. Alba and Nee 2003, 176. See also Alba and Foner 2015, 25–26.

18. Budiman 2020; Batalova, Hanna, and Levesque 2021. Asians include those from East and Southeast Asia, South Asia, and Central Asia.

19. Gonzalez-Barrera 2015; Massey, Durand, and Pren 2016; Budiman 2020; Zong and Batalova 2018.

20. Chishti, Hipson, and Ball 2015. See also Lee 2019.

21. Foner 1973.

22. Massey et al. 1993.

23. This subsequent legislation included the 1980 Refugee Act, establishing the criteria for admission of refugees and immigration based on humanitarian relief and giving presidents the authority to set annual ceilings for the number of refugee entries; the 1986 Immigration Reform and Control Act, providing a path to legalization for many (ultimately nearly three million) undocumented people; and the Immigration Act of 1990, raising the annual numerical limit on family-sponsored immigrant visas, creating the diversity visa lottery, and enacting new high-skilled visa categories (Waters and Pineau 2015, 65–66; see also Donato and Amuedo-Dorantes 2020). That congressional legislation since 1965 expanded the legal influx has a lot to do with what political scientist Aristide Zolberg (1999) calls the strange bedfellows of immigration politics: business interests eager for cheap and mobile labor combined with the work of ethnic and civil rights groups, religious bodies, and immigrant-rights organizations to promote the continuation of or growth in legal immigration levels.

24. Martin 2014; Donato and Amuedo-Dorantes 2020. One factor contributing to soaring immigration in the last half century is that the 1965 law and subsequent amendments exempted immediate relatives of US citizens (spouses, parents, and unmarried children under twenty-one) from the annual worldwide and per country numerical limits applying to other family as well as employment categories. This exemption helps explain why the number of green cards

issued in many years has exceeded the annual flexible worldwide cap, which after a series of legislative modifications, stood at 675,000 at the beginning of the twenty-first century (for details on how the US legal immigration system works, see Gelatt 2019).

25. Donato and Amuedo-Dorantes 2020; Batalova, Hanna, and Levesque 2021; Chishti and Bolter 2020. The 1850 Census was the first to collect data on nativity.

26. American Immigration Council 2020; Budiman 2020; Blizzard and Batalova 2019b; Gelatt 2019; Waters and Pineau 2015, 130–31.

27. This figure does not include tourists or other short-term visitors (Batalova, Hanna, and Levesque 2021).

28. Donato and Amuedo-Dorantes 2020; Blizzard and Batalova 2019b. Exchange visitor visas are for those approved to participate in work-and-study-based exchange visitor programs.

29. Alba and Foner 2015, 32–33; Batalova, Blizzard, and Bolter 2020; Bier 2020; Blizzard and Batalova 2019b; Pierce and Gelatt 2018; Waters and Pineau 2015. In recent years, roughly half the green cards issued annually have gone to immigrants already in the United States who have adjusted from another status such as temporary worker or international student (Gelatt 2019).

30. Warren 2017, 2019.

31. Capps et al. 2020; Batalova, Hanna, and Levesque 2021.

32. Waters and Pineau 2015, 43.

33. Zolberg 2006, 240, 264. After 1917, a literacy test was required of all immigrants over sixteen at Ellis Island, reading thirty to forty words in English or their native language, although it had little impact on the admission of European immigrants.

34. In addition, most people fleeing their home countries are unable to access humanitarian protection such as refugee or asylum status (American Immigration Council 2019).

35. Gelatt 2019.

36. Krogstad, Passel, and Cohn 2019.

37. Massey, Durand, and Pren 2016; Alba and Foner 2015, 38–39.

38. De Genova 2004; Massey, Durand, and Malone 2002; Massey and Pren 2012; Sandoval-Strausz 2019, 132.

39. Capps et al. 2020.

40. Waters and Pineau 2015, 36.

41. Batalova, Hanna, and Levesque 2021; Foner 2013a.

Chapter 2. The Racial Order

1. Passel and Cohn 2008.

2. In using the term "race," I refer to the belief that visible differences or putative ancestry define groups or categories of people in ways that are seen to be innate or unchangeable. Ethnicity is more about differences based on culture and a sense of common origins, and is often characterized as optional for most Americans (Foner and Fredrickson 2004; Foner, Deaux, and Donato 2018; Cornell and Hartmann 2007; Waters 1990).

3. This chapter draws on my earlier publications and collaborations, especially Foner, Deaux, and Donato 2018. See also Alba and Foner 2015; Foner 2000, 2005.

4. Fox and Guglielmo 2012, 334. See also Perlmann 2018, 67–68.

5. López 1996.

6. Fox and Guglielmo 2012, 343.

7. Jacobson 1998, 6; Lee 2019, 114; Alba 2020.

8. Perlmann 2005, 11.

9. Lee 2019, 125, 134; Ross 1914, 95; Grant 1916.

10. *New York: A Collection from Harper's Magazine* 1991, 304.

11. Cited in Jacobson 1998, 178.

12. Barker, Dodd, and Commager 1937, cited in Fitzgerald 1979, 79–80.

13. Alba 2009; Foner 2000, 2005.

14. Alba 2009, 75.

15. See, for example, Guterl 2001.

16. Alba 2009, 80; DeParle 2019. See also Gerstle 2001.

17. Abrajano and Hajnal 2015, 54.

18. Espiritu 1997, 109.

19. Wollenberg 1995.

20. Lee 2019, 181. See also Kraut 2016.

21. Lee and Zhou 2015.

22. Krogstad and Radford 2018.

23. Lee and Zhou 2014, 8; Lee and Zhou 2015. See also Tran, Lee, Khachikian, and Lee 2018.

24. Alba and Foner 2015, 210.

25. Kambhampaty 2020; Zhou 2004.

26. Feinberg 2020; Chishti and Bolter 2020.

27. Chinese American woman quoted in Zhou 2004, 35; Wu 2013, 2; Tuan 1998.

28. Budiman and Ruiz 2021; Kasinitz 2021.

29. Lee and Zhou 2014, 8.

30. Okamoto 2014, 43–46, 48. See also Espiritu 1992; Lee and Ramakrishnan 2020.

31. Okamoto 2014.

32. Fischer 2014.

33. Brown 2014; Cohn 2010; Flores, Lopez, and Krogstad 2019; Frey 2015; Haub 2012; Rumbaut 2006, 2011. In this book, I use the terms Latino and Hispanic interchangeably. About a third of Hispanics in the United States are immigrants, and two-thirds are US born (Batalova, Hanna, and Levesque 2021).

34. Itzigsohn 2004, 199. See also Rumbaut 2006.

35. Mora 2014, 16.

36. Foner, Deaux, and Donato 2018; Itzigsohn 2004.

37. Rumbaut 2011.

38. See Kibria, Bowman, and O'Leary 2014, 129; Fox and Guglielmo 2012.

39. Roth 2012, 64.

40. Foner 2005, 24.

41. Kibria, Bowman, and O'Leary 2014, 126.

42. Telles and Sue 2019, 2; Noe-Bustamante, Flores, and Shah 2019.

43. Ortiz and Telles 2012; Pew Research Center 2015b.

44. Fox and Guglielmo 2012, 367.

45. Cited in Fox and Guglielmo 2012, 367.

46. The discussion in this and the following paragraph draws on Alba and Foner 2015, 107.

47. Jiménez 2010.

48. Dowling 2014; Pew Research Center 2019b. See also Valdez and Golash-Boza 2017.

49. López and Stanton-Salazar 2001, 75.

50. Hamilton 2019.

51. Vickerman 2001, 237, 242; Hamilton 2019, 193.

52. Anderson and López 2018; Hamilton 2019.

53. Vickerman 2001, 255.

54. Anderson 2015; Vickerman 2001; Hamilton 2019. In only three of the ten metropolitan areas with the largest Black populations were Black immigrants a double-digit share of the overall Black population in 2013. Following Miami–Fort Lauderdale–West Palm Beach and New York–Newark–Jersey City, the Washington, DC, metropolitan area was in third place, with 15 percent of the area's Blacks being foreign born. In the other seven metropolitan areas, Black immigrants' share of the Black population was much smaller, such as 8 percent in the Atlanta area, 4 percent in Chicago, and only 1 percent in Detroit (Anderson 2015). On Somalis in Lewiston, Maine, see Anderson 2019; Besteman 2016. On East Africans in Minneapolis, see Chambers 2017; Guenther, Pendaz, and Makene 2011. On Africans in Fargo, North Dakota, see Erickson 2020.

55. Clerge 2019, 17, 197, 209–10.

56. Kasinitz 1992. This first wave began around 1900 and ended in the mid-1920s. By 1930, a little under a hundred thousand foreign-born Blacks lived in the United States, with the vast majority coming from the Caribbean; in 2016, around two million Black immigrants from the Caribbean lived in the United States (Kasinitz 1992; Anderson and López 2018).

57. Vickerman 2001, 254.

58. Portes and Armony 2018, 156–57. See also Etienne 2020; Stepick et al. 2003.

59. See, for example, Waters 1999.

60. Batalova and Feldblum 2020, based on an analysis of 2018 Census data.

61. Vickerman 2016, 77; Sall 2020.

62. Vickerman 2016, 77; 2013.

63. Hamilton 2019, 72–73; Waters and Kasinitz 2015.

64. Alba and Foner 2015, 75–80. As a large literature demonstrates, confinement to predominantly, often virtually all-Black or racial minority neighborhoods in the United States limits, among other things, access to good schools while increasing exposure to crime and reducing informal contacts with Whites.

65. Clerge 2019, 231.

66. Alba and Foner 2015, 209–10, 104; Hamilton 2019, 221–22.

67. Hamilton 2019, 214.

68. Foner 2018; Foner, Deaux, and Donato 2018; Waters 2014; Pager 2007.

69. Waters 2001, 213. See also Clerge 2019, 143.

70. Vickerman 2016, 77.

71. Vickerman 2016, 78.

72. Foner 2018.

73. Bashi Bobb and Clarke 2001, 233; Foner 2018.

74. Quoted in Imoagene 2017, 142.

75. See Waters 1999; Foner 2001.

76. According to an analysis of national surveys spanning the 2010–16 period, about 30 to 40 percent of White Americans have a strong racial identity, and 20 percent have a strong level of group consciousness as Whites as well as feel a sense of discontent over the status of their racial group (Jardina 2019, 261–62). In this book, I use the terms Whites and non-Hispanic Whites interchangeably. The term Hispanic on the Census has given rise to the category non-Hispanic White, which is used frequently in government reports and academic studies. It is a catchall category for all those who identify as Whites but whose ancestry does not include a Spanish-speaking nation (Foley 2004, 341).

77. McDermott and Samson 2005.

78. Alba 2020, 25.

79. Hochschild 2016; Alba 2020.

80. Painter 2016; Jardina quoted in Chotiner 2019.

81. Craig and Richeson 2018.

82. Political scientist Deborah Schildkraut quoted in Edsall 2020. See also Alba 2020.

83. Jardina 2019, 3–4.

84. Quoted in Jiménez and Horowitz 2013, 859. See also Jiménez 2017.

85. Quoted in Chow 2017. See also Tehranian 2009.

86. Quoted in Wiltz 2014.

87. Alba 2009, 217.

88. Alba 2020, 6; 2009. For alternative predictions about the future of the racial order, see Bonilla-Silva 2004; Gans 2012; Kaufmann 2019; Lee and Bean 2010; Marrow 2011.

89. On the early twentieth-century period, see Ngai 2004, 3. Before World War I, as Ngai (2006) notes, statutes of limitations of one to five years meant that even those in the United States unlawfully did not live forever with the specter of deportation.

90. Alba 2020, chapter 7.

91. Alba 2020, 2009; Alba and Foner 2015.

92. Alba 2020, 184. The study analyzes those in the top quartile of jobs, ranked in terms of their median earnings.

93. Alba and Nee 2003, 132.

94. Alba and Foner 2015. For a personal account of multiethnic and multiracial mixing in colleges and neighborhoods, see Mehta 2019, 236–42.

95. Cornell and Hartmann 2007, 257.

96. Alba 2020, chapter 4.

97. Jilani 2020. See also Törngren, Irastorza, and Rodríguez-García 2021.

98. Alba 2020, chapter 4.

99. Williams 2012, 2019; Friedersdorf 2019; Gans 2012, 268.

100. Alba 2020.

101. Lee and Bean 2010.

102. Pew Research Center 2015b.

103. Pew Research Center 2015b, 58.

104. Alba 2016, 2020; Myers and Levy 2018.

105. Alba 2016, 2020.

Chapter 3. Changing Cities and Communities

1. These figures, from the New York City Planning Population FactFinder, are for the Auburndale neighborhood based on 2013–17 American Community Survey data.

2. Singer 2004, 2015.

3. Foner 2013b; Singer 2004.

4. Foner 2013c; Sandoval-Strausz 2019, 12.

5. Singer 2015.

6. Singer 2015.

7. Singer 2004, 2015; Wikipedia 2020.

8. Singer 2013, 80.

9. Singer 2013, 87, 89; Frey 2015, 164.

10. Singer 2013, 87. This represented a change from 1980, when similar shares of immigrants lived in the cities and suburbs of the largest metropolitan areas in the United States.

11. Rothstein 2017.

12. Price and Singer 2008. On immigration's role in the changing racial and ethnic composition of suburban Dallas, see Brettell 2008.

13. Odem 2008, 110–18. See also Waters and Pineau 2015, 218–19.

14. Vitiello and Sugrue 2017b, 3; Frey 2019a; Eltagouri 2017.

15. Quoted in Dickey 2007. See also Waters and Pineau 2015, 326–32.

16. Sampson 2017, 12–13.

17. According to one analysis, the decline in the murder rate between 1980 and 2010 was greater in metropolitan areas with a high percentage of foreign born than in those where the foreign-born share was small. The result was that in 2010, homicide rates were higher in the metropolitan areas with small foreign-born populations (Adelman et al. 2017, 67).

18. Sampson 2017, 19–20; Waters and Pineau 2015, 330–32. See also Rumbaut, Dingeman, and Robles 2019; Adelman et al. 2017. One study concludes, on the basis of an analysis of Census data, that the neighborhood segregation of immigrants has a protective effect on violent crime in places that have structural resources such as low poverty rates and educational opportunities (Feldmeyer, Harris, and Scroggins 2015).

19. Kallick 2015. See also Fiscal Policy Institute 2012.

20. Orleck 1987, 2013; Sandoval-Strausz 2017, 137–38; Emmanuel 2015.

21. Porter 2018.

22. Lichter 2012, 4. One study shows that the influx of Hispanics in nonmetropolitan areas has mostly slowed, not reversed, population loss. Only about one in ten (nearly two hundred) of the nonmetropolitan counties in this analysis grew in 2010–17 because Hispanic increases offset non-Hispanic population declines (Lichter and Johnson 2020).

23. Carr, Lichter, and Kefalas 2012.

24. See, for example, Parrado and Kandel 2008.

25. Vezner 2017; Mathema, Svajlenka, and Hermann 2018; Lichter 2012, 10, 14.

26. Carr, Lichter, and Kefalas 2012, 42–43.

27. In 2010, Whites remained a majority—68 percent—of suburban residents, but this was a drop from 93 percent in 1970. For the changing racial composition of central cities and suburbs, 1970–2010, based on an analysis of 287 metropolitan statistical areas, see Massey and Tannen 2018, 1600–601. See also Batalova, Hanna, and Levesque 2021.

28. Foner 2013b; Sandoval-Strausz 2019, 180; *The Economist* 2017.

29. Frey 2015, 159.

30. Frey 2015, 54.

31. The 1960 figures are from Miami-Dade Department of Planning and Zoning, "Demographic Profile, 1960–2000."

32. Portes and Armony 2018; Portes and Stepick 1993; City of Los Angeles, Department of City Planning 2015; Schneider 2008.

33. Wikipedia 2021. Hialeah and Miami, Florida were also among these cities.

34. Frey 2015, 54–55.

35. On Winston-Salem, North Carolina, see J. Jones 2019. On Nashville, see Winders 2008, 257. On Charlotte, see Jones-Correa 2016.

36. Frey 2015, chapter 5.

37. Anderson 2015; Anderson and López 2018.

38. Rischin 1962, 76; Hapgood (1902) 1967, 113; Odencrantz 1919, 12; Luconi 2001, 27.

39. Zukin 2010.

40. Foner 2000.

41. Price and Singer 2008, 149–50.

42. Alba and Foner 2015, 71.

43. Moore 1981; Goldstein 2006; Gans 1957.

44. Matsumoto 2018.

45. Zhou, Chin, and Kim 2013, 373.

46. Jiménez 2017, 20.

47. Fong 1994; Zhou, Chin, and Kim 2013, 370–79.

48. The discussion of the decline of all-White neighborhoods draws on Alba and Foner 2015, 93–94. On contemporary super-diversity, see Foner 2017; Foner, Duyvendak, and Kasinitz 2019.

49. Alba 2020, 192.

50. Logan and Zhang 2010. See also Zhang and Logan 2016.

51. The twenty-four metropolitan regions included many of the largest metropolises: New York (plus Newark, Jersey City, Bergen-Passaic, and Trenton), Chicago, and Los Angeles; San Francisco, Sacramento, San Diego, Bakersfield, Oakland, Riverside, Stockton, and Vallejo; Dallas, Fort Worth, Houston, College Station, and Galveston; and Miami, Denver, Colorado Springs, and Las Vegas (Logan and Zhang 2010, 1080–82).

52. Alba and Foner 2015, 94. According to a recent analysis, the average White resident in the hundred-largest metropolitan areas lived in a less White neighborhood in 2014–19 than in 2000, although Whites almost everywhere continued to live in mostly White neighborhoods (Frey 2021a).

53. Putnam 2007.

54. Carr, Lichter, and Kefalas 2012; Hirschman and Massey 2008.

55. Pettigrew and Tropp 2006.

56. Wessendorf 2014.

57. Alba and Foner 2017; Sandoval-Strausz 2019, 317.

58. See, for example, Menjívar 2003.

59. Foner 2013b. Over one hundred Chicago-area Catholic churches, by one account, now offer Spanish-language Mass to congregants (on the history of Mexicans' involvement in the Catholic church in Chicago, see Kanter 2020).

60. Pew Research Center 2017b, 2015a; Alba and Foner 2015, 131. A small proportion of Muslims, about one in seven, are African Americans.

61. Berglund 2015.

62. Waters and Pineau 2015, 318.

63. Wuthnow 2005, 217–20.

64. Hamilton 2019, 70. See also Pew Research Center 2017b.

65. See, for example, Bilici 2012; Pew Research Center 2017b; Karam 2020; Waters and Pineau 2015, 323.

66. Pew Research Center 2017a.

67. Pew Research Center 2017b; Eck 2001, 232; Chappell 2018.

68. Pew Research Center 2017b.

69. Alba and Foner 2015, 134.

70. Gerstle 2015, 37.

71. Alba and Foner 2015, 134–35.

72. Gerstle 2015, 50.

73. Custodio 2010; McDonnell and Hill 1993; Gershberg, Danenberg, and Sanchez 2004; Harrington 2018.

74. Zhou and Kim 2006; Yin 2017.

75. Salomone 2010, 23, 25. See also Baker 2011.

76. Foner 2000, 207.

77. Salomone 2010, 157–58.

78. Suárez-Orozco, Suárez-Orozco, and Todorova 2008, 370.

79. Salomone 2010, 190–91; Salomone 2021.

80. Foner 2000.

81. Moore et al. 2017, 126; McGuinness 2013.

82. Quoted in Bell 2017; Eldred 2018; Brenner et al. 2018.

83. de Graauw 2015.

84. See de Graauw 2014.

85. Provine et al. 2016, 1–2, 13, 148. See also Golash-Boza 2011.

86. Provine et al., 2, 30, 113. The national surveys were conducted in 2007–10.

87. Provine et al., 80–88.

Chapter 4. The Economy

1. American Immigration Council 2017; Batalova 2020.

2. Blau and Mackie 2017, 6.

3. Batalova, Hanna, and Levesque 2021. The civilian labor force is comprised of civilians sixteen and older who were either employed or unemployed, but looking for work in the week prior to participation in the American Community Survey or decennial Census.

4. In the period from 2003 through 2013, the employment rate (percentage of individuals employed during the week they were surveyed by the Current Population Survey) for all foreign-born males was 86 percent, 83 percent for second-generation males, and 82 percent for males in the third and higher generations. The average employment rate of foreign-born men with less than twelve years of schooling exceeded that of men in the second generation by 21 points and men in the third and higher generations by 26 percentage points. Among women, immigrants had a lower employment rate (61 percent) than the native born (roughly 72 percent for both the second generation and the third and higher generations) (Waters and Pineau 2015, 264–65).

5. Bennett 2020; Waters and Pineau 2015, 266; Bean et al. 2014.

6. DeSilver 2017. See also Eckstein and Peri 2018.

7. Eckstein and Peri 2018, 5–6.

8. Gonzalez-Rivera 2016.

9. Jacoby 2012.

10. Waldinger and Lichter 2003.

11. Foner 2005, 171–72; Foner 1973.

12. Foner 1994; Kolker 2018.

13. Hagan, Hernández-León, and Demonsant 2015.

14. Hondagneu-Sotelo 2001, 8.

15. Hondagneu-Sotelo 2001, 8; Garip 2017, 76; Milkman 2020, 113–14.

16. Hondagneu-Sotelo 2001, 8.

17. Kaufman 2000, 364.

18. Batalova 2020.

19. Ortman, Velkoff, and Hogan 2014.

20. Cortés and Tessada 2011.

21. Batalova, Hanna, and Levesque 2021. This figure (35 percent) refers to those ages sixteen years and older.

22. Kallick 2013, 76–77.

23. Batalova 2020; American Immigration Council 2018.

24. In 2018, 22 percent of foreign-born physicians and surgeons were Indian, followed by those from China / Hong Kong (6 percent) (Batalova 2020).

25. Myers and Pitkin 2013.

26. Sturtevant 2017.

27. Porter 2019; Siniavskaia 2018. In 2016, according to a home builders' association study, immigrants accounted for one in four construction workers in the country; in some jobs like roofing, the share of immigrants was over 40 percent.

28. Kerr and Kerr 2018.

29. Kosten 2018; Kerr and Kerr 2018; Hathaway 2017. See also Kallick 2015.

30. Waldinger 1986, 268.

31. Kallick 2015, 2, 9, 34.

32. Hirschman and Mogford 2009, 917.

33. Hirschman and Mogford 2009.

34. Florida 2017.

35. Anderson 2018.

36. Eckstein and Peri 2018, 10.

37. Eckstein and Peri 2018, 11. According to a recent study, nearly half of the CEO founders of New York City's high-tech firms were immigrants or second generation, with a robust Asian and western European presence (Nee and Drouhot 2020).

38. Hunt and Gauthier-Loiselle 2010; Blau and Mackie 2017, 255–58.

39. Blau and Mackie 2017. See also Peri and Sparber 2020.

40. Portes and Armony 2018, 67, 11.

41. Waldinger 1996, 12.

42. Hilgers 2014; Liang and Zhou 2018; Liang et al. 2018.

43. Eckstein and Nguyen 2018; Eckstein and Peri 2018.

44. Eckstein and Nguyen 2011; Min 2013. By 2016, according to the Census Bureau, New York City alone had over four thousand nail salons (Kim 2020).

45. Eckstein and Nguyen 2011, 645.

46. "Meat, Beef and Poultry Processing Industry in the US" 2019.

47. Hirschman and Massey 2008, 9.

48. Parrado and Kandel 2008, 106.

49. Milkman 2020, 84–96.

50. Milkman 2020, 94–95.

51. Parrado and Kandel 2008; Fremstad, Rho, and Brown 2020. Both studies are based on analysis of data on the animal slaughtering and processing industry (William Kandel, personal communication).

52. Milkman 2020, 84–85, 128.

53. Milkman 2020, 129, 142, 144–51. Contemporary worker centers, Milkman notes, have parallels with late nineteenth- and early twentieth-century labor reform groups and settlement houses.

54. Krogstad, Passel, and Cohn 2019.

55. Orrenius and Zavodny 2009; Milkman 2020.

56. Moyce and Schenker 2018.

57. Molteni 2020.

58. Gelatt 2020, 6, 11.

59. Quoted in Hoban 2017.

60. Blau and Mackie 2017, 5.

61. Peri 2017.

62. Blau and Mackie 2017, 6.

63. Blau and Mackie 2017, 5–6, 228.

64. Lim 2001; Waldinger and Lichter 2003.

65. Waldinger and Lichter 2003, 208–9.

66. Giovanni Peri and Chad Sparber cited in Porter 2017. On native workers' shift out of low-wage and precarious jobs in fields such as meatpacking that used to have high wages, health

coverage, benefits, and employment security in the context of employer efforts to weaken unions, deregulation policies, and subcontracting, see Milkman 2020. As many US-born workers abandoned the degraded jobs and sought employment in more desirable sectors, they were replaced by immigrants.

67. Hirschman and Mogford 2009.

68. Roberts and Wolf 2018. High-tech industries were those having high concentrations of science, technology, engineering, and mathematics occupations.

Chapter 5. The Territory of Culture: Immigration, Popular Culture, and the Arts

1. Lee 2008, 25–26.

2. Lee 2008, 9, 26. The process in which elements from immigrants' home country cultures and those of the long-established native born blend into something new in the US social, economic, and political context is often labeled creolization (Foner 1997; Gabaccia 1998). Another view, associated with new assimilation theory, stresses how mainstream American institutions and customs expand to accommodate cultural alternatives, usually after being "Americanized" to some extent (Alba and Nee 2003).

3. Ray 2016, 106, 109.

4. Gabaccia 1998, 148.

5. Gabaccia 1998, 3; Butler 2018.

6. Nathan 2008; Gabaccia 1998, 4.

7. Gabaccia 1998, 4–5.

8. Nathan 2008.

9. "Consumption of Bagels in the U.S. 2020" 2020.

10. Ray 2016, 105.

11. Ray 2016, 108.

12. Lee 2008, 10; Coe 2009; Hayford 2011.

13. Chen 2014; Liu 2015.

14. Lee 2008, 257, 82–83; Liu 2015.

15. Guest 2011; Hilgers 2014; Liang and Zhou 2018.

16. Liu 2015.

17. Pierson 2015.

18. Liu 2015, 138; Goldfield 2020, 13.

19. Arellano 2012, 269; Ray 2016, 93.

20. Gabaccia 1998, 165; Arellano 2012, 202, 221; Hyslop 2017.

21. Quoted in Friesen 2012. See also Pilcher 2012.

22. Arellano 2012, 150, 145–46.

23. Arellano 2012, 4, 2.

24. Ray 2016, 107.

25. Gabaccia 1998, 202–3.

26. Shah 2020.

27. Halter 2000, 9.

28. Gabaccia 1998, 226.

29. League of American Orchestras 2016; Paarlberg 2012.

30. Roth 1959; Bellow 1953; Jen 1991; Díaz 2007; Lahiri 2003.

31. Hunt, Ramon, and Tran 2019, 21.

32. Chin et al. 2017; Force 2018; Smith, Choueiti, and Pieper 2016.

33. Laurino 2000; Alba and Kasinitz 2006.

34. Kasinitz 1992. On the San Francisco Carnival, representing Afro-Caribbeans, Brazilians, and Latin Americans, but targeted at a predominantly White audience, see Hintzen 2001, 46.

35. Jiménez 2017, 82.

36. Shutika 2011, 31; personal communication from Shutika, January 3, 2021.

37. Jiménez 2017, 85.

38. French 2005.

39. Portman was born in Israel, while Sheen is the grandchild of immigrants. The five earlier era film stars mentioned, with one exception (Bancroft, the granddaughter of Italian immigrants), were children of immigrants.

40. "'Big Sick' Creators Nanjiani and Gordon on Turning Their Courtship into a Movie," NPR, June 23, 2017.

41. Wides-Munoz 2010; González 2013.

42. Nussbaum 2015.

43. Chiang 2018.

44. "Comic Ramy Youssef on Being an 'Allah Carte' Muslim" 2019.

45. Mora 2014; Krogstad and Lopez 2017; Valdes 2015; Business Wire 2019.

46. Like O'Neill, celebrated American playwright Arthur Miller was the son of an immigrant father—in Miller's case, from eastern Europe.

47. Lahiri 2003; Díaz 2007; Nguyen 2015; Adichie 2013.

48. Witchel 2012.

49. See, for example, Beah 2014; Lai 2011; Nguyen 2015; Jin 1999, 2004.

50. Grande 2006; Mbue 2016; Ko 2017. See also Alvarez 2020; Bulawayo 2013; Urrea 2018.

51. See, for example, Adichie 2013; Danticat 1994; Gyasi 2020.

52. Marshall (1959) 1981; Sandomir 2019.

53. See, for example, Díaz 2007; Jen 1991; Lahiri 2003; Lee 2007. On the second generation, see Foner and Dreby 2010; Kasinitz et al. 2008.

54. Kasinitz 2014, 266–75.

55. Study in Royal Society Open Science reported in Thompson 2015. Rap is one of the elements of hip-hop. In addition to music, hip-hop often refers to a cultural form including, among other things, dance, poetry, clothing styles, and graffiti art (Kasinitz 2014, 280).

56. Kasinitz 2014, 280–82; Rubin and Melnick 2007; Vickerman 2013.

57. Quoted in Okura 2013.

58. Public Broadcasting Service 2017. Puerto Ricans who move to the mainland United States, it should be noted, are migrants, not immigrants; those born in Puerto Rico are US citizens by birth. For a critical view of corporate influences on Latino/a performers who have been marketed as global icons of Latinidad and subject to demands to make their music more palatable to wider audiences, see Cepeda 2014; Dávila 2014.

59. "Carlos Santana Biography," n.d.

60. Purdum 2018a, 2018b.

61. Purdum 2018a.

62. Kasinitz 2014, 282.

63. Kasinitz 2016, 3.

64. Piepenburg 2016.

65. Brantley 2015.

66. Gabaccia 1998, 228, 230–31.

67. Czekalinski and Nhan 2012.

68. Hirschman 2013, 42.

69. Hirschman 2005; Kasinitz 2014; Kasinitz et al. 2008.

Chapter 6. Electoral Politics

1. Dawsey 2018.

2. Meyerson 2002, 23.

3. Sides, Tesler, and Vavreck 2018, 13, 26. Whites in this chapter, to emphasize, refer to non-Hispanic Whites.

4. Abramowitz 2018, 58.

5. Abrajano and Hajnal 2015.

6. Sterne 2001, 59; Gerstle and Mollenkopf 2001, 26.

7. Abramowitz 2018, 18; Meyerson 2002, 23; Sterne 2001, 59.

8. Schickler 2016; Meyerson 2002.

9. Starr 1997; Meyerson 2002; Abramowitz 2018, 22, 25.

10. Sides, Tesler, and Vavreck 2018; Abramowitz 2018.

11. Abrajano and Hajnal 2015, 80–81; Sides, Tesler, and Vavreck 2018, 26. In the 2019 Pew Research Center (2020) survey, non-Hispanic White registered voters identified with or leaned Republican by a substantial margin, 53 percent, vs. 42 percent who leaned Democratic.

12. Pew Research Center 2020; Abrajano and Hajnal 2015, 6, 11, 42.

13. Pew Research Center 2020; Sides, Tesler, and Vavreck 2018, 26. The Pew survey data refer to Democratic and Democratic-leaning as well as Republican and Republican-leaning registered voters.

14. Abramowitz 2018, 13.

15. Abramowitz 2018, x.

16. Alba and Foner 2017; Alba 2020, 30–33.

17. Pew Research Center 2020.

18. Pew Research Center 2020; Budiman, Noe-Bustamante, and Lopez 2020. See also Frey 2015, 2018.

19. Griffin, Frey, and Teixeira 2020; Pew Research Center 2020.

20. Batalova, Hanna, and Levesque 2021.

21. Batalova, Hanna, and Levesque 2021; Passel and Cohn 2019.

22. Waters and Kasinitz 2015.

23. Ngai 2004.

24. Chavez 2008.

25. Brown, Jones, and Becker 2018.

26. Jardina 2019, 267.

27. Hochschild 2016, 143, 137–39.

28. Sides, Tesler, and Vavreck 2018, 8.

29. Alba and Foner 2017. See also Norris and Inglehart 2019.

30. Abrajano and Hajnal 2015, 27.

31. Jardina 2019, 222–28.

32. Abramowitz 2018, 140; Sides, Tesler, and Vavreck 2018, 90–93.

33. B. Jones 2019. Only 11 percent of the Democrats viewed immigrants as a burden. The survey combines Democrats and Democratic-leaning respondents, on the one hand, and Republicans and Republican-leaning respondents, on the other.

34. Jardina 2019. See also King and Smith 2020.

35. Lee 2019, 7–9.

36. Sandoval-Strausz 2019, 335.

37. Boissoneault 2017; Daniels 2004; Kraut 2016; Lee 2019; Zolberg 2006.

38. Daniels 2004; Lee 2015; Foner 2005.

39. Daniels 2004, 52.

40. Abrajano and Hajnal 2015, 2; Hernández 2006.

41. Massey, Durand, and Malone 2002.

42. Klein 2018; Anderson 2020.

43. Cited in Matthews 2015.

44. Fuchs 1990.

45. Foner 2000, 165–66.

46. López 2015, 4; Baker 2018; Withers 2018.

47. President George W. Bush, remarks on signing the Immigration Act, 1990; President Bill Clinton, commencement address at Portland State University, 1998; President Barack Obama, remarks in an address to the nation on immigration, 2014.

48. During Trump's presidency, the US Citizen and Immigration Services even removed a passage from its official mission statement that described "America's promise as a nation of immigrants."

49. Edsall 2019; see also Lee 2019, 323.

50. Bouie 2019; Leonhardt and Philbrick 2018; Silva 2018.

51. See, for example, Glazer and Moynihan 1970; McNickle 1993; Mollenkopf 2014.

52. By 1890, the Irish had captured most of the Democratic Party organizations in northern and midwestern cities; an 1894 list of Irish party bosses includes John Kelly and Richard Croker in New York City, Hugh McLaughlin in Brooklyn, Mike McDonald in Chicago, Pat Maguire in Boston, William Sheehan in Buffalo, and "Little Bob" Davis in Jersey City (Erie 1988, 4, 2).

53. Erie 1988, 51–53.

54. Quoted in McNickle 1993, 9.

55. McNickle 1993, 2; Mollenkopf and Sonenshein 2009, 77; Foner 2014, 38–39.

56. In 1910, Jewish and Italian immigrants together accounted for nearly a fifth of the city's population; by 1920, foreign-born Jews and Italians along with their US-born children made up about 43 percent of the city (Foner 2000).

DeParle, Jason. 2019. "What Makes an American." *New York Times*, August 9.

DeSilver, Drew. 2017. "Immigrants Don't Make Up a Majority in Any U.S. Industry." Pew Research Center, March 16.

Díaz, Junot. 2007. *The Brief Wondrous Life of Oscar Wao*. New York: Penguin.

Dickey, Christopher. 2007. "Do Immigrants Make U.S. Safer?" *Newsweek*, November 27.

Donato, Katharine, and Catalina Amuedo-Dorantes. 2020. "The Legal Landscape of U.S. Immigration: An Introduction." *RSF: The Russell Sage Foundation of the Social Sciences* 6:1–16.

Donato, Katharine, and Shirin Hakimzadeh. 2006. "The Changing Face of the Gulf Coast: Immigration to Louisiana, Mississippi, and Alabama." *Migration Information Source*, January 1.

Dowling, Julie. 2014. *Mexican Americans and the Question of Race*. Austin: University of Texas Press.

Eck, Diana. 2001. *A New Religious America: How a "Christian Country" Has Become the World's Most Religiously Diverse Nation*. New York: HarperCollins.

Eckstein, Susan, and Thanh-Nghi Nguyen. 2011. "The Making and Transnationalization of an Ethnic Niche: Vietnamese Manicurists." *International Migration Review* 45:639–74.

Eckstein, Susan, and Giovanni Peri. 2018. "Immigrant Niches and Immigrant Networks in the U.S. Labor Market." *RSF: The Russell Sage Foundation Journal of the Social Sciences* 4:1–17.

The Economist. 2017. "Latinos Have Become Chicago's Second Largest Ethnic Group." October 5.

Edsall, Thomas. 2019. "Trump Has a Gift for Tearing Us Apart." *New York Times*, December 11.

———. 2020. "Trump Hasn't Given Up on Divide and Conquer." *New York Times*, April 29.

Eldred, Sheila. 2018. "With Scarce Access to Interpreters, Immigrants Struggle to Understand Doctors' Orders." NPR, August 18.

Eltagouri, Marwa. 2017. "For Many Midwestern Cities with Shrinking Populations Immigration Is a Lifeline." *Chicago Tribune*, September 18.

Emmanuel, Adeshina. 2015. "On Chicago's Southwest Side, Immigrants Have Breathed New Life into Communities." *Chicago Reporter*, November 16.

Epps, Bernard. 2018. "The Citizenship Clause Means What It Says." *Atlantic*, October 30.

Erickson, Jennifer. 2020. *Race-ing Fargo: Refugees, Citizenship, and the Transformation of Small Cities*. Ithaca, NY: Cornell University Press.

Erie, Stephen. 1988. *Rainbow's End: Irish-Americans and the Dilemmas of Urban Machine Politics, 1840–1985*. Berkeley: University of California Press.

Espiritu, Yen Le. 1992. *Asian American Panethnicity: Bridging Institutions and Identities*. Philadelphia: Temple University Press.

———. 1997. *Asian American Women and Men*. Thousand Oaks, CA: Sage.

Etienne, Vadricka. 2020. "Rather Be Known as Haitian: Identity Construction of the Ethnically-Identified Second Generation." *Ethnic and Racial Studies* 42:2158–75.

European Commission. 2018. *A Comparative Analysis of Non-Discrimination Law in Europe, 2018*. Brussels: European Commission.

Feinberg, Ayal. 2020. "Hate Crimes against Asian Americans Have Been Declining for Years. Will the Coronavirus Change That?" *Washington Post*, April 13.

Feldmeyer, Ben, Casey Harris, and Jennifer Scroggins. 2015. "Enclaves of Opportunity or 'Ghettos of Last Resort?' Assessing the Effects of Immigrant Segregation on Violent Crime Rates." *Social Science Research* 52:1–17.

Feldstein, Martin S. 2017. "Why Is Growth Better in the United States than in Other Industrial Countries." NBER Working Paper. No. 23221, National Bureau of Economic Research, March.

Fiscal Policy Institute. 2009. *Immigrants and the Economy.* New York: Fiscal Policy Institute.

———. 2012. *Immigrant Small Business Owners: A Significant and Growing Part of the Economy.* New York: Fiscal Policy Institute.

Fischer, Claude. 2014. "Where Did 'Hispanics' Come From?" *Berkeley Blog,* March 29.

Fitzgerald, David Scott, and David Cook-Martin. 2014. *Culling the Masses: The Democratic Origins of Racist Immigration Policy in the Americas.* Cambridge, MA: Harvard University Press.

Fitzgerald, Frances. 1979. *America Revised.* New York: Vintage.

Flores, Antonio, Mark Hugo Lopez, and Jens Manuel Krogstad. 2019. "Hispanic Population Reached New High in 2018, but Growth Has Slowed." Pew Research Center, July 8.

Florida, Richard. 2017. "Without Immigrants, the Fortune 500 Would Be the Fortune 284." Bloomberg CityLab, December 5.

Foley, Neil. 2004. "Straddling the Color Line: The Legal Construction of Hispanic Identity in Texas." In *Not Just Black and White: Historical and Contemporary Perspectives on Immigration, Race, and Ethnicity in the United States,* edited by Nancy Foner and George M. Fredrickson, 341–57. New York: Russell Sage Foundation.

Foner, Nancy. 1973. *Status and Power in Rural Jamaica: A Study of Educational and Political Change.* New York: Teachers College Press.

———. 1994. *The Caregiving Dilemma: Work in an American Nursing Home.* Berkeley: University of California Press.

———. 1997. "The Immigrant Family: Cultural Legacies and Cultural Changes." *International Migration Review* 31:891–904.

———. 2000. *From Ellis Island to JFK: New York's Two Great Waves of Immigration.* New Haven, CT: Yale University Press.

———, ed. 2001. *Islands in the City: West Indian Migration to New York.* Berkeley: University of California Press.

———. 2005. *In a New Land: A Comparative View of Immigration.* New York: NYU Press.

———. 2006. "Then and Now or Then to Now: Immigration to New York in Contemporary and Historical Perspective." *Journal of American Ethnic History* 25:33–47.

———. 2013a. "Immigration Past and Present." *Daedalus* (Summer): 16–25.

———. 2013b. "Introduction: Immigrants in New York City in the New Millennium." In *One Out of Three: Immigrant New York in the Twenty-First Century,* edited by Nancy Foner, 1–34. New York: Columbia University Press.

———, ed. 2013c. *One Out of Three: Immigrant New York in the Twenty-First Century.* New York: Columbia University Press.

———. 2014. "Immigration History and the Remaking of New York." In *New York and Amsterdam: Immigration and the New Urban Landscape,* edited by Nancy Foner, Jan Rath, Jan Willem Duyvendak, and Rogier van Reekum, 29–51. New York: NYU Press.

———. 2017. "What's New about Super-Diversity? A Research Comment." *Journal of American Ethnic History* 36:49–57.

———. 2018. "Race in an Era of Mass Migration: Black Migrants in Europe and the United States." *Ethnic and Racial Studies* 41:1113–30.

———. 2019. "The Uses and Abuses of History: Understanding Contemporary U.S. Immigration." *Journal of Ethnic and Migration Studies* 45:4–20.

Foner, Nancy, and Richard Alba. 2018. "Being Muslim in the United States and Western Europe: Why Is It Different?" In *Growing Up Muslim in Europe and the United States*, edited by Mehdi Bozorgmehr and Philip Kasinitz, 21–38. New York: Routledge.

Foner, Nancy, Kay Deaux, and Katharine Donato. 2018. "Introduction: Immigration and Changing Identities." *RSF: The Russell Sage Journal of the Social Sciences* 4:1–25.

Foner, Nancy, and Joanna Dreby. 2010. "Relations between the Generations in Immigrant Families." *Annual Review of Sociology* 37:545–64.

Foner, Nancy, Jan Willem Duyvendak, and Philip Kasinitz. 2019. "Introduction: Super-diversity in Everyday Life." *Ethnic and Racial Studies* 42:1–16.

Foner, Nancy, and George M. Fredrickson. 2004. "Immigration, Race, and Ethnicity in the United States: Social Constructions and Social Relations in Historical and Contemporary Perspective." In *Not Just Black and White: Historical and Contemporary Perspectives on Immigration, Race, and Ethnicity in the United States*, edited by Nancy Foner and George M. Fredrickson, 1–22. New York: Russell Sage Foundation.

Foner, Nancy, and Leo Lucassen. 2012. "Legacies of the Past." In *The Changing Face of World Cities: Young Adult Children of Immigrants in Europe and the United States*, edited by Maurice Crul and John H. Mollenkopf, 26–43. New York: Russell Sage Foundation.

Foner, Nancy, Jan Rath, Jan Willem Duyvendak, and Rogier van Reekum, eds. 2014. *New York and Amsterdam: Immigration and the New Urban Landscape*. New York: NYU Press.

Fong, Eric. 1994. *The First Suburban Chinatown: The Remaking of Monterey Park, California*. Philadelphia: Temple University Press.

Force, Thessaly. 2018. "Why Do Asian-Americans Remain Largely Unseen in Film and Television." *New York Times*, November 6.

Fox, Cybelle, and Thomas Guglielmo. 2012. "Defining America's Racial Boundaries: Blacks, Mexicans, and European Immigrants: 1890–1945." *American Journal of Sociology* 118:327–79.

Fremstad, Shawn, Hye Jin Rho, and Hayley Brown. 2020. "Meatpacking Workers Are a Diverse Group Who Need Better Protections." Center for Economic and Policy Research, April 29.

French, Philip. 2005. "The Actress Who Graduated with Dignity." *Guardian*, June 11.

Frey, William H. 2015. *Diversity Explosion: How New Racial Demographics Are Remaking America*. Washington, DC: Brookings Institution Press.

———. 2018. "2018 Exit Polls Show Greater White Support for Democrats." Brookings, November 8.

———. 2019a. "As Americans Spread Out, Immigration Plays a Crucial Role in Local Population Growth." Brookings, April 22.

———. 2019b. "Less than Half of US Children Under 15 Are White, Census Shows." Brookings, June 24.

———. 2020a. "Reducing Immigration Will Not Stop America's Rising Diversity, Census Projections Show." Brookings, February 19.

———. 2020b. "The 2010s May Have Seen the Slowest Population Growth in U.S. History, Census Data Show." Brookings, January 3.

———. 2021a. "Neighborhood Segregation Persists for Black, Latino or Hispanic, and Asian Americans." Brookings, April 6.

———. 2021b. "Turnout in 2020 Election Spiked among Both Democratic and Republican Voting Groups, New Census Data Shows." Brookings, May 5.

Friedersdorf, Conor. 2019. "Unraveling Race: Thomas Chatterton Williams Wants to Discard Traditional Racial Categories." *Atlantic*, November 5.

Friesen, Katy June. 2012. "Where Do Tacos Come From?" *Smithsonian Magazine*, May 3.

Fuchs, Lawrence. 1990. *The American Kaleidoscope.* Hanover, NH: University Press of New England.

Gabaccia, Donna. 1998. *We Are What We Eat: Ethnic Food and the Making of Americans.* Cambridge, MA: Harvard University Press.

———. 2010. "Nations of Immigrants: Do Words Matter?" *Pluralist* 5:5–31.

Gans, Herbert. 1957. "Progress of a Suburban Jewish Community: Park Forest Revisited." *Commentary* (February): 113–22.

———. 1979. "Symbolic Ethnicity: The Future of Ethnic Groups and Cultures in America." *Ethnic and Racial Studies* 2:1–20.

———. 2012. "'Whitening' and the Changing American Racial Hierarchy." *Du Bois Review* 9:267–79.

Garip, Filiz. 2017. *On the Move: Changing Mechanisms of Mexico-U.S. Migration.* Princeton, NJ: Princeton University Press.

Gelatt, Julia. 2019. "Explainer: How the U.S. Legal Immigration System Works." Migration Policy Institute, April.

———. 2020. "Immigrant Workers: Vital to the U.S. COVID-19 Response, Disproportionately Vulnerable." Migration Policy Institute, March.

Gershberg, Alec Ian, Anne Danenberg, and Patricia Sanchez. 2004. *Beyond Bilingual Education: New Immigrants and Public School Policies in California.* Washington, DC: Urban Institute Press.

Gerstle, Gary. 2001. *American Crucible: Race and Nation in the Twentieth Century.* Princeton, NJ: Princeton University Press.

———. 2015. "The Contradictory Character of American Nationality: A Historical Perspective." In *Fear, Anxiety, and National Identity: Immigration and Belonging in North America and Western Europe*, edited by Nancy Foner and Patrick Simon, 33–58. New York: Russell Sage Foundation.

Gerstle, Gary, and John H. Mollenkopf. 2001. "The Political Incorporation of Immigrants, Then and Now." In *E Pluribus Unum? Contemporary and Historical Perspectives on Immigrant Incorporation*, edited by Gary Gerstle and John H. Mollenkopf, 1–32. New York: Russell Sage Foundation.

Glazer, Nathan, and Daniel Patrick Moynihan. 1970. *Beyond the Melting Pot.* 2nd ed. Cambridge, MA: MIT Press.

Golash-Boza, Tanya. 2011. *Immigration Nation: Raids, Detentions, and Deportations in Post-9/11 America.* New York: Routledge.

Goldfield, Hannah. 2020. "A New Kind of Hot Chicken, from Pecking House." *New Yorker*, December 4.

Goldstein, Judith. 2006. *Inventing Great Neck: Jewish Identity and the American Dream.* New Brunswick, NJ: Rutgers University Press.

González, Tanya. 2013. "A Mainstream Dream: Latinas/os on Primetime Television." In *Latinos and American Popular Culture*, edited by Patricia M. Montilla, 1–20. Santa Barbara, CA: Praeger.

Gonzalez-Barrera, Anna. 2015. "More Mexicans Leaving than Coming to the U.S." Pew Research Center, November 19.

Gonzalez-Rivera, Christian. 2016. "Where Immigrant New Yorkers Go to Work." Center for an Urban Future, October.

Grande, Reyna. 2006. *Across a Hundred Mountains*. New York: Atria.

Grant, Madison. 1916. *The Passing of the Great Race*. New York: Scribner's.

Greenberg, Stanley. 2019. *R.I.P. GOP: How the New America Is Dooming the Republicans*. New York: Thomas Dunne Books.

Griffin, Rob, William H. Frey, and Ruy Teixeira. 2020. "America's Electoral Future: The Coming Generational Transformation." Brookings, October 19.

Guenther, Katja M., Sadie Pendaz, and Fortunata Songora Makene. 2011. "The Impact of Intersecting Dimensions of Inequality and Identity on the Racial Status of Eastern African Immigrants." *Sociological Forum* 26:98–120.

Guest, Kenneth. 2011. "From Mott Street to East Broadway: Fuzhounese Immigrants and the Revitalization of New York's Chinatown." *Journal of Chinese Overseas* 7:22–44.

Guterl, Matthew Pratt. 2001. *The Color of Race in America: 1900–1940*. Cambridge, MA: Harvard University Press.

Gyasi, Yaa. 2020. *Transcendent Kingdom*. New York: Knopf.

Hackett, Conrad. 2017. "Five Facts about the Muslim Population in Europe." Washington, DC: Pew Research Center.

Hagan, Jacqueline Maria, Rubén Hernández-León, and Jean-Luc Demonsant. 2015. *Skills of the "Unskilled": Work and Mobility among Mexican Migrants*. Berkeley: University of California Press.

Halter, Marilyn. 2000. *Shopping for Identity: The Marketing of Ethnicity*. New York: Schocken.

Hamilton, Tod. 2019. *Immigration and the Remaking of Black America*. New York: Russell Sage Foundation.

Handlin, Oscar. 1959. *Immigration as a Factor in American History*. Englewood Cliffs, NJ: Prentice Hall.

Hapgood, Hutchins. (1902) 1967. *The Spirit of the Ghetto*. Cambridge, MA: Harvard University Press.

Harrington, Theresa. 2018. "Innovative High School for New Immigrant Students a Model in California." EdSource, May 20.

Hathaway, Ian. 2017. "Almost Half of All Fortune 500 Companies Were Founded by American Immigrants or Their Children." Brookings Institution, December 4.

Haub, Carl. 2012. "Changing the Way U.S. Hispanics Are Counted." Population Reference Bureau, November 7.

Hayford, Charles. 2011. "Who's Afraid of Chop Suey?" *Education about Asia* 16 (Winter): 7–12.

Hernández, Kelly Lytle. 2006. "The Crimes and Consequences of Illegal Immigration: A Cross-Border Examination of Operation Wetback, 1943–1954." *Western Historical Quarterly* (Winter): 421–44.

Hilgers, Lauren. 2014. "The Kitchen Network: America's Underground Chinese Workers." *New Yorker*, October 13.

Hintzen, Percy. 2001. *West Indian in the West: Self-Representations in an Immigrant Community*. New York: NYU Press.

Hirschman, Charles. 2005. "Immigration and the American Century." *Demography* 42:595–620.

———. 2013. "The Contributions of Immigrants to American Culture." *Daedalus* 142:26–47.

Hirschman, Charles, and Douglas S. Massey. 2008. "Places and Peoples: The New American Mosaic." In *New Faces in New Places: The Changing Geography of American Immigration*, edited by Douglas S. Massey, 1–22. New York: Russell Sage Foundation.

Hirschman, Charles, and Elizabeth Mogford. 2009. "Immigration and the American Industrial Revolution from 1880 to 1920." *Social Science Research* 38:897–920.

Hoban, Brennan. 2017. "Do Immigrants 'Steal' Jobs from American Workers?" Brookings, August 24.

Hochschild, Arlie. 2016. *Strangers in Their Own Land: Anger and Mourning on the American Right*. New York: New Press.

Hondagneu-Sotelo, Pierrette. 2001. *Domestica: Immigrant Workers Cleaning and Caring in the Shadows of Affluence*. Berkeley: University of California Press.

Hunt, Darnell, Ana-Christina Ramón, and Michael Tran. 2019. *Hollywood Diversity Report 2019: Old Story, New Beginning*. Los Angeles: UCLA Division of Social Sciences.

Hunt, Jennifer, and Marjolaine Gauthier-Loiselle. 2010. "How Much Does Immigration Boost Innovation?" *American Economic Journal: Macroeconomics* 2:31–56.

Huntington, Samuel. 2004. *Who Are We? The Challenges to America's National Identity*. New York: Simon and Schuster.

Hyslop, Gill. 2017. "Top US Salty Snack Brands in 2017." Bakeryandsnacks.com.

Imoagene, Onoso. 2017. *Beyond Expectations: Second-Generation Nigerians in the United States and Britain*. Berkeley: University of California Press.

"International Migrant Stock 2015." 2015. United Nations Department of Economic and Social Affairs, Population Division.

Itzigsohn, José. 2004. "The Formation of Latino and Latina Panethnic Identities." In *Not Just Black and White: Historical and Contemporary Perspectives on Immigration, Race, and Ethnicity in the United States*, edited by Nancy Foner and George M. Fredrickson, 197–216. New York: Russell Sage Foundation.

Jacobson, Matthew Frye. 1998. *Whiteness of a Different Color: European Immigrants and the Alchemy of Race*. Cambridge, MA: Harvard University Press.

———. 2006. *Roots Too: White Ethnic Revival in Post–Civil Rights America*. Cambridge, MA: Harvard University Press.

Jacoby, Tamar. 2012. "Without Immigrant Labor, the Economy Would Crumble." *New York Times*, April 17.

Jardina, Ashley. 2019. *White Identity Politics*. New York: Cambridge University Press.

Jen, Gish. 1991. *Typical American*. Boston: Houghton Mifflin.

Jilani, Seema. 2020. "My Daughter Passes for White." *New York Times*, February 28.

Jiménez, Tomás. 2010. *Replenished Ethnicity: Mexican Americans, Immigration, and Identity*. Berkeley: University of California Press.

Laurence, Jonathan, and Justin Vaisse. 2006. *Integrating Islam: Political and Religious Challenges in Contemporary France*. Washington, DC: Brookings Institution Press.

Laurino, Mario. 2000. "From the Fonz to the Sopranos, Not Much Evolution." *New York Times*, December 24.

League of American Orchestras. 2016. *Racial/Ethnic and Gender Diversity in the Orchestra Field*. New York: League of American Orchestras.

Lee, Erika. 2015. *The Making of Asian America: A History*. New York: Simon and Schuster.

———. 2019. *America for Americans: A History of Xenophobia in the United States*. New York: Basic Books.

Lee, Jennifer, and Frank Bean. 2010. *The Diversity Paradox: Immigration and the Color Line in Twenty-First Century America*. New York: Russell Sage Foundation.

Lee, Jennifer, and Karthick Ramakrishnan. 2020. "Who Counts as Asian." *Ethnic and Racial Studies* 43:1733–56.

Lee, Jennifer, and Min Zhou. 2014. "From Unassimilable to Exceptional: The Rise of Asian Americans and 'Stereotype Promise.'" *New Diversities* 16:7–22.

———. 2015. *The Asian American Achievement Paradox*. New York: Russell Sage Foundation.

Lee, Jennifer, and Monika Yadav. 2020. "The Rise of Anti-Asian Hate in the Wake of Covid-19." Social Science Research Council, May 21.

Lee, Jennifer 8. 2008. *The Fortune Cookie Chronicles: Adventures in the World of Chinese Food*. New York: Twelve.

Lee, Min Jin. 2007. *Free Food for Millionaires*. New York: Grand Central Publishing.

Leonhardt, David, and Ian Prasad Philbrick. 2018. "Donald Trump's Racism: The Definitive List, Updated." *New York Times*, January 15.

Liang, Zai. 2021. "Spatial Diffusion of Low-Skilled Chinese Immigrants in the U.S. and Challenges of Covid-19." Paper presented at the annual meeting of the Eastern Sociological Society, February 19.

Liang, Zai, and Bo Zhou. 2018. "The Rise of Market-Based Job Search Institutions and Job Niches for Low-Skilled Chinese Immigrants." *RSF: The Russell Sage Foundation Journal of the Social Sciences* 4:78–95.

Liang, Zai, Jiejin Li, Glenn Deane, Zhen Li, and Bo Zhou. 2018. "From Chinatown to Every Town: New Patterns of Employment for Low-Skilled Chinese Immigrants in the United States." *Social Forces* 97:893–920.

Lichter, Daniel T. 2012. "Immigration and the New Racial Diversity in Rural America." *Rural Sociology* 77:3–35.

Lichter, Daniel T., and Kenneth M. Johnson. 2020. "A Demographic Lifeline? Immigration and Hispanic Population Growth in Rural America." *Population Research and Policy Review* 39:785–803.

Lim, Nelson. 2001. "On the Back of Blacks? Immigrants and the Fortunes of African Americans." In *Strangers at the Gates: New Immigrants in Urban America*, edited by Roger Waldinger, 186–227. Berkeley: University of California Press.

Liptak, Adam. 2013. "Smaller States Find Outsize Clout Growing in Senate." *New York Times*, March 10.

Liu, Haiming. 2015. *From Canton Restaurant to Panda Express: A History of Chinese Food in the United States*. New Brunswick, NJ: Rutgers University Press.

Livingston, Gretchen. 2019a. "Hispanic Women No Longer Account for the Majority of Immigrant Births in the U.S." Pew Research Center, August 8.

———. 2019b. "Is U.S. Fertility at an All-Time Low? Two of Three Measures Point to Yes." Pew Research Center, May 2.

Lobo, Arun Peter, and Joseph J. Salvo. 2013. "A Portrait of New York's Immigrant Mélange." In *One Out of Three: Immigrant New York in the Twenty-First Century*, edited by Nancy Foner, 35–63. New York: Columbia University Press.

Logan, John, and Wenquan Zhang. 2010. "Global Neighborhoods: New Pathways to Diversity and Separation." *American Journal of Sociology* 115:1069–109.

López, David E., and Ricardo D. Stanton-Salazar. 2001. "Mexican Americans: A Second Generation at Risk." In *Ethnicities: Children of Immigrants in America*, edited by Rubén G. Rumbaut and Alejandro Portes, 57–90. Berkeley: University of California Press.

López, Ian Haney. 1996. *White by Law: The Legal Construction of Race*. New York: NYU Press.

———. 2015. *Dog Whistle Politics*. New York: Oxford University Press.

Luconi, Stefano. 2001. *From Paesani to White Ethnics: The Italian Experience in Philadelphia*. Albany: SUNY Press.

Marrow, Helen. 2011. *New Destination Dreaming: Immigration, Race, and Legal Status in the Rural American South*. Stanford, CA: Stanford University Press.

Marshall, Paule. (1959) 1981. *Brown Girl, Brownstones*. New York: Feminist Press.

Martin, Philip. 2014. *Trends in Migration to the U.S.* Washington, DC: Population Reference Bureau, May 19.

Massey, Douglas S., ed. 2008. *New Faces in New Places: The Changing Geography of American Immigration*. New York: Russell Sage Foundation.

Massey, Douglas S., Joaquin Arango, Graeme Hugo, Ali Kouaouci, Adela Pellegrino, and J. Edward Taylor. 1993. "Theories of International Migration: A Review and Appraisal." *Population and Development Review* 19:431–66.

Massey, Douglas S., Jorge Durand, and Nolan Malone. 2002. *Beyond Smoke and Mirrors: Mexican Immigration in an Era of Economic Integration*. New York: Russell Sage Foundation.

Massey, Douglas S., Jorge Durand, and Karen A. Pren. 2016. "Why Border Enforcement Backfired." *American Journal of Sociology* 121:1557–600.

Massey, Douglas S., and Karen A. Pren. 2012. "Unintended Consequences of US Immigration Policy: Explaining the Post-1965 Surge from Latin America." *Population and Development Review* 38:1–29.

Massey, Douglas S., and Jonathan Tannen. 2018. "Suburbanization and Segregation in the United States: 1970–2010." *Ethnic and Racial Studies* 41:1594–611.

Matsumoto, Noriko. 2018. *Beyond the City and the Bridge: East Asian Immigration in a New Jersey Suburb*. New Brunswick, NJ: Rutgers University Press.

Mathema, Silva, Nicole Prchal Svajlenka, and Anneliese Hermann. 2018. "Revival and Opportunity: Immigrants in Rural America." Center for American Progress, September.

Matthews, Dylan. 2015. "Woodrow Wilson Was Extremely Racist—Even by the Standards of His Time." *Vox*, November 20.

Mbue, Imbolo. 2016. *Behold the Dreamers*. New York: Random House.

McCann, James, and Michael Jones-Correa. 2020. *Holding Fast: Resilience and Civic Engagement among Latino Immigrants*. New York: Russell Sage Foundation.

McDermott, Monica, and Frank L. Samson. 2005. "White Racial and Ethnic Identity in the United States." *Annual Review of Sociology* 31:245–61.

McDonnell, Lorraine, and Paul Hill. 1993. *Newcomers in American Schools: Meeting the Needs of Immigrant Youth*. Santa Monica, CA: Rand.

McGuinness, Margaret M. 2013. *Called to Serve: A History of Nuns in America*. New York: NYU Press.

McNickle, Chris. 1993. *To Be Mayor of New York*. New York: Columbia University Press.

"Meat, Beef and Poultry Processing Industry in the US—Market Research Report." 2019. IBIS-World, November.

Mehta, Suketu. 2019. *This Land Is Our Land: An Immigrant's Manifesto*. New York: Farrar, Straus and Giroux.

Menjívar, Cecilia. 2003. "Religion and Immigration in Comparative Perspective: Catholic and Evangelical Salvadorans in San Francisco, Washington, D.C., and Phoenix." *Sociology of Religion* 64:21–45.

Mentzelopoulou, Maria Margarita, and Costica Dumbrava. 2018. "Acquisition and Loss of Citizenship in EU Member States: Key Trends and Issues." European Parliamentary Research Service, July.

Meyerson, Harold. 2002. "The Rising Latino Tide." *American Prospect*, November 18.

Millhiser, Ian. 2019. "The Astounding Advantage the Electoral College Gives to Republicans." *Vox*, September 17.

Milkman, Ruth, 2020. *Immigrant Labor and the New Precariat*. Cambridge, UK: Polity.

Min, Pyong Gap. 2013. "Koreans: Changes in New York in the Twenty-First Century." In *One Out of Three: Immigrant New York in the Twenty-First Century*, edited by Nancy Foner, 148–75. New York: Columbia University Press.

Mohamed, Basheer. 2018. "New Estimates Show U.S. Muslim Population Continues to Grow." Washington, DC: Pew Research Center.

Mollenkopf, John H. 2014. "The Rise of Immigrant Influence in New York City Politics." In *New York and Amsterdam: Immigration and the New Urban Landscape*, edited by Nancy Foner, Jan Rath, Jan Willem Duyvendak, and Rogier van Reekum, 203–29. New York: NYU Press.

Mollenkopf, John H., and Manuel Pastor, eds. 2016. *Unsettled Americans: Metropolitan Context and Civic Leadership for Immigrant Integration*. Ithaca, NY: Cornell University Press.

Mollenkopf, John H., and Raphael J. Sonenshein. 2009. "The New Urban Politics of Integration: A View from the Gateway Cities." In *Bringing Outsiders In: Transatlantic Perspectives on Immigrant Political Incorporation*, edited by Jennifer L. Hochschild and John H. Mollenkopf, 74–92. Ithaca, NY: Cornell University Press.

———. 2013. "New York City and Los Angeles: Government and Political Influence." In *New York and Los Angeles: The Uncertain Future*, edited by David Halle and Andrew A. Beveridge, 137–53. New York: Oxford University Press.

Molotsky, Irvin. 1988. "Senate Votes to Compensate Japanese-American Internees." *New York Times*, April 21.

Molteni, Megan. 2020. "Why Meatpacking Plants Have Become Covid-19 Hot Spots." *Wired*, May 7.

Moore, Deborah Dash. 1981. *At Home in America: Second Generation New York Jews*. New York: Columbia University Press.

Moore, Deborah Dash, Jeffrey S. Gurock, Annie Polland, Howard B. Rock, and Daniel Soyer. 2017. *Jewish New York: The Remarkable Story of a City and a People.* New York: NYU Press.

Mora, G. Cristina. 2014. *Making Hispanics: How Activists, Bureaucrats, and Media Constructed a New American.* Chicago: University of Chicago Press.

Moses, Paul. 2018. "When Rudy Giuliani Sided with New York's Immigrants." *Newsday,* July 1.

Moyce, Sally, and Marc Schenker. 2018. "Migrant Workers and Their Occupational Health and Safety." *Annual Review of Public Health* 39:351–65.

Myers, Dowell, and Morris Levy. 2018. "Racial Population Projections and Reactions to Alternative News Accounts of Growing Diversity." *Annals of the American Academy of Political and Social Science* 677:215–28.

Myers, Dowell, and John Pitkin. 2013. "Immigrant Contributions to Housing Demand in the United States: A Comparison of Recent Decades and Projections to 2020 for the States and Nation." Research Institute for Housing America Research Paper No. 13–01, February.

Nathan, Joan. 2008. "A Short History of the Bagel." *Slate,* November 12.

National Association of Latino Elected and Appointed Officials (NALEO). 2019. *National Directory of Latino Elected Officials.* Los Angeles: NALEO Educational Fund.

Nee, Victor, and Lucas Drouhot. 2020. "Immigration, Opportunity, and Assimilation in a Technology Economy." *Theory and Society* 49:965–90.

New American Economy. 2020a. "Covid-19: Immigrants Are Essential in Securing U.S. Food Supply Chain." New American Economy Research Fund, April 16.

———. 2020b. "Immigration and Covid-19." New American Economy Research Fund, March 26.

New York: A Collection from Harper's Magazine. 1991. New York: Gallery Books.

Ngai, Mai M. 2004. *Impossible Subjects: Illegal Aliens and the Making of Modern America.* Princeton, NJ: Princeton University Press.

———. 2006. "How Grandma Got Legal." *Los Angeles Times,* May 16.

Nguyen, Viet Thanh. 2015. *The Sympathizer.* New York: Grove Press.

Noe-Bustamante, Luis, Antonio Flores, and Sono Shah. 2019. "Facts on Hispanics of Mexican Origin in the United States, 2017." Pew Research Center, September 16.

Norris, Pippa, and Ronald Inglehart. 2019. *Cultural Backlash: Trump, Brexit, and Authoritarian Populism.* New York: Cambridge University Press.

Nussbaum, Emily. 2015. "Home Cooking." *New Yorker,* March 9.

Odem, Mary E. 2008. "Unsettled in the Suburbs: Latino Immigration and Ethnic Diversity in Metro Atlanta." In *Twenty-First Century Gateways: Immigrant Incorporation in Suburban America,* edited by Audrey Singer, Susan W. Hardwick, and Caroline B. Brettell, 105–36. Washington, DC: Brookings Institution Press.

Odencrantz, Louise. 1919. *Italian Women in Industry: A Study of Conditions in New York City.* New York: Russell Sage Foundation.

Okamoto, Dina. 2014. *Redefining Race: Asian American Panethnicity and Shifting Ethnic Boundaries.* New York: Russell Sage Foundation.

Okura, Lynn. 2013. "Gloria Estefan Tells Oprah How She's Stayed True to Her Music." *Huffington Post,* August 8.

Orleck, Annelise. 1987. "The Soviet Jews: Life in Brighton Beach, Brooklyn." In *New Immigrants in New York,* edited by Nancy Foner, 272–304. New York: Columbia University Press.

———. 2013. "Soviet Jews: The Continuing Russification of Jewish New York." In *One Out of Three: Immigrant New York in the Twenty-First Century*, edited by Nancy Foner, 90–119. New York: Columbia University Press.

Orrenius, Pia, and Madeline Zavodny. 2009. "Do Immigrants Work in Riskier Jobs?" *Demography* 46:535–51.

Ortiz, Vilma, and Edward Telles. 2012. "Racial Identity and Racial Treatment of Mexican Americans." *Race and Social Problems* 4:41–56.

Ortman, Jennifer M., Victoria A. Velkoff, and Howard Hogan. 2014. *An Aging Nation: The Older Population in the United States*. Washington, DC: US Census Bureau, May.

Paarlberg, Michael Ahn. 2012. "Can Asians Save Classical Music." *Slate*, February 2.

Pager, Devah. 2007. *Marked: Race, Crime, and Finding Work in an Era of Mass Incarceration*. Chicago: University of Chicago Press.

Painter, Nell Irvin. 2016. "What Whiteness Means in the Trump Era." *New York Times*, November 12.

Parrado, Emilio A., and William Kandel. 2008. "New Hispanic Migrant Destinations: A Tale of Two Industries." In *New Faces in New Places: The Changing Geography of American Immigration*, edited by Douglas S. Massey, 99–123. New York: Russell Sage Foundation.

Passel, Jeffrey S., and D'Vera Cohn. 2008. "U.S. Population Projections: 2005–2050." Pew Research Center, February 11.

———. 2019. "Mexicans Decline to Less than Half the Unauthorized Immigrant Population for the First Time." Pew Research Center, June 12.

Peri, Giovanni. 2017. "The Impact of Immigration on Wages of Unskilled Workers." *Cato Journal* 37:449–60.

Peri, Giovanni, and Chad Sparber. 2020. "Presidential Executive Actions Halting High Skilled Immigration Hurt the US Economy." UC Davis Global Migration Center, July.

Perlmann, Joel. 2005. *Italians Then, Mexicans Now: Immigrant Origins and Second-Generation Progress, 1890–2000*. New York: Russell Sage Foundation.

———. 2018. *America Classifies the Immigrants: From Ellis Island to the 2020 Census*. Cambridge, MA: Harvard University Press.

Pettigrew, Thomas, and Linda Tropp. 2006. "A Meta-Analytic Test of Intergroup Contact Theory." *Journal of Personality and Social Psychology* 90:751–83.

Pew Forum on Religion and Public Life. 2012. "Faith on the Move: The Religious Affiliation of International Migrants." Washington, DC: Pew Research Center.

Pew Research Center. 2015a. *America's Changing Religious Landscape*. Washington, DC: Pew Research Center.

———. 2015b. *Multiracial in America: Proud, Diverse, and Growing in Numbers*. Washington, DC: Pew Research Center.

———. 2017a. *Americans Express Increasingly Warm Feelings toward Religious Groups*. Washington, DC: Pew Research Center.

———. 2017b. *U.S. Muslims Concerned about Their Place in Society, but Continue to Believe in the American Dream*. Washington, DC: Pew Research Center.

———. 2019a. *Generation Z Looks a Lot Like Millennials on Key Social and Political Issues*. Washington, DC: Pew Research Center.

———. 2019b. *Race in America 2019*. Washington, DC: Pew Research Center.

———. 2020. *In Changing U.S. Electorate, Race and Education Remain Stark Dividing Lines*. Washington, DC: Pew Research Center.

Piepenburg, Erik. 2016. "Why 'Hamilton' Has Heat." *New York Times*, June 12.

Pierce, Sarah, and Julia Gelatt. 2018. "Evolution of the H1-B: Latest Trends in a Program on the Brink of Reform." Issue Brief. Migration Policy Institute.

Pierson, David. 2015. "Panda Express' Billionaire CEO Dishes Up a Stir-Fry Empire." *Los Angeles Times*, January 11.

Pilcher, Jeffrey M. 2012. *Planet Taco: A Global History of Mexican Food*. New York: Oxford University Press.

Porter, Eduardo. 2017. "The Danger from Low-Skilled Immigrants: Not Having Them." *New York Times*, August 8.

———. 2018. "The Hard Truths of Trying to 'Save' the Rural Economy." *New York Times*, December 14.

———. 2019. "Short of Workers, U.S. Builders and Farmers Crave More Immigrants." *New York Times*, April 3.

Portes, Alejandro. 2012. "Tensions That Make a Difference: Institutions, Interests, and the Immigrant Drive." *Sociological Forum* 27:563–78.

Portes, Alejandro, and Ariel Armony. 2018. *The Global Edge: Miami in the Twenty-First Century*. Berkeley: University of California Press.

Portes, Alejandro, and Alex Stepick. 1993. *City on the Edge: The Transformation of Miami*. Berkeley: University of California Press.

Price, Marie, and Audrey Singer. 2008. "Edge Gateways: Immigrants, Suburbs, and the Policies of Reception in Metropolitan Washington." In *Twenty-First Century Gateways: Immigrant Incorporation in Suburban America*, edited by Audrey Singer, Susan W. Hardwick, and Caroline B. Brettell, 137–70. Washington, DC: Brookings Institution Press.

Provine, Doris Marie, Monica W. Varsanyi, Paul G. Lewis, and Scott H. Decker. 2016. *Policing Immigrants: Local Law Enforcement on the Front Lines*. Chicago: University of Chicago Press.

Public Broadcasting Service. 2017. *Latin Music USA*. May 5.

Purdum, Todd. 2018a. "'Oklahoma' Was the 'Hamilton' of Its Day." *New York Times*, March 31.

———. 2018b. *Something Wonderful: Rodgers and Hammerstein's Broadway Revolution*. New York: Henry Holt.

Putnam, Robert. 2007. "E Pluribus Unum: Diversity and Community in the Twenty-First Century." *Scandinavian Political Studies* 30:137–74.

Railton, Ben. 2017. "DACA, the 1924 Immigration Act, and American Exclusion." *Huffington Post*, September 7.

Ray, Krishnendu. 2016. *The Ethnic Restaurateur*. London: Bloomsbury Academic.

Rischin, Moses. 1962. *The Promised City: New York's Jews, 1870–1914*. Cambridge, MA: Harvard University Press.

Roberts, Brian, and Michael Wolf. 2018. "High-Tech Industries: An Analysis of Employment, Wages, and Output." *Beyond the Numbers* 7 (May).

Rooduijn, Matthijs. 2015. "The Rise of the Populist Radical Right in Western Europe." *European View* 14:3–11.

Ross, Edward A. 1914. *The Old World and the New*. New York: Century.

Roth, Philip. 1959. *Goodbye, Columbus, and Five Short Stories*. Boston: Houghton Mifflin.

Roth, Wendy. 2012. *Race Migrations: Latinos and the Cultural Transformation of Race*. Stanford, CA: Stanford University Press.

Rothstein, Richard. 2017. *The Color of Law*. New York: Liveright.

Rubin, Rachel Lee, and Jeffrey Melnick. 2007. *Immigration and American Popular Culture*. New York: NYU Press.

Rumbaut, Rubén G. 2006. "The Making of a People." In *Hispanics and the Future of America*, edited by Marta Tienda and Faith Mitchell, 16–65. Washington, DC: National Academies Press.

———. 2011. "Pigments of Our Imagination: The Racialization of the Hispanic-Latino Category." *Migration Information Source*, April 27.

Rumbaut, Rubén G., Katie Dingeman, and Anthony Robles. 2019. "Immigration and Crime and Criminalization of Immigration." In *The Routledge International Handbook of Migration Studies*, 2nd ed., edited by Steven J. Gold and Stephanie J. Nawyn, 472–82. New York: Routledge.

Salomone, Rosemary. 2010. *True American: Language, Identity, and the Education of Immigrant Children*. Cambridge, MA: Harvard University Press.

———. 2021. *The Rise of English: Global Politics and the Power of Language*. New York: Oxford University Press.

Sall, Dialika. 2020. "Selective Acculturation among Low-Income Second-Generation West Africans." *Journal of Ethnic and Migration Studies* 46:2199–217.

Sampson, Robert J. 2017. "Immigration and the New Social Transformation of the American City." In *Immigration and Metropolitan Revitalization in the United States*, edited by Domenic Vitiello and Thomas J. Sugrue, 11–24. Philadelphia: University of Pennsylvania Press.

Sandomir, Richard. 2019. "Paule Marshall, Influential Black Novelist Dies, at 90." *New York Times*, August 16.

Sandoval-Strausz, A. K. 2017. "*Migrantes*, Barrios, and *Infraestructura*: Transnational Processes of Urban Revitalization in Chicago." In *Immigration and Metropolitan Revitalization in the United States*, edited by Domenic Vitiello and Thomas J. Sugrue, 133–53. Philadelphia: University of Pennsylvania Press.

———. 2019. *Barrio America: How Latino Immigrants Saved the American City*. New York: Basic Books.

Sargent, Greg. 2018. "Trump's Hard-Core Base Will Not Rule This Country Forever." *Washington Post*, August 10.

Schickler, Eric. 2016. *Racial Realignment: The Transformation of American Liberalism, 1932–1965*. Princeton, NJ: Princeton University Press.

Schneider, Jack. 2008. "Escape from Los Angeles: White Flight from Los Angeles and Its Schools, 1960–1980." *Journal of Urban History* 34:995–1012.

Schultz, Kevin. 2011. *Tri-Faith America*. New York: Oxford University Press.

Shah, Khushbu. 2020. "Best New Chefs 2020." *Food & Wine*, May 12.

Shutika, Debra Lattanzi. 2011. *Beyond the Borderlands: Migration and Belonging in the United States and Mexico*. Berkeley: University of California Press.

Sides, John, Michael Tesler, and Lynn Vavreck. 2018. *Identity Crisis: The 2016 Presidential Campaign and the Battle for the Meaning of America*. Princeton, NJ: Princeton University Press.

Silva, Christianna. 2018. "Trump's Full List of 'Racist' Comments about Immigrants, Muslims, and Others." *Newsweek*, January 11.

Singer, Audrey. 2004. "The Rise of New Immigrant Gateways." Brookings, February 1.

———. 2013. "Contemporary Immigrant Gateways in Historical Perspective." *Daedalus* (Summer): 76–91.

———. 2015. "A Typology of Immigrant Gateways, 2014." Brookings, December.

Singer, Audrey, Susan Hardwick, and Caroline Brettell, eds. 2008. *Twenty-First Century Gateways: Immigrant Incorporation in Suburban America*. Washington, DC: Brookings Institution Press.

Siniavskaia, Natalia. 2018. "Immigrant Workers in the Construction Labor Force." National Association of Home Builders, January 2.

Smith, Paul. 2020. "'Use It or Lose It': The Problem of Purges from the Registration Rolls of Voters Who Don't Vote Regularly." American Bar Association, February 10.

Smith, Stacy L., Marc Choueiti, and Katherine Pieper. 2016. *Inclusion or Invisibility? Comprehensive Annenberg Report on Diversity in Entertainment*. Los Angeles: Institute for Diversity and Empowerment at Annenberg.

Smith, Zadie. 2001. *White Teeth*. New York: Vintage.

Starr, Paul. 1997. "An Emerging Democratic Majority." *American Prospect*, November–December.

Stepick, Alex, Guillermo Grenier, Max Castro, and Marvin Dunn. 2003. *This Land Is Our Land: Immigrants and Power in Miami*. Berkeley: University of California Press.

Sterne, Evelyn Savidge. 2001. "Beyond the Boss: Immigration and American Political Culture, 1880–1940." In *E Pluribus Unum? Contemporary and Historical Perspectives on Immigrant Incorporation*, edited by Gary Gerstle and John H. Mollenkopf, 33–66. New York: Russell Sage Foundation.

Stubbs, Nathan. 2021. "Leap of Faith: Lafayette's Newest Immigrant Restaurants Plant Deeper Roots during the Pandemic." *Current*, February 11.

Sturtevant, Lisa. 2017. *Home in America: Immigrants and Housing Demand*. Washington, DC: Urban Land Institute.

Suárez-Orozco, Carola, Marcelo Suárez-Orozco, and Irina Todorova. 2008. *Learning in a New Land: Immigrant Students in American Society*. Cambridge, MA: Harvard University Press.

Tehranian, John. 2009. *Whitewashed: America's Invisible Middle Eastern Minority*. New York: NYU Press.

Telles, Edward, and Christina Sue. 2019. *Durable Ethnicity: Mexican Americans and the Ethnic Core*. New York: Oxford University Press.

Thompson, Derek. 2015. "1991: The Most Important Year in Pop Music History." *Atlantic*, May 8.

Törngren, Sayaka Osanami, Nahikari Irastorza, and Dan Rodríguez-García. 2021. "Understanding Multiethnic and Multiracial Experiences Globally: Towards a Conceptual Framework of Mixedness." *Journal of Ethnic and Migration Studies* 47:763–81.

Tran, Van C., Jennifer Lee, Oshin Khachikian, and Jess Lee. 2018. "Hyper-Selectivity, Racial Mobility, and the Remaking of Race." *RSF: The Russell Sage Foundation Journal of the Social Sciences* 4:188–209.

Tuan, Mia. 1998. *Forever Foreigners or Honorary Whites?* New Brunswick, NJ: Rutgers University Press.

Tucker, Todd. 2019. "Fixing the Senate: Equitable and Full Representation for the 21st Century." Roosevelt Institute, March 18.

Urrea, Luis Alberto. 2018. *The House of Broken Angels*. Boston: Little, Brown and Company.

US Bureau of Labor Statistics. 2021. *Occupational Outlook Handbook*. Washington, DC: US Department of Labor.

US Census Bureau. 2018. "Older People Projected to Outnumber Children for First Time in U.S. History." March 13.

Valdes, Marcela. 2015. "Jorge Ramos's Long Game." *New York Times Magazine*, September 25.

Valdez, Zulema, and Tanya Golash-Boza. 2017. "U.S. Ethnic and Racial Relations in the Twenty-First Century." *Ethnic and Racial Studies* 40:2081–209.

Vezner, Tad. 2017. "Worthington, Minn. Was Dying: Then, Enter the Immigrants." *Twin Cities Pioneer Press*, February 3.

Vickerman, Milton. 2001. "Tweaking a Monolith: The West Indian Immigrant Encounter with 'Blackness.'" In *Islands in the City: West Indian Migration to New York*, edited by Nancy Foner, 237–57. Berkeley: University of California Press.

———. 2013. "Jamaicans: Balancing Race and Ethnicity." In *One Out of Three: Immigrant New York in the Twenty-First Century*, edited by Nancy Foner, 176–99. New York: Columbia University Press.

———. 2016. "Black Immigrants, Perceptions of Difference, and the Abiding Sting of Blackness." *Journal of American Ethnic History* 36:71–81.

Vitiello, Domenic, and Thomas J. Sugrue, eds. 2017a. *Immigration and Metropolitan Revitalization in the United States*. Philadelphia: University of Pennsylvania Press.

———. 2017b. "Introduction: Immigration and the New American Metropolis." In *Immigration and Metropolitan Revitalization in the United States*, edited by Domenic Vitiello and Thomas J. Sugrue, 1–10. Philadelphia: University of Pennsylvania Press.

Waldinger, Roger. 1986. "Immigrant Enterprise: A Critique and Reformulation." *Theory and Society* 15:249–85.

———. 1996. *Still the Promised City? African-Americans and New Immigrants in Postindustrial New York*. Cambridge, MA: Harvard University Press.

———, ed. 2001. *Strangers at the Gates: New Immigrants in Urban America*. Berkeley: University of California Press.

Waldinger, Roger, and Mehdi Bozorgmehr, eds. 1996. *Ethnic Los Angeles*. New York: Russell Sage Foundation.

Waldinger, Roger, and Michael Lichter. 2003. *How the Other Half Works: Immigration and the Social Organization of Labor*. Berkeley: University of California Press.

Waldman, Paul. 2020. "If Joe Biden Wins, Immigration Reform May Actually Be Possible." *Washington Post*, May 19.

Wallace, Sophia J. 2014. "Representing Latinos: Examining Descriptive and Substantive Representation in Congress." *Political Research Quarterly* 67:917–29.

Warren, Robert. 2017. "DHS Overestimates Visa Overstays for 2016; Overstay Population Growth Near Zero during the Year." *Journal on Migration and Human Security* 5:768–79.

———. 2019. "US Undocumented Population Continued to Fall from 2016 to 2017 and Visa Overstays Significantly Exceeded Illegal Crossings for the Seventh Consecutive Year." *Journal on Migration and Human Security* 7:19–22.

Waters, Mary C. 1990. *Ethnic Options: Choosing Identities in America.* Berkeley: University of California Press.

———. 1999. *Black Identities: West Indian Immigrant Dreams and American Realities.* Cambridge, MA: Harvard University Press.

———. 2001. "Growing Up West Indian and African American: Gender and Class Differences in the Second Generation." In *Islands in the City: West Indian Migration to New York,* edited by Nancy Foner, 193–215. Berkeley: University of California Press.

———. 2014. "Nativism, Racism, and Immigration in New York City." In *New York and Amsterdam: Immigration and the New Urban Landscape,* edited by Nancy Foner, Jan Rath, Jan Willem Duyvendak, and Rogier van Reekum, 143–69. New York: NYU Press.

Waters, Mary C., and Philip Kasinitz. 2015. "The War on Crime and the War on Immigrants: Racial and Legal Exclusion in the Twenty-First Century United States." In *Fear, Anxiety, and National Identity: Immigration and Belonging in North America and Western Europe,* edited by Nancy Foner and Patrick Simon, 115–43. New York: Russell Sage Foundation.

Waters, Mary C., and Marisa Pineau, eds. 2015. *The Integration of Immigrants into American Society.* Washington, DC: National Academies Press.

Weil, Patrick. 2001. "Access to Citizenship: A Comparison of Twenty-Five Nationality Laws." In *Citizenship Today: Global Perspectives and Practices,* edited by T. Alexander Aleinikoff and Douglas Klusmeyer, 17–35. Washington, DC: Carnegie Endowment for International Peace.

Wessendorf, Susanne. 2014. *Commonplace Diversity: Social Relations in a Super-Diverse Context.* Basingstoke, UK: Palgrave Macmillan.

Wides-Munoz, Laura. 2010. "'Ugly Betty' Broke New Ground for Latinos, Gays." Boston.com, April 9.

Wikipedia. 2020. "List of Cities by Foreign-Born Population." https://en.wikipedia.org/wiki/List_of_United_States_cities_by_foreign-born_population.

———. 2021. "List of U.S. Cities with Large Hispanic Populations." https://en.wikipedia.org/wiki/List_of_U.S._cities_with_large_Hispanic_populations.

Williams, Thomas Chatterton. 2012. "As Black as We Wish to Be." *New York Times,* March 16.

———. 2019. "The Singular Power of Writing: An Interview with Thomas Chatterton Williams." *Los Angeles Review of Books,* April 12.

Wilson, Walter Clark. 2010. "Descriptive Representation and Latino Interest Bill Sponsorship in Congress." *Social Science Quarterly* 91:1043–62.

Wiltz, Teresa. 2014. "Lobbying for a 'MENA' Category on U.S. Census." *USA Today,* August 13.

Winders, Jamie. 2008. "Nashville's New 'Sonido': Latino Migration and the Changing Politics of Race." In *New Faces in New Places: The Changing Geography of American Immigration,* edited by Douglas S. Massey, 249–73. New York: Russell Sage Foundation.

———. 2013. *Nashville in the New Millennium: Immigrant Settlement, Urban Transformation, and Social Belonging.* New York: Russell Sage Foundation.

Witchel, Alex. 2012. "The Man Who Can Make Bruce Lee Talk." *New York Times,* November 7.

Withers, Rachel. 2018. "George H. W. Bush's 'Willie Horton' Ad Will Always Be the Reference Point for Dog-Whistle Racism." *Vox,* December 1.

Wollenberg, Charles M. 1995. "'Yellow Peril' in the Schools (I and II)." In *The Asian American Educational Experience: A Sourcebook for Teachers and Students*, edited by Don T. Nakanishi and Tina Yamano Nishida, 3–29. New York: Routledge.

Wu, Ellen D. 2013. *The Color of Success: Asian Americans and the Origins of the Model Minority*. Princeton, NJ: Princeton University Press.

Wuthnow, Robert. 2005. *America and the Challenges of Religious Diversity*. Princeton, NJ: Princeton University Press.

Yin, Alice. 2017. "Asian Test-Prep Centers Offer Asian Parents Exactly What They Want: 'Results.'" *New York Times*, October 25.

Zallman, Leah, Karen E. Finnegan, David U. Himmelstein, Sharon Touw, and Steffie Woolhandler, 2018. "Care for America's Elderly and Disabled People Relies on Immigrant Labor." *Health Affairs* 38:919–26.

Zhang, Jenny. 2020. "The Path to Survival Is Even More Complicated for Immigrant-Owned Mom-and-Pop Businesses." Eater.com, May 6.

Zhang, Wenquan, and John Logan. 2016. "Global Neighborhoods: Beyond the Multiethnic Metropolis." *Demography* 53:1933–53.

Zhou, Min. 2004. "Are Asian Americans Becoming 'White'?" *Contexts* 3:29–37.

Zhou, Min, Margaret M. Chin, and Rebecca Y. Kim. 2013. "The Transformation of Chinese American Communities: New York vs. Los Angeles." In *New York and Los Angeles: The Uncertain Future*, edited by David Halle and Andrew A. Beveridge, 358–84. New York: Oxford University Press.

Zhou, Min, and Susan Kim. 2006. "Community Forces, Social Capital, and Educational Achievement: The Case of Supplementary Education in the Chinese and Korean Immigrant Communities." *Harvard Educational Review* 76:1–29.

Zolberg, Aristide R. 1999. "Matters of State: Theorizing Immigration Policy." In *The Handbook of International Migration: The American Experience*, edited by Charles Hirschman, Philip Kasinitz, and Josh DeWind, 71–93. New York: Russell Sage Foundation.

———. 2006. *A Nation by Design: Immigration Policy in the Fashioning of America*. Cambridge, MA: Harvard University Press.

Zong, Jie, and Jeanne Batalova. 2018. "Mexican Immigrants in the United States." *Migration Information Source*, October 11.

Zukin, Sharon. 2010. *Naked City: The Death and Life of Authentic Urban Places*. New York: Oxford University Press.

Zúñiga, Víctor, and Rubén Hernández-León, eds. 2005. *New Destinations: Mexican Immigration in the United States*. New York: Russell Sage Foundation.

INDEX

Page numbers in italics refer to illustrations.